BY WALLACE STEVENS

Poetry

HARMONIUM (1923, 1931, 1937)*

THE MAN WITH THE BLUE GUITAR,
including IDEAS OF ORDER
(1936, 1937; *in one volume,* 1952)*

PARTS OF A WORLD (1942, 1951)*

TRANSPORT TO SUMMER (1947)*

THE AURORAS OF AUTUMN (1950)*

THE COLLECTED POEMS OF WALLACE STEVENS (1954)

OPUS POSTHUMOUS: *Poems, Plays, Prose* (1957)

THE PALM AT THE END OF THE MIND (1971)

Prose

THE NECESSARY ANGEL:
Essays on Reality and the Imagination (1951)

THE LETTERS OF WALLACE STEVENS (1966)

* Included in *The Collected Poems of Wallace Stevens*

*These are Borzoi Books,
published by Alfred A. Knopf
in New York.*

SOUVENIRS
AND
PROPHECIES

SOUVENIRS
AND
PROPHECIES

The Young Wallace Stevens

HOLLY STEVENS

Alfred A. Knopf
New York
1977

THIS IS A BORZOI BOOK
PUBLISHED BY ALFRED A. KNOPF, INC.

Library of Congress Cataloging in Publication Data

Stevens, Holly Bright.   Souvenirs and prophecies.

An account of Stevens' early life,
incorporating his journal and other writings.
Includes bibliographical references.
1. Stevens, Wallace, 1879–1955—Biography—Youth.
I. Stevens, Wallace, 1879–1955.   II. Title.
PS3537.T4753Z7673   811'.5'2 [B]   76–13732
ISBN 0–394–48715–X

Manufactured in the United States of America
First Edition

INTRODUCTION

Ten years ago, when I was editing my father's correspondence, very few letters were available for the years before he began courting my mother and writing to her regularly. It then seemed appropriate to excerpt from the journals he had kept, beginning in the fall of 1898, to indicate his activities and states of mind during the period for which we had no, or few, other words of his own.

The journals have haunted me ever since, for it seemed to me that they must contain some key to understanding the development from boy, to man, to major poet. They are intimate in the best sense, as they express the innermost thoughts and essential nature of Wallace Stevens in his formative years; they are included here, in full, to give a sharper and more personal focus than any amount of excerpting could provide.

When I began to work on this book, as a Senior Fellow of the National Endowment for the Humanities (and I am grateful for the grant that enabled me to spend a full, uninterrupted year getting started), I had several projects in mind: annotation of the journals; collection and study of the juvenilia; further study of the letters, including new ones that had shown up since publication of my edition; and meeting and talking with people, friends and relatives of my father's, who had known him well, particularly those who had known him before I did, in an effort to turn up information about his life and the sort of person he was. Because he did not publish poetry professionally until 1914–15, and his first book was not published until he was forty-four (in 1923, the year before I was born), his early years had a special interest; I felt that a concentration there could lead to a better understanding of the development of Stevens' poetic thought and of his ultimate role as one of America's major poets.

Close study of the journals revealed that he used much of the material entered there throughout his life; there are many connections between them and poems written years later. This is not so true in the case of the juvenilia, but the poems, in particular, give an insight into the working of the young poet's mind, as do some of the anecdotes I have heard. Thus ordinary annotation seemed insufficient; what did seem essential was to interweave the available material (even though that made necessary the repetition of a good deal that has been previously published) and some of my own speculations, to provide a background for what my father has described far better than I ever could, in "Effects of Analogy" (1948):

> A man's sense of the world is born with him and persists, and penetrates the ameliorations of education and experience of life. His species is as fixed as his genus. For each man, then, certain subjects are congenital. Now the poet manifests his personality, first of all by his choice of subject. Temperament is a more explicit word than personality and would no doubt be the exact word to use, since it emphasizes the manner of thinking and feeling. It is agreeable to think of the poet as a whole biological mechanism and not as a subordinate mechanism within that larger one. . . .
>
> What is the poet's subject? It is his sense of the world. For him, it is inevitable and inexhaustible. If he departs from it he becomes artificial and laborious and while his artifice may be skillful and his labor perceptive no one knows better than he that what he is doing, under the circumstances, is not essential to him. It may help him to feel that it may be essential to someone else. But this justification, though it might justify what he does in the eyes of all the world, would never quite justify him in his own eyes. There is nothing of selfishness in this. It is often said of a man that his work is autobiographical in spite of every subterfuge. It cannot be otherwise. . . .
>
> The truth is that a man's sense of the world dictates his subjects to him and that this sense is derived from his personality, his temperament, over which he has little control and possibly none, except superficially. It is not a literary problem. It is the problem of his mind and nerves. These sayings are another form of the saying that poets are born not made. A poet writes of twilight because he shrinks from noonday.

A poem that has often been called autobiographical by critics, "The Comedian as the Letter C" (1922), opens:

> Nota: man is the intelligence of his soil,
> The sovereign ghost.

And we can note the consistency of these lines with what Stevens said in his essay more than twenty-five years later. At the beginning of part IV of the poem, he changes the line, but not the consistency:

> Nota: his soil is man's intelligence.
> That's better.

It is in this section that we find the lines:

> He, therefore, wrote his prolegomena,
> And, being full of the caprice, inscribed
> Commingled souvenirs and prophecies.
> He made a singular collation.

From those souvenirs and prophecies we finally find:

> The image must be of the nature of its creator.
> It is the nature of its creator increased,
> Heightened. It is he, anew, in a freshened youth
> And it is he in the substance of his region,
> Wood of his forests and stone out of his fields
> Or from under his mountains.

I hope that my "commingling" will provide a "sense of the world" of Wallace Stevens.

HOLLY STEVENS

November 1975
Guilford, Connecticut

SOUVENIRS
AND
PROPHECIES

I

The house where my father was born, in the 300 block of North Fifth Street in Reading, Pennsylvania, is still standing, as are its neighbors, although for the most part they are no longer residences but mainly professional offices and, on the ground floors, are occasionally used for various commercial purposes. The architecture above eye level has not changed; but the elms and horse-chestnut trees that used to arch the street are gone, and the street is no longer dirt. As Stevens says in "The Rock" (1950):

> It is an illusion that we were ever alive,
> Lived in the houses of mothers, arranged ourselves
> By our own motions in a freedom of air.

> Regard the freedom of seventy years ago.
> It is no longer air. The houses still stand,
> Though they are rigid in rigid emptiness.

> Even our shadows, their shadows, no longer remain.

The shadows of family and place are an important part of my father's soil; we might call them the "sovereign ghosts," and in his "intelligence" they do remain. Although the tower on Mount Penn, which dominates Reading to the east, is not the same tower that was there in the nineteenth century, and the Oley Valley is hard to see today because of the smog, we will find an important sense of place in the journals of Wallace Stevens.

As to family, when my father wrote in "Less and Less Human, O Savage Spirit" (1944):

> If there must be a god in the house, must be,
> Saying things in the rooms and on the stair,

> Let him move as the sunlight moves on the floor,
> Or moonlight, silently, as Plato's ghost

> Or Aristotle's skeleton. Let him hang out
> His stars on the wall. He must dwell quietly.

we can imagine that he may have been thinking of his own father, who

wasn't a man given to pushing his way. He needed what all of us need, and what most of us don't get: that is to say, discreet affection. So much depends on ourselves in that respect. I think that he loved to be at the house with us, but he was incapable of lifting a hand to attract any of us, so that, while we loved him as it was natural to do, we also were afraid of him, at least to the extent of holding off. The result was that he lived alone. The greater part of his life was spent at his office; he wanted quiet and, in that quiet, to create a life of his own.

If that was true of my grandfather, and I can easily imagine it was since I have heard that he would not even talk on the telephone at home, it certainly was true of my father and of our house as I grew up; we held off from each other—one might say that my father lived alone. He says it himself in a poem written in 1945:

> The house was quiet and the world was calm.
> The reader became the book; and summer night
>
> Was like the conscious being of the book.
> The house was quiet and the world was calm.
>
> The words were spoken as if there was no book,
> Except that the reader leaned above the page,
>
> Wanted to lean, wanted much most to be
> The scholar to whom his book is true, to whom
>
> The summer night is like a perfection of thought.
> The house was quiet because it had to be.
>
> The quiet was part of the meaning, part of the mind:
> The access of perfection to the page.
>
> And the world was calm. The truth in a calm world,
> In which there is no other meaning, itself
>
> Is calm, itself is summer and night, itself
> Is the reader leaning late and reading there.

And again, he once wrote to a friend, "At home, our house was rather a curious place, with all of us in different parts of it, reading."

If it is true, as a cousin told me, that my grandfather looked upon open expressions of affection or other emotions as a sign of weakness, and that he thought of himself "as a Sphinx; like he was the patriarch, but that was it"; surely we find my father's echo of that when he refers to

> the impersonal person, the wanderer,
> The father, the ancestor, the bearded peer,
> The total of human shadows bright as glass.

in "Things of August" (1949). Or, as he says in "Esthétique du Mal" (1944):

> The son
> And the father alike and equally are spent,
> Each one, by the necessity of being
> Himself, the unalterable necessity
> Of being this unalterable animal.

"The father" (my grandfather), Garrett Barcalow Stevens, was born on September 29, 1848, a middle child of the large family of Benjamin and Elizabeth Barcalow Stevens. Benjamin was a well-respected citizen of the area, a large landholder, and a pillar in the Dutch Reformed Church. For a large part of his life he was associated with the Feasterville Sabbath School; he was also treasurer of the Society for the Prosecution of Horse Thieves after the Civil War. Born in 1808, he lived to the age of eighty-six, dying in 1894 when his grandson Wallace was fifteen, and thus had had an opportunity to know him. Indeed, he refers to visiting his grandfather's farm often, and recalled:

> Neshaminy is a little place seven or eight miles from Doylestown. To the west of it lies the country through which the Perkiomen Creek runs. This creek, when I was a boy, was famous for its bass. It almost amounts to a genealogical fact that all his life long my father used to fish in Perkiomen for bass, and this can only mean that he did it as a boy.

One of the sources of the Neshaminy Creek rises on the Stevens farm; later the Neshaminy feeds into the Perkiomen. When we remember that Indians had not disappeared from this part of Pennsylvania in the nineteenth century, we find something new has been added to these lines,

> The wood-doves are singing along the Perkiomen.
> The bass lie deep, still afraid of the Indians.

and to the title of the poem from which they come, "Thinking of a Relation Between the Images of Metaphors."

It must have been immediately after finishing his own education that Garrett Barcalow Stevens left the farm to become a schoolteacher, for he was "appointed to his first place when only 17 years of age." He must have been well above average in intelligence, and ambitious as well, for

> after three years' experience [he] decided to take up the legal profession. He came to Reading in 1870, became a student in the law office of John S. Richards and was admitted to practice in the Berks Courts on Aug. 12, 1872.

As a law clerk, he probably did not earn much more than he had as a teacher ($100 a year plus chores was the typical stipend at the time), but a profession was open to him where he could, and would, earn considerably more. Nevertheless, his first two years in Reading must have been difficult, and he must have exerted a good deal of self-discipline. Not only did his clerkship take up six days of the week but, in order to pass the bar examinations, he had to be able to translate at sight both Latin and Greek; classical languages were not taught in country schools at that time, so he must have taught himself in whatever spare time he could find. Or, possibly, he had private tutoring and, if so, it may have been through his tutor that he met the woman he was to marry: Margaretha Catharine Zeller, known as Kate. We know that they had met and become friends before Christmas of 1871, for at that time Garrett gave her a copy of *The Poetical Works of Alexander Pope*, inscribing the date and his "Compliments." She was a schoolteacher in Reading, having, like Garrett, become one at an early age. She was only fifteen when her father died, and she had to begin earning her own living as soon as she was qualified. In 1872, the same year that Garrett was admitted to the bar, her mother died, and at the age of twenty-four she was on her own.

Four years later, Garrett and Kate were married, on November 9, 1876. Local newspaper reports at the time imply a certain jovial familiarity with my grandfather and indicate that during his first four years of law practice he became a popular man about town, was politically active, had journalistic connections, and saved enough money to be what might be termed "comfortably situated." One report tells us that

> Mr. Stevens came within an ace of being nominated by the Democracy of this city for the Legislature. . . . As a lawyer Mr. Stevens is winning much esteem and his energy and application make him a useful attorney and citizen. As a speaker and writer he is brilliant and powerful. . . .

and, referring to Kate's maiden name, contains an outrageous pun:

> He has furnished his house complete from "Zeller" to "Garrett" too and we won't undertake to foretell what such a man may accomplish in the future.

According to the newspaper, the young couple moved into a house at 307 North Fifth Street; by the time my father was born they were living a few houses farther north, at 323, a typical brick row house, with front door and two windows on the first floor, and three windows on each of the second and third floors, all facing west. As my father wrote to Tom McGreevy in 1948,

> The house in which I was born and lived as a boy faced the west and wherever I have lived if the house faced any other way I have always been pulling it round on an axis to get it straight.

That same year he wrote a poem that includes the poignant line, "I live in Pennsylvania"; the significance of the subtitle of the second section of the poem, "The Westwardness of Everything," is enhanced when we learn that his room at home had been on the third floor front—facing west.

It is a large house and must have been ample for the growing Stevens family. The first child, Garrett Barcalow, Jr., was born on December 19, 1877, followed by my father on October 2, 1879, and then a third son, John Bergen, on December 9, 1880. An infant was stillborn in 1883 (and possibly two other children, who may have been twins, were born to the couple but did not survive), before the arrival of two daughters, Elizabeth, on July 19, 1885, and Mary Katharine, also known as Catharine, on April 25, 1889. All the children's names were family names except my father's; he once wrote a friend saying that he had been named after a prominent politician of the time, [George] Wallace Delamater, but it seems more likely that he was named for the minister who had married his parents, Wallace Rackcliffe, pastor of the First Presbyterian Church in Reading, where Kate was a member. Possibly he was named for both, each parent agreeing to the name for a different reason.

It is difficult to find information about my father's childhood, almost a hundred years later, but not impossible. From the Reading newspapers we learn that the month of his birth, October 1879, was a period of drought: by the 16th the receiving reservoir was empty. A yellow fever epidemic was raging in Pennsylvania and other eastern states, but an "era of general prosperity in business enterprises" was indicated under the heading, "A Glance at the Historical Events of the Waning Year." The first words we have from Wallace Stevens come only when he is fifteen, in letters he wrote home to his mother while spending part of the summer of 1895 in the country at Ephrata; his only reminiscence of childhood does not occur until 1909, in a letter to his future wife.

But even if we were willing to accept a gap of almost fifteen years, we would expect to find some information in school records; unfortunately a fire at the high school shortly after my father's graduation destroyed whatever was there. It is only when we turn to the newspapers that we at least find various lists of class standings and other data, which give an indication of his abilities as a student; we also find quotations from the orations he gave while in school, and some other pertinent information. As to what life was like, growing up at 323 North Fifth Street, we must take Wallace Stevens' later word for it:

> My father was quite a good egg; agreeable, active. He was of Holland Dutch descent, and his father and his grandfather had been farmers. We were all great readers, and the old man used to delight in retiring to the room called the library on a Sunday afternoon to read a five- or six-hundred page novel. The library was no real institution, you understand; just a room with some books where you could go and be quiet. My mother just kept house and ran the family. When I was younger I always used to think that I got my practical side from my father, and my imagination from my mother.

As I grew up our house was quiet too, but Sunday afternoons became devoted to listening to the New York Philharmonic orchestra concerts on the radio, and Saturday afternoons to opera, either on the radio or on records. At other times we read, and my mother "just kept house" and worked in the garden or played the piano. Like his father before him, mine did not entertain business associates at home; he needed a quiet place "to create a life of his own":

> His place, as he sat and as he thought, was not
> In anything that he constructed, . . .
>
> It was here. This was the setting and the time
> Of year. Here in his house and in his room,
> In his chair. . . .

That was important, "at least when the weather was bad."

My father's brother John was only a year younger than he was, and three years younger than the firstborn, Garrett. Their close ages made great companions of the boys, though Wallace (known as Pat) was probably resented at first by Garrett (known as Buck), and John probably hated being "the baby," as he was until his sister Elizabeth was born some months before his fifth brithday. Nevertheless they spent a good deal of time together, at least until Buck left Reading to enter Yale in the fall of 1895; the competition between Pat and John probably intensified at about that time, after my father missed a year of school and the brothers became classmates.

> We thought alike
> And that made brothers of us in a home
> In which we fed on being brothers,

and they were mischievous brothers as well. Once, at the Stevens farm, they discovered an old musket in the attic and paraded around with it rather recklessly, much to the dismay of their grandmother and a visiting cousin. When a street light on North Fifth Street shone into a neighbor's window, who then painted it green to reduce the glare, Pat would steal out at night, shinny up the pole, and scrape the paint off, thus awakening the neighbor, who would paint it again the next day. This cycle apparently was repeated several times before Pat was caught. Another story about the Stevens boys relates that when a steeple was being erected on a nearby church, they used to climb up and hide in the scaffolding. They would sit there, chewing tobacco, and at an opportune moment, often when a prominent citizen was passing below, would expectorate. According to the story, they were never caught. And, like all boys, they stole fruit from a neighbor's tree; when discovered, they called out as they ran away, "God helps those who help themselves!"

Their education, at least that of the two younger boys, did not begin in the public schools of Reading. They first entered a private kindergarten run by a French lady, which was located only three blocks from home, at the corner of Walnut and Sixth streets. Of the several kindergartens in Reading at the time, the only one that fits the description was run by a Mrs. Adele Ruenzler, who, with her husband, was also for some time a neighbor of the Stevenses on North Fifth Street. Her curriculum included both French and German, and it seems highly likely that Wallace's first exposure to those languages came when he was very young, long before the elementary courses he took in 1897–98, his first year at college. While an early knowledge of German might be expected, because it was a language commonly used in Reading, an equally early knowledge of French is a surprising possibility, which may have some bearing on his feeling for this language later in life. For example, in a book published in France in 1929, Stevens is quoted as saying:

> La légèreté, la grâce, le son et la couleur du français ont eu sur moi une influence indéniable et une influence précieuse.

In the *Adagia* he notes, "French and English constitute a single language"; and he enlarges on that in a letter to Bernard Heringman in 1953:

> I still think that English and French are the same language, not etymologically nor at sea level. But at sea level it is not possible to communicate with many people who speak English in English. You have to take my statement as applying only in the areas in which it would in fact apply. What a great many people fail to see is that one uses French for the pleasure that it gives.

Following kindergarten the boys went to one of the best parochial schools in town, which was attached to St. John's Evangelical Lutheran Church on Walnut Street. All the church records of the time are written in German, but presumably the school was run in English; unfortunately, no school records remain. For one year of his elementary school career my father was a student at the parochial school attached to St. Paul's

Lutheran Church in the Williamsburg section of Brooklyn, where his uncle was pastor, but again no records remain. When I visited the church I was struck by the multitude of men in the nearby streets who looked like bearded rabbis; a Lutheran church seemed out of place, and I thought of my father's line,

> Read, rabbi, the phases of this difference.

On Monday, September 12, 1892 (shortly before his thirteenth birthday), Wallace Stevens was enrolled at Reading Boys' High School as a member of Class D (the freshman class), taking the classical curriculum. The required courses included Latin, algebra, arithmetic, analytical grammar and composition, English classics, physical geography, and history of Greece. We do not have his grades for each course, but at the end of the year his rating was only 5.88 on a scale that ran from zero to ten. A long-standing rule was that pupils who did not attain a rating of at least 6.50 had to remain in the same class for another year. Writing to Byron Vazakas in 1937, my father referred to "having flunked a year because of too many nights out." But Louis Heizmann, who lived across the street on North Fifth, recalled that my father was seriously ill one year and was not promoted because he had missed a great deal of school. For whatever reason, when Pat reentered high school the following autumn it was with his brother John as a classmate. At the end of 1893–94 Pat made the honor roll in two of his courses: history of Greece and physical geography; John was not listed on the honor roll, but, after all, he had taken the courses only once.

Each year included three terms, and by the close of the second term in Class C, during 1894–95, John was catching up: his rating was 7.93, while Pat's was 8.37. Only one student in the class had a higher rating, and he also led the honor roll at the end of the year; by that time neither Stevens boy was included. It is hard to tell which courses caused their individual downfalls; the curriculum included Greek, Latin (Caesar), algebra, geometry, physics, English (with composition), and history of Rome.

A third Stevens boy was also missing from the honor roll that year, but nevertheless Garrett Barcalow Stevens, Jr., graduated as president of the class of 1895. It was his class that published the first newspaper ever issued at the high school, *Dots and Dashes*. Volume I, no. 1, appeared in January 1895; it included a column, "The Tattler," which the second number, published in February, claimed "will hereafter be an important department. . . ." Among the "Tattler" staff is listed, for Class C, "W. Stevens."

By the March issue, reporters had also been appointed from the Girls' High School, and "Tattler" had become a permanent feature, described as containing "breezy personals, suggestions, bright sayings, jokes, etc."

Unfortunately, none of the contributions is signed, and no articles else-where in the paper are attributed to "W. Stevens" during its existence, al-though he continues to be listed on the masthead as a member of the "reportorial staff" through the final issue in June 1895. My guess is that his first published writing appears somewhere in this school paper, though I would hesitate to claim any particular item as his. Nor do I understand why the paper was not continued by succeeding classes. But a clue as to what he may have contributed can be found in the memoirs of Edwin De Turck Bechtel, known as Ned, who was a member of the class of 1898 at the school, as recorded by his widow:

> Whenever Ned met Wallace Stevens, the poet, who had been a class ahead of him, they told uproarious tales of Skib's treatment of stupid pupils. Ned said that "at high school Wallace was a whimsical, un-predictable young enthusiast, who lampooned Dido's tear-stained adventures in the cave, or wrote enigmatic couplets to gazelles."

"Skib" was the high school principal, Martin E. Scheibner, a remarkable man, who was, according to Mrs. Bechtel,

> teacher of Greek, Latin and Moral Philosophy. Ned wrote of him: "He was an imaginative, well-educated Russian nobleman, who had fled because of some political offense against the Czarist regime. He cajoled us into translating Homer and Virgil at sight, and in his en-thusiasm introduced us to other classic authors."

The anonymous memorial note on my father in *The Century Association Year-Book* for 1956 includes a similar description of Scheibner, adding that "he had a lasting influence on Stevens," and I wouldn't be surprised if it had been written by Bechtel, whose friendship with my father, after some years in abeyance, was resumed during the 1940's.

At the end of Pat and John's third year together in high school, John stood second in his class; according to the local newspaper, Wallace Stevens was "absent from examination, sick," and so was not rated. The curriculum that year had consisted of courses in Greek (Xenophon), Latin (Virgil), geometry, rhetoric, composition, and (optionally) physics. At the end of the second term, in March, John had been ranked second in the class, and Pat third; only the ubiquitous Erle Meredith, who always came in first, was ahead of them. It was at this time that one of the local newspapers carried an announcement of a competitive examination of Class B students for the *Reading Eagle* Prize. This was an annual affair, and the prize was given for the best essay written on a subject announced by the principal only at the time of the examination, when the essays were then written under his supervision. Careful reading of the *Eagle* does not disclose the subject assigned; but my father won the contest, for two books that he never discarded bore the inscription "The Reading Eagle Prize for best essay in rhetorical contest of Class B, Boys High School, awarded to

Wallace Stevens, March, 1896." Even though not at the top of the honor roll, he was winning academic honors. One can imagine the strong rivalry between him and his brother John. Undoubtedly their father was also urging them to do well, for he must have been sorely disappointed during that winter when his eldest son flunked out of Yale after only four months' attendance.

The boys were all together that summer, visiting their grandmother Stevens at Ivyland; following the death of her husband, she had moved to this town where one of her daughters lived. In the fall, Garrett entered law school at Dickinson College in Carlisle, Pennsylvania; Pat and John returned to high school for their final year, in Class A. The curriculum included, under Greek, two terms on the *Iliad* and one on Herodotus; under Latin, two terms on Cicero and one on Livy or Sallust; English literature, American literature, elocution, and something called "Mental Philosophy." Of these, the one that seems to have had the most immediate effect on my father was elocution; it was offered in the first term, which began during the presidential campaign between Bryan and McKinley, when oratory seemed all-important. Harriet Monroe, who was present at the Democratic convention that summer in Chicago, described William Jennings Bryan as "a dark-haired young man of powerful build with a voice like the Bull of Bashan." That would hardly have applied to my father, but on December 22, 1896, he delivered an oration at the "Alumni night" exercises at the high school, which was well received according to the newspaper report:

> Wallace Stevens took the "Greatest need of the age," for his topic, and handled it exceeding well. . . . Rev. Dr. Gaul, of the judges, reported that they awarded the prize for oratory to Wallace Stevens. The judges were unanimous. Then the boys in the audience broke loose, clapped their hands and applauded. The winner is a son of Garrett B. Stevens and a favorite in the school, as was proven by the send-off his classmates gave him. When he received his medal he bowed his thanks. Then the boys gave him the school yell and a cheer.

The newspaper included the text of the oration in its account, noting that my father took "opportunity" as his answer to "the greatest need." Despite its schoolboy rhetoric, it was a convincing and imaginative piece of work for a young man barely seventeen years old.

Six months later, at graduation, he addressed the public again, with an oration entitled "The Thessalians." The newspaper reported that he "spoke as though he were a veteran speaker," and that his "patriotic sentiments were rewarded with loud acclamation." The commencement exercises were held in the Academy of Music on Thursday, June 24, 1897, and included "musical interludes"; the eclectic nature of the event is indicated by the fact that my father's patriotic oration was immediately preceded by a gavotte called "Fairy Bells."

Although neither John nor Pat received "honorable mention," both graduated "with merit," and looked forward to college: John had been accepted at the University of Pennsylvania, and Pat at Harvard. One more event in their high school lives remained, however. A week after the formal exercises, a graduation celebration was held at the Rajah Temple in Reading. The boys' mother was one of the "patronesses" for the "banquet and social." The menu consisted of "consommé, spiced oysters, sweetbread pâtés, deviled crabs, barbecue chicken, bread sticks, peas, French potatoes, chicken salad, assorted nuts, olives, fancy ices, berries, fancy cakes, coffee, lemonade." There was a concert by the Germania Orchestra, which also provided music for dancing at nine o'clock; one of the three "floor managers" was Wallace Stevens. We can wonder what his duties were; at any rate, the school year ended on a festive note.

When my father entered Harvard that fall, his father began writing to him regularly and presumably wrote to all his sons, though none of the other correspondences have been found. The taciturnity and reserve that typified Garrett Barcalow Stevens at home dissolved into real warmth in his letters, though they are often full of strictures and advice. Apparently my father arrived in Cambridge before the official opening day for the Class of 1901, September 30, 1897, because the first letter addressed to him there was postmarked September 27. It reports on my father's brothers, noting that Garrett "has some ideas now that would have made him good at New Haven"; as to John, it indicates that he was not sure he had made the right choice and was jealous of Wallace for being at Harvard; and it includes the warning that many "kick at the application essential to success." There was also a reminder:

> Grandmother Stevens finishes her 86th year on the 15th of Oct.—having been born in 1811. A congratulatory line from you—with any flower fern or fancy from any of our old Ghost haunted celebrities would tickle her. She preserves her fancy for these things—and a sprig of Ivy from Old South Church—would make her give you a ginger cake—though she loves you for my sake.

The letter reached my father at 54 Garden Street in Cambridge, a rooming house run by the daughters of Theophilus Parsons, who had been Dane Professor of Law at Harvard from 1848 to 1870. The ladies' clientele ranged from young instructors, through graduate students, to freshmen; the other two members of the class of 1901 who lived there in 1897–98 were Arthur Pope, who later became chairman of the art department at Harvard and director of the Fogg Museum (I still have a watercolor by Pope, which used to hang in the front hall of our home on Westerly Terrace in Hartford), and Harold Hastings Flower, who became a lawyer. This was to be my father's home for the next three years, at least during the school months, and there is a sense of his surroundings in a letter he wrote in 1948 to William Carlos Williams, on learning that Williams was to receive the Russell Loines Award in Poetry from the American Academy and National Institute of Arts and Letters.

> When I went to Cambridge Russell Loines was living in the attic of the house in which I was to live. This house was an old-fashioned dwelling. It was owned by three old maid daughters of Theophilus Parsons who in his day was a professor at the Law School. Loines had come to Harvard after leaving Columbia principally in order to become a member of Charles Eliot Norton's class in Dante. In those days Loines was very much of a poet, not that he wrote a great deal of poetry—but he was intensely interested in it and thought about it constantly. His room was lighted by a long slanting trap window in the roof. There was only one other window. It was heated by a little Franklin stove. It required about all the time of an old colored man to keep that and the other stoves and numerous grates in the house going. That room meant everything to Loines. I am not sure whether he remained in Cambridge to go to the Law School. In any event, the following spring he gave up his room and I took it. I kept it only a single year. Then I took a room below it on the second floor because there was more space and because it was more convenient.

A letter from Loines to his mother gives another glimpse of the atmosphere of the house. (The reference to "the Popes" includes Arthur and his brother, Herbert, a third-year law student; "Stevenson" is not a mistake for my father's name, but a mistake in spelling the name of Henry Thew Stephenson, class of 1898.)

> The Sabbath is well spent, and the last act must be a few lines to you, though they will doubtless cross your letter again. It has been a rainy, indoor day, fit for reading and writing letters. We had a beer and song night in this room last night, all the men in the house who were not away, and a very sociable two hours we made of it. The Popes favored us with a varied programme of topical songs. They have good voices. Flower and I read a while after the others left, and it was nigh one o'clock before I was in bed. The cheerful patter of the rain this morning was a pleasant accompaniment to sleep to, and I didn't stir my stumps till nearly half-past nine. After breakfast I sat down to write letters, then read Marcus Aurelius till lunch-time. Took Flower down to lunch with me. A nice boy, I'm getting very much attached to him. It's a good thing for him to have the serious minds of Stevenson and myself in the house.

While there is no mention of Wallace Stevens, he is there at the party; and in the house, possibly in that same room, as seen in a comment by Arthur Pope:

I recall especially his bursting out of his room to recite a new combination of words or a new metaphor that he had just invented, and to share his delight which was most infectious.

It is clear, from a letter his father wrote to him a month after school had opened, that he lived modestly during his first year away from home.

> Don't you want your exchequer replenished soon? You are doing well—I have no bill from anybody yet, neither from Bursar, nor anyone at Cambridge—and I suppose I had better get my bank account so heeled as to meet something in that line shortly. I hear of some fellows who have seen you and who say you seem very contented and quite determined to show good reports when the summing up is done, and who speak well of your surroundings and opportunities.
>
> If you find that you may have carved out too much work for yourself, be candid with your adviser; and do whatever strict application—with a fair regard for due exercise—can accomplish for one never knows, in these poor business times, whether *opportunities* ever return.
>
> Keep me advised of the state of your finances and of your health. I remember that Miss Parsons said that when one of her boys was ill or homesick that she coaxed them to eat with her—and you have said that she has extended her kind attentions. Does this mean that you smoke too strong tobacco?

It is hard to believe that he was restless, or dissatisfied, in his first year away from home—at Harvard, where he had wanted to be, and where the opportunities that he and his father valued were so abundant. Homesick, perhaps; but if that was the case then why did he not return to Reading occasionally? As he wrote to his friend Tom McGreevy in 1948:

> When I was a boy and used to go home from college, I used to feel as if it was going back to mother earth and I would return to college not only invigorated in the normal way but rather furiously set up and independent.

But perhaps it also made him feel independent not to go home at all during that first year, despite some poignant pleading at Christmastime from his father, who mentioned, "All the other Reading boys coming home." He may well have regretted his decision, for many years later he wrote to José Rodríguez Feo:

> Years ago when I was in Cambridge I decided to stay up there one Christmas because it was a pretty long trip to go home to Pennsylvania. Besides, I wanted to attend one of the receptions which Charles

Eliot Norton used to give every Christmas to students who remained in Cambridge. It was a very forlorn experience. When the time came to go to the reception I said to myself the hell with it and spent the time sitting by the fire.

He also wrote to his future wife, in 1909, saying that his "first year away from home, at Cambridge, made an enormous difference in everything." And my cousins have told me that when he finally did come home for the summer, he had assumed "airs" and a Harvard accent that were quite a source of amusement to the other members of the family.

One of the things that Wallace Stevens was doing in Cambridge was writing poetry, possibly under the influence of Russell Loines. The January issue of a magazine established the previous autumn at Reading Boys' High School, *The Red and Black*, led off with his first known published poem.

AUTUMN

Long lines of coral light
And evening star,
One shade that leads the night
On from afar.

And I keep, sorrowing,
This sunless zone,
Waiting and resting here,
In calm above.

The author is given only as "W.S., '97," but no one else in the class had those initials. As further evidence, the words "above" and "alone" look very much alike in my father's handwriting and may easily have been misread by the typesetter; "alone" would seem to be the appropriate last word for this poem, to rhyme with "zone."

Not all was "forlorn experience" in a "sunless zone," however. There were parties at 54 Garden Street, sometimes given by the landladies. In January we learn from one of my grandfather's letters:

Miss Parsons speaks approvingly of your manners and shows that she likes you—and wants to see you get along nicely—and mentions the little sociable which she has planned for your entertainment on the 21st; and I shall be tickled indeed to know how you tripped the light fantastic and passed bonbons as lunch. Oh—My—but these days away from the sight of some kid who'd bawl, "Look at Pat," are full of light and love and in the after life, when brooding hours hang their pall upon us—They seem like dreams. Happy indeed those who know how to make lasting friends with them.

But life was not all poetry and parties. Study was the major purpose of being at Harvard and, presumably, Wallace was diligent, for, as a special student, he could choose whatever courses he wished. One course that particularly pleased his father was government, which included "Leading Principles of Constitutional Law" in the second semester; he commented,

> Glad to see that you have taken up Government. For someday they will want to make you a school Director or Member of Councils. . . . Get all such books as are essential to a complete understanding of the subjects. There is a small publication on the U.S. Constitution that I used to know by heart when I was about 15 and it made a politician of me—for I hardly ever could get over the first line: "We, *the people,* of the United States in order to form a more perfect Union &c." For the darned thing had to be ratified by *separate* States and not by the whole people. But you cannot know too much on this subject since you are one day to be President &c &c.

My father was once asked to become a director of a private school, but he never became President; was it because he only received a "B" for the course instead of an "A"?

He did receive "A"s for the two English courses he took during his freshman year. One, English-A, "Rhetoric and English Composition," had several instructors, including Charles Townsend Copeland, who became a friend of my father's at some point during his college years, possibly then, and Pierre LaRose, a close friend of George Santayana's, who may have introduced Stevens to Santayana. But it has been impossible to determine which section my father was in. The other English course, no. 28, "History and Development of English Literature in Outline," also had several instructors; looking over the list it seems quite likely that my father drew Barrett Wendell, whose lectures at the Lowell Institute, published in 1891, certainly would have interested the young Stevens, particularly the one called "Elegance."

He also received an "A" for an elementary course in French prose and composition, a "B" for a similar course in German (the teacher, who was also my father's adviser, was Max Poll), and a "B" for an introductory course in medieval and modern European history. With this solid program, Garrett Barcalow Stevens had little to worry about when he wrote to his son saying that he wanted to educate

> a real live boy who means to crowd the men on the front bench in whatever place he goes—and who, at school, is getting his equipment ready.
>
> For life is either a pastoral dream—the ideal of the tramp, or superannuated village farmer—Or it is the wild hurly burly activity of the fellows who make the world richer and better by their being

in it: the fellows whose services make the rest furnish them subsistence and yield them honor, whose services are *always* needed.

As the year drew to a close, his father wrote again, anticipating Wallace's return to Reading for the summer.

> I have no particular job waiting for you—but after you get rested we will find something to assist in keeping afloat.

It has been said that Wallace Stevens worked as a reporter during his summer vacations, and this certainly seems possible because his father was a close friend of the editor of the *Reading Times*, Tom Zimmerman. But my father does not refer to such a job himself, and close reading of the *Times* does not disclose anything that might readily be attributed to him. Nevertheless, it is easy to imagine him, as a young man, participating to some extent in the activities of this story from the *Times*, headlined "At Kuechler's Roost."

> A party of members of the Reading Press club, to the number of about twenty, enjoyed through the courtesy of the United Traction company and the Mt. Penn gravity company a trip to "Kuechler's Roost" yesterday afternoon. The party left Sixth and Penn at 3.55 in a special car and the gravity station at 4.10, arriving at the point designated about 4.30. After greeting "Mine Host" Kuechler the party sat under the grape vines and enjoyed a good look at Dame Nature who put on one of her prettiest smiles. Games and other recreation was indulged in and 5 o'clock the party sat down under the spreading trees and enjoyed one of the most delicious suppers that could have been produced anywhere on earth. Pure mountain air is a splendid appetizer and hunger is a splendid chef and there were no dyspeptics round that table judging from the hearty laughter that greeted every bon mot, repartee or jolly good story, which like good wine, improves with age. It was noticed at the station that several members of the party had cork-screws, but they were not needed because all the bottles had patent stoppers. After feasting and enjoying the scenery and incidentally several good cigars, the party returned home shortly after 7 o'clock delighted with the trip to "the loveliest spot which mortal man has ever laid his eyes upon."

Kuechler's rustic shack on Mount Penn, surrounded by vineyards from which he made his own wine, was a popular summer resort; he also provided excellent meals, and often entertained local notables from Reading, including Tom Zimmerman and Garrett Barcalow Stevens. At Kuechler's death, some six years later, both men celebrated his establishment and his hospitality in verse; on the occasion just reported my father may well have been included in the group, whether or not he was working for the *Times*. If he ever did so, it seems likely that it was this summer, since his journal places him elsewhere in succeeding years.

II

It was after his return to college in the fall of 1898 that Wallace Stevens began to keep a journal. The label on the front of the stenographer's notebook that he used reads,

Wallace Stevens.
54 Garden street. Notes.

The first inside page reads,

Varii Imagorerum.
If I live I ought to speak my mind.
Jowett.

After a few pages that are missing, the journal resumes.

(Jowett: Life & Letters 165)

People will find out at last that there is something more valuable in the world than human life as they are beginning to find out that there is something more valuable than the abstract idea of freedom on the Slavery Question.

Benjamin Jowett, the English scholar and theologian, a student of Kant and Hegel, translator of Plato and Thucydides, had died in 1893 after serving for several years as vice-chancellor of Oxford University. At Harvard there was strong interest in his work at this time; there was even a "Jowett Club," although my father was not listed as one of its members. But certainly he shared that interest, as evidenced by the fact that he owned Jowett's translation of Plato's *Dialogues* and kept it throughout his life (it was sold by the family in 1959), and by the compatibility of the next journal entry.

VI. I find the first volume of Abbott and Campbell's "Life and Letters of Jowett" rather incoherent. As a matter of fact the material being less it should have been easier to classify and arrange than that of the large second volume which shows compactness and judgment despite its length. On page 153 Vol. II are some thoughts on poetry which I must put down here: "True poetry is the remembrance of youth, of love, of the noblest thoughts of man, of the greatest deeds of the past.—The reconciliation of poetry, as of religion, with truth, may still be possible. Neither is the element of pleasure to be excluded. For when we substitute a higher pleasure for a lower we raise men in the scale of existence.

How often he must have thought of this, how many years he must have mulled it over, consciously or not, before he used "It Must Give Pleasure" as the subtitle of the third part of "Notes Toward a Supreme Fiction," first published in 1942.

The journal continues, still referring to Jowett:

Of poetry which falls short of this high vocation he speaks with strong condemnation:—"It is, in Plato's language, a flattery, a sophistry, a strain, in which, without any serious purpose, the poet lends wings to his fancy and exhibits his gifts of language and metre—Such an one ministers to the weaker side of human nature; he idealizes the sensual; he sings the strain of love in the latest fashion; instead of raising men above themselves he brings them back to the 'tyranny of the many masters' from which all his life long he has been praying to be delivered."

In a leap forward in time, here is Stevens writing to Ronald Lane Latimer in 1936:

I dare say that the orderly relations of society as a whole have a poetic value, but the idea sounds like something for a choral society, or for Racine. It is hard to say what so vast an amplification would bring about. For my own part, I take such things for granted. Of course, this is merely one more romantic evasion in place of the thinking it out in which one ought to indulge. That remark just touches an old idea, and that is that poetry must limit itself in respect to intelligence. There is a point at which intelligence destroys poetry.

Thus, "thinking it out" is also a thinking back, to Jowett and beyond.

The next entries in the journal are the first ones to be dated, so presumably the Jowett entries were written earlier in the fall of 1898.

Dec. 4.
I wish that like Eugénie de Guérin I might write something about which I could say, "Ceci n'est pas pour le public; c'est de l'intime, c'est de l'âme, c'est pour un."

Dec. 8.

Last night I read several of Francis Turner Palgrave's "Essays on Art." The style is one of rather dainty thoughtfulness and sentiment. It shows that Palgrave was convinced of many ideals and was a man of delicate tastes. At the same time it shows no especial vigor or originality. It is a summing up of the best. Palgrave believes with Ruskin that the quality of an artist's work depends on the quality of his mind. Thus if a man have poetical depths his conceptions will be poetical also; and that, while designing, he may be engaged singly with technique, the finished painting will have something more than this mere technique—the poetical inspiration and feeling.

It may be of interest to compare that with excerpts from my father's essay "The Relations Between Poetry and Painting," written fifty-three years later, in 1951.

> Now, a poet looking for an analogy between poetry and painting and trying to take the point of view of a man whose center is poetry begins with a sense that the technical pervades painting to such a degree that the two are identified. This is untrue, since, if painting was purely technical, that conception of it would exclude the artist as a person. . . . The point is that the poet does his job by virtue of an effort of the mind.

Stevens had written to Latimer in 1936, saying, "There is a point at which intelligence destroys poetry," and in that same letter, noting that Latimer, as "The Alcestis Press," had published Stevens' *Ideas of Order* the previous year, is the following:

> You ask whether I should continue to write if no one but myself would ever see my work. There is no reason to believe that anyone will ever see any more of my work; you may change your mind about another book. Anyone who has known a number of poets must have been struck by their extraordinary egotism. There is not the slightest doubt that egotism is at the bottom of what a good many poets do. However, there are other theories about that: for instance, there is the theory that writing poetry is a sexual activity.

Note these lines from "Le Monocle de Mon Oncle" (1918):

> If sex were all, then every trembling hand
> Could make us squeak, like dolls, the wished-for words.

The letter to Latimer goes on:

> The truth is that egotism is at the bottom of everything everybody does, and that, if some really acute observer made as much of egotism as Freud has made of sex, people would forget a good deal about sex

and find the explanation for everything in egotism. I write poetry because I want to write it.

We are likely to give many incorrect explanations for what we do instinctively. It is very easy for me to say that I write poetry in order to formulate my ideas and to relate myself to the world. That is why I think I write it, though it may not be the right reason. That being so, I think that I should continue to write poetry whether or not anybody ever saw it, and certainly I write lots of it that nobody ever sees. We are all busy thinking things that nobody ever knows about. If a woman in her room is such an exciting subject of speculation, a man in his thoughts is equally exciting.

There is something similar in "Men Made Out of Words," written ten years after the letter, in 1946:

> What should we be without the sexual myth,
> The human revery or poem of death?
>
> Castratos of moon-mash—Life consists
> Of propositions about life. The human
>
> Revery is a solitude in which
> We compose these propositions, torn by dreams,
>
> By the terrible incantations of defeats
> And by the fear that defeats and dreams are one.
>
> The whole race is a poet that writes down
> The eccentric propositions of its fate.

As Marianne Moore once wrote my father, "poetry is best defined by writing it."

And, indeed, Stevens was writing it; his first poem to appear in *The Harvard Advocate* was in the issue of November 28, 1898.

WHO LIES DEAD

> Who lies dead in the sea,
>   All water 'tween him and the stars,
> The keels of a myriad ships above,
>   The sheets on a myriad spars?
>
> Who lies dead in the world,
>   All heavy of heart and hand,
> The blaze of a myriad arms in sight,
>   The sweep of a myriad band?

He wrote another poem on that date. From his journal:

Since I have been reading [Edward] Fitzgerald's letters, as well as Jowett's, and see how clearly they illustrate the man, I have felt a new attitude growing up in me. What was cold is warming up and as long as I feel that I am really sincere just so long I shall dare to be candid with myself.

A page and a half of the journal have been cut out here before the following:

Dec. 15.
Advocate appeared today with "Vita Mea." Written Nov. 28.

VITA MEA

With fear I trembled in the House of Life,
Hast'ning from door to door, from room to room,
Seeking a way from that impenetrable gloom
Against whose walls my strength lay weak from strife,
All dark! All dark! And what sweet wind was rife
With earth, or sea, or star, or new sun's bloom,
Lay sick and dead within that place of doom,
Where I went raving like the winter's wife.

"In vain, in vain," with bitter lips I cried;
"In vain, in vain," along the hall-ways died
And sank in silences away. Oppressed
I wept. Lo! through those tears the window-bars
Shone bright, where Faith and Hope like long-sought stars
First gleamed upon that prison of unrest.

17 December.

V.

SELF-RESPECT

Sun in the heaven,
Thou are the cause of my mirth,
Star in the evening
Thine is my province since birth;
Depths of the sky
Yours are the depths of my worth.

This poem apparently did not satisfy the young poet, for it has been erased, though still legible. There is no trace of I through IV, unless they are the verses referred to in a letter Wallace received from his father a few days before the Christmas recess was to begin.

Your lines run prettily in the Stanzas sent and we may soon expect the shades of Longfellow to seem less grey. I'll talk it over prosily with you when I see you.

This year Wallace did go home for Christmas, and he took his journal with him. The first entry written in Reading begins on the same page where "Self-Respect" has been erased.

VI.

December 27.   Reading, Pa.

Yesterday afternoon I took a walk alone over Mount Penn starting from Stony Creek and going through the trees to the Tower and down from that to the city, avoiding paths as much as possible. The edge of the woods from Stony Creek was very tangled with long, green, thorny tendrils of wild-roses. The ground at that foot of the hill was marshy in spots, elsewhere the leaves were matted and laid by the weight of a snow which had melted. Clusters of green ferns spread here and there. There were some brilliant spots of moss and every now and then I would start at a piece of dead white birch stirred by my foot which looked very much like a frozen snake. I found a large snail, some yellow dandelions and a weed of some sort—heavy—grey on the face but deep purple on the under side. At the top of the hill I sat down on a pile of rocks with my back to the city and my face towards a deep, rough valley in the East. The city was smoky and noisy but the country depths were prodigiously still except for a shout now and then from some children in the woods on the slope of the hill and once the trembling rumble of an unnatural train down on the horizon. I forget what I was thinking of—except that I wondered why people took books into the woods to read in summertime when there was so much else to be read there that one could not find in books. I was also struck by the curious effect of the sunlight on the tops of the trees while so much darkness lay under the limbs. Coming home I saw the sun go down behind a veil of grime. It was rather terrifying I confess from an allegorical point of view. But that is usually the case with allegory.

Apparently my father worked over this entry later, as several words and phrases have been revised in his hand; it also seems that he had originally intended to write a poem here, following "Self-Respect," as indicated by the number VI. But not until 1946, in "Credences of Summer," do we find the fitting lines:

> It is the natural tower of all the world,
> The point of survey, green's green apogee,
> But a tower more precious than the view beyond,
> A point of survey squatting like a throne

Axis of everything, green's apogee
And happiest folk-land, mostly marriage hymns.
It is the mountain on which the tower stands,
It is the final mountain. Here the sun,
Sleepless, inhales his proper air, and rests.
This is the refuge that the end creates.

It is the old man standing on the tower,
Who reads no book.

A line has been drawn across the page before the journal entry continues:

In the evening Lee Smith, [Ed] Livingood, Will Dunyan and I called on the Savages. We talked about Livingood's theory that a man who writes poetry, in many cases will be found to be a poor singer, that an artist may not enjoy poetry, that an orator may not enjoy music—in short that any emotion expressed in one form of art tends to exclude the possibility of its expression through any other.

Recalling Stevens' use of Dante Gabriel Rossetti's phrase "House of Life" in "Vita Mea," and his reference to Ruskin when discussing poets and painters, it is possible to imagine his part in the discussion, since Rossetti was both poet and painter and had Ruskin as a patron.

He did not pick up his journal again until after his return to Cambridge, and we might note here the courses that he was taking during his second year. Though it appears unlikely from the verses he wrote, he received an "A" for English 22, composition, which was taught by Barrett Wendell, among others. There were two half-year courses in English literature as well, which ranged from the death of Dryden (1700) to the publication of the *Lyrical Ballads* at the end of the eighteenth century. One of the two instructors in the second term was Charles Townsend Copeland, and if my father had not met him before then, this is when they probably became friends, for "Copey" did not teach any other English courses that my father took. It was, incidentally, only for that second term that Wallace garnered an "A," having received a "B" for the first semester, which ended with the death of Swift. He also took an elementary course in economics and one in European history (since the middle of the eighteenth century); for these he received his lowest grade at Harvard: "C" in each; he did better in French literature (Corneille to Balzac) and composition, for which he received a "B," and a German course, "Goethe and His Time," for which he received a "B+."

He was apparently dissatisfied with his journal in January, for the entries are spotty. A page begins: "Verse is not poetry: it is the vehicle to poetry." Beneath this a line has been drawn and, beneath that, the date, "Jan. 9—1899," has been entered. The rest of the page has been cut out.

The next page begins, "Jan. 18. Poetry is Man." The rest of the page has been cut out. The following page begins, "Jan. 21—"; again the rest has been cut out, as is the case with the next page, headed "Jan. 24." The page following that one opens:

> Do not direct your efforts toward some alien perfection when it happens to agree with your own conviction & ideal.

Beneath that sentence a line has been drawn, and the entry below the line has a good many words crossed out, so that what was originally written is illegible. What remains reads:

> 24. I must endeavor to get at Goethe's philosophy—Livingood is familiar with a great deal of it already—consciously or unconsciously. It will be a great pleasure to generations who become more and more intimately acquainted with his work to become more and more deeply interested in the human being. As a genius he differs from Shakespere in being a nucleus for his productions—Shakespere being a non-entity about which cluster a great many supreme plays and poems.

> 24. Labor conquers everything except itself.

The page following that is headed "Jan. 30. Song," but what followed has been excised, and there are no entries during February in this notebook.

In January he had had a short story, "Her First Escapade," published in *The Harvard Advocate;* his next contribution, a typically sophomoric attempt at autobiography, gives an idea of what might have been in his journal if he had not temporarily abandoned it.

A DAY IN FEBRUARY.

The warm afternoon beat against his windows courageously, and his face was hidden in a book whose leaves were following one another to the end. He was unconsciously enjoying the sun upon his back, though he probably imputed his good humor to the philosophy he was reading, and was quite unaware that, after all, any philosophy was a sin on such a day. When he first came to college, he had been tall and fresh, but, as he piled up theme upon theme and thesis upon thesis, a slight bend became noticeable in his shoulders, and he felt empty and unambitious; for the few steps that carried him every day to two or three recitations were not to be compared with the walks he had taken at home, alone on the roads, free and high spirited.

But somehow his former buoyancy would occasionally assert itself, like a clear spot in the confusion of his studies, and then he would wonder at the change that had taken place—the change from his old life of poetic impulse to this new existence of libraries and lectures. And when the philosophy had run out, and the book had been put on his shelves, he thrust his hands into his pockets and walked to the window. The afternoon was still full and diaphanous, and he stood there longer, perhaps, than he had intended; for he knew that whatever time he gave to the mere gazing at things was lost to Science and his own Wisdom.

It was unaccountable, but suddenly he threw the window open. A deep stream of sweet air poured into his room, suffusing him with a pleasure in it and a delight which was downright treachery to his courses. He was thinking to himself that this was one of those first warm days, premonitions of Spring, which stray into the calendar now and then despite the weather bureau; and with that thought came others of a certain hill in Pennsylvania, of a certain grove of maples, and of a certain house which he knew as home on vacations and in summer time. He also thought that now would be a good time to rest an hour and be himself again. But the wind that was so sweet to him was gone. It had blown into the dry corners, rustled the curtains, passed over his pictures, and turned over the things on his table—the things which had frightened and driven it away, things covered with economic calculations and mathematical designs. That made him remember that it was still winter.

But winter or no winter, he found that his work was disagreeable and he lost faith in it. What did he care to know of the religion of the mound builders, or of the antiquity of a legend which was not worth the telling? Of what interest to him was it to know the technical kind of reasoning that had induced Caesar to adorn Rome with theatres, when he felt the throbbing in his blood of new life, new love? His industry seemed worthless so far as he himself was concerned; it seemed like the building of a house of cards when what he desired were castles in Spain. It is not to be wondered at, therefore, that this tall, eager form that had been buried in philosophy a moment ago, suddenly buttoned up its coat, threw on a cap, and started out of doors.

On the street all the old fervor came back into his blood, his face, his gait. He swung along under the trees, feeling as though he had accomplished some meritorious deed, like a knight in street clothes. He saw fellows with whom he had been accustomed to review History and compose English, and he nodded in a high, exuberant way. When he found the houses getting thin, he turned back again, his eyes bright, his cheeks burning. The work he had left seemed shallow, and he resolved that after this he would be less Faust than Pan. Then, when he was in his room again, he pitched a stack of writing into a waste basket and, bowing to an imaginary person, he said: "Ah, old man, old fellow, you don't know, you haven't any idea how glad I am to meet you again."

Another version of this, far from sophomoric, may be seen in these lines from "Extracts from Addresses to the Academy of Fine Ideas," written over forty years later (1940):

> On an early Sunday in April, a feeble day,
> He felt curious about the winter hills
> And wondered about the water in the lake.
> It had been cold since December. Snow fell, first,
> At New Year and, from then until April, lay
> On everything. Now it had melted, leaving
> The gray grass like a pallet, closely pressed;
> And dirt. The wind blew in the empty place.
> The winter wind blew in an empty place—
> There was that difference between the and an,
> The difference between himself and no man,
> No man that heard a wind in an empty place.
> It was time to be himself again, to see
> If the place, in spite of its witheredness, was still
> Within the difference. He felt curious
> Whether the water was black and lashed about
> Or whether the ice still covered the lake. There was still
> Snow under the trees and on the northern rocks,
> The dead rocks not the green rocks, the live rocks. If,
> When he looked, the water ran up the air or grew white
> Against the edge of the ice, the abstraction would
> Be broken and winter would be broken and done,
> And being would be being himself again,
> Being, becoming seeing and feeling and self,
> Black water breaking into reality.

The March 13 *Advocate* included a poem that may first have been a part of the journal; the next page after the one headed "Jan. 30. Song" is headed "March 1. Song," with a circled comment, "weak." The rest of the page has been cut out, but possibly a version of the published "Song" had been written there.

> She loves me or loves me not,
>   What care I?—
> The depth of the fields is just as sweet
>   And sweet the sky.
>
> She loves me or loves me not,
>   Is that to die?—
> The green of the woods is just as fair,
>   And fair the sky.

At this point my father began to keep a second notebook. Titled on the cover, "English 22—Long Theme—2nd hf-yr Wallace Stevens, Sp." in ink, and below that "Notes." in pencil, the first inside page reads "1899 & 1900." The first entry, which has a page to itself, reads:

> "But my flag is not unfurl'd
> On the Admiral-staff, and to philosophise
> I dare not yet"

Two pages following that one are missing—perhaps a false start at the "long theme," which appears to be a series of sonnets—before coming to a page dated February 22, where the following sonnet appears; it was published five months later in *The Harvard Monthly* over the pseudonym John Morris, 2nd.

I.

> I strode along my beaches like a sea,
> The sand before me stretching firm and fair;
> No inland darkness cast its shadow there
> And my long step was gloriously free.
> The careless wind was happy company
> That hurried past and did not question where;
> Yet as I moved I felt a deep despair
> And wonder of the thoughts that came to me.
>
> For to my face the deep wind brought the scent
> Of flowers I could not see upon the strand;
> And in the sky a silent cloud was blent
> With dreams of my soul's stillness; and the sand,
> That had been naught to me, now trembled far
> In mystery beneath the evening star.

The second sonnet, dated February 23 in the notebook, was not published until May 1900, when it appeared in *East & West*, a "Monthly Magazine of Letters," founded at Columbia University in New York.

II.

> Come, said the world, thy youth is not all play,
> Upon these hills vast palaces must rise,
> And over this green plain that calmly lies
> In peace, a mighty city must have sway.
> These weak and murmuring reeds cannot gainsay
> The building of my wharves; this flood that flies

Unfathomed clear must bear my merchandise,
And sweep my burdens on their seaward way.

No cried my heart, this thing I cannot do,
This is my home, this plain and water clear
Are my companions faultless as the sky—
I cannot, will not give them up to you.
And if you come upon them I shall fear,
And if you steal them from me I shall die.

The third sonnet, dated February 24, apparently never was published, as perhaps the poet may later have wished about those that were, with their adolescent echoings of Keats and Shelley.

III.

When I think of all the centuries long dead,
The cities fall'n to dust, the kingdoms won
And in a moment lost again, the sun
That in a high and cloudless heaven led
Sad days of vanished beauty ere they fled,
Sad days so far and fair to muse upon,—
The earth grown grey and covered with the run
And progress of her years' unending tread.

Then my youth leaves me, and the blood
Leaps in its ardor like a flood.
Others with hot and angry pride, I cry,
Others in their thin covered dust may lie
And give their majesty to some pale bud
But not—if strength of will abides—not I.

The next page has been cut out of the notebook, and presumably had on it the first version of a fourth sonnet, which, as my father notes in April, had originally been written on February 25. The fifth sonnet, dated February 27, is on the following page; like the third, it never appeared in print.

V.

The rivers flow on idly in their light
The world is sleeping, and the golden dower
Of heaven is silent as a languorous flower
That spreads its deepness on the tender night.
The distant cities glimmer pale and bright
Each like a separate far and flaring bower

Noiseless and undisturbed in resting power
Filled with the semblance of a vaster might.

Upon this wide and star-kissed plain, my life
Is soon to feel the stir and heat of strife.
Let me look on then for a moment here
Before the morn wakes up my lust for wrong,
Let me look on a moment without fear
With eyes undimmed and youth both pure and strong.

The next sonnet, which Harold Bloom has called "pure Shelley," was published almost immediately, in the March issue of *The Harvard Monthly*. It is dated "March 1 & 2" in the notebook.

VI.

If we are leaves that fall upon the ground
To lose our greenness in the quiet dust
Of forest-depths; if we are flowers that must
Lie torn and creased upon a bitter mound
No touch of sweetness in our ruins found;
If we are weeds whom no one wise can trust
To live an hour before we feel the gust
Of Death, and by our side its last keen sound

Then let a tremor through our briefness run,
Wrapping it in with mad, sweet sorcery
Of love; for in the fern I saw the sun
Take fire against the dew; the lily white
Was soft and deep at morn; the rosary
Streamed forth a wild perfume into the light.

Again showing a strong Shelleyan influence, the seventh sonnet, dated March 7, was included in the April 10 issue of *The Harvard Advocate*.

VII.

There shines the morning star! Through the forlorn
And silent spaces of cold heaven's height
Pours the bright radiance of his kingly light,
Swinging in revery before the morn.
The flush and fall of many tides have worn
Upon the coasts beneath him, in their flight
From sea to sea; yet ever on the night
His clear and splendid visage is upborne.

Like this he pondered on the world's first day,
Sweet Eden's flowers heavy with the dew;
And so he led bold Jason on his way
Sparkling forever in the galley's foam;
And still he shone most perfect in the blue
All bright and lovely on the hosts of Rome.

Slowing the pace a bit, the next sonnet is not dated until March 12, and the notebook indicates that it was revised on March 17, and again on March 30. The revisions still did not bring it up to a satisfactory level and it was not published.

VIII.

The soul of happy youth is never lost
In fancy on a page; nor does he dream
With pitiful eyes on tender leaves that turn
With mournful history of beings crossed
In their desires; nor is he rudely tossed
By energy of tears for the warm beam
Of endless love that doth already seem
All cold and dead with Time's destroying frost.

For his own love is better than the tale
Of other love gone by; and he doth feel
As fair as Launcelot in rustling mail,
Hard-driven flowers bright against his steel,
Passing through gloomy forests without fear
To keep sweet tryst with still-eyed Guenevere.

The ninth sonnet, also dated March 12, has become the most famous of the sequence, since it is the one to which George Santayana wrote a sonnet in response, after reading it. It was first published in *The Harvard Monthly* for May 1899.

IX.

Cathedrals are not built along the sea;
The tender bells would jangle on the hoar
And iron winds; the graceful turrets roar
With bitter storms the long night angrily;
And through the precious organ pipes would be
A low and constant murmur of the shore
That down those golden shafts would rudely pour
A mighty and a lasting melody.

And those who knelt within the gilded stalls
Would have vast outlook for their weary eyes;
There, they would see high shadows on the walls
From passing vessels in their fall and rise.
Through gaudy windows there would come too soon
The low and splendid rising of the moon.

The next four sonnets, written March 27, March 30, April 4, and April 12, were not successful, nor were they published.

X.

Yet mystery is better than the light
That comes up briefly in the gloom, and goes
Before it well defines the thing it shows,
Leaving it doubly darkened; and the sight
That seeks to pierce a never-ending flight
Of dim and idle visions had best close
Its many lids; the heavy-petalled rose
Lies still and perfect in the depth of night.

So youth is better than weak, wrinkled age
Looking with patience on a single beam
Of fancied morn; and no disturbing gleam
Most futile and most sinister in birth
Mars the high pleasure of youth's pilgrimage
Passing with ardor through the happy earth.

XI.

I found it flaming in the scarlet rose.
Hast thou not seen? I found it in the bed
Of blue forgetmenots. Hast thou not read?
And in the bluer bed of ocean goes
Its mystery forever, yet who knows?
And down the yellow valleys to the head
Of Earth, and in the breast of youth, and dead
Drear winter breaking-up in spring-time snows—

In these I found it—life's whole history—
Nor cared to guess what lay beyond, as though
This were the last—as though the mystery
Of rose-depths, or the sea, or earth, or slow
Transforming winter ended here—and did
Not point to things in greater mystery hid.

XII.

I sang an idle song of happy youth,
A simple and a hopeful roundelay
That thoughtlessly ran through a sweet array
Of cadences, until I cried "Forsooth,
My song, thou art unjewelled and uncouth,
I will adorn thee like the month of May,
With loveliness and fervor; and thy way
Shall be a spiritual reach for Truth."

Ah well, my youth is ending, and the one,
Effaceless memory of its eager years
Is that I also strove to sing what none
Have sung; and that when I had calmed my fears,
Laid by my hopes and viewed what I have done,
My weary eyes were filled with bitter tears.

XIII.

How sweet it is to find an asphodel
Along the margin of the winter sea;
More dear than any idle pearl could be,
Cast up in beauty of imperfect spell
From ruins of some olden caravel.
Because of it the world grows fair to me
And like it I could live forever free
From bitter thought of earthly parable.

Dear youth, thou also art a pleasant flow'r,
A tall, fair figure in the sullen plain,
With beauty rising in thee hour by hour—
Shining about thee like long-ripened grain;
And at thy feet with undiminished pow'r
Roll the huge waters of an endless main.

The next sonnet clearly indicates that my father had been reading the *Rubáiyát of Omar Khayyám*, as noted by Robert Buttel and confirmed by the fact that he had acquired a copy of the book the previous autumn. Written on April 13, 1899, the sonnet appeared in *The Harvard Advocate* the following spring over the pseudonym R. Jerries.

XIV.

And even as I passed beside the booth
Of roses, and beheld them brightly twine

To damask heights, taking them as a sign
Of my own self still unconcerned with truth;
Even as I held up in hands uncouth
And drained with joy the golden-bodied wine,
Deeming it half-unworthy, half-divine,
From out the sweet-rimmed goblet of my youth;

Even in that pure hour I heard the tone
Of grievous music stir in memory,
Telling me of the time already flown
From my first youth. It sounded like the rise
Of distant echo from dead melody,
Soft as a song heard far in Paradise.

On April 14 the journal notes, "No. IIII written Feb. 25 & Mar. 30. Replaced by this," before going on to the last sonnet of the series. Like most of the others, it was not published by Stevens.

Through dreary winter had my soul endured
With futile striving and grave argument
Brief sunless days of bitter discontent,
Until, at length, to all its griefs inured
It ceased from idle turmoil, and secured
A new and rich repose; each hour was blent
With easeful visions of the Orient
And cities on uncertain hills immured.

It seemed as though upon a mournful world
A pure-voiced robin had sent forth a ray
Of long-impending beauty, to allay
Her wild desire; as though her deep unrest
Was in a moment's minstrelsy uphurled
Sweet-startling from her heavy-laden breast.

No wonder Stevens wrote to Donald Hall, in 1950, "Some of one's early things give one the creeps." But even though the sonnets are derivative and sentimental, they are technically competent; if they were submitted as his "long theme" for English 22, as I suspect they were, we should remember that he received an "A" for the course.

Four pages have been cut out of the notebook following the last sonnet, and the next page carries a journal entry dated the following summer. It seems appropriate, then, to return to the first notebook, which he took up again on March 18. The page is headed with that date, followed by a circled comment, "silly," and, after the first line of what follows, a circled "very."

You say this is the iris?
And that faery blue
Is the forget-me-not?
And that golden hue
Is but a heavy rose?
And these four long-stemmed blooms
Are purple tulips that enclose
So and so many leaves?
Their names are tender mumbling
For you who know
Naught else; through my own soul
Their wonders nameless go.

An interesting preface to Stevens' use of "forgetmenots" and roses, or "rose-depths," in Sonnet XI.

III

A month or so earlier, at the beginning of the second semester, Stevens had been appointed to the staff of *The Harvard Advocate*. One of his colleagues, Murray Seasongood, provides the first known description of my father from one of his contemporaries:

> I used to see him rather frequently and sometimes we would take long walks together. He was always very modest, simple and delightful . . . a large, handsome, healthy, robust, amiable person, with light curly hair and the most friendly of smiles and dispositions. To keep up with his rolling, vigorous gait and animated, frank and amusing talk, while striding alongside of him was both a feat and a privilege. He was modest, almost diffident, and very tolerant and kindly towards, alike, his colleagues and contributors of manuscripts. Even then a magnificent craftsman, he could write noble sonnets, odes and mighty lines in the traditional forms of poetry.

The modesty is shown in a comment my father made fifty-five years later during an interview:

> I suppose I wrote some poetry of an elementary sort in my younger days, but nothing that has any significance. When I was at Harvard I used to write an occasional poem for the *Advocate* and often sign some fictitious name. You see, I was the editor of the magazine, and often one had to furnish much of the material himself.

He did not become editor until the following year, but at the time he joined the staff his father wrote to congratulate him.

> Glad to hear from you and to learn that you had been given a place on the *Advocate*. The feeling that what one publishes is more important than what one thinks or writes will be with you to compress your likings into what your readers will like—and the experience will be a good one. It is all right to talk gush and nonsense, but to see it in cold type don't seem worth while; and yet—there will be but

half a column in the *Advocate* if you suppress all that is not brilliant and philosophical—

It was in a philosophical, Paterian vein that Stevens made his next journal entry, on March 28.

> Art for art's sake is both indiscreet and worthless. It opposes the common run of things by simply existing alone and for its own sake, because the common run of things are all parts of a system and exist not for themselves but because they are indispensable. This argument is apparent to the reason but it does not convince the fancy—which in artistic matters is often the real thing to be dealt with. Take therefore a few specific examples, such as the sun which is certainly beautiful and mighty enough to withstand the trivial adjective artistic. But its beauty is incidental and assists in making agreeable a monotonous machine. To say that stars were made to guide navigators etc. seems like stretching a point; but the real use of their beauty (which is not their excuse) is that it is a service, a food. Beauty is strength. But art—art all alone, detached, sensuous for the sake of sensuousness, not to perpetuate inspiration or thought, art that is mere art—seems to me to be the most arrant as it is the most inexcuseable rubbish.
>
> Art must fit with other things; it must be part of the system of the world. And if it finds a place in that system it will likewise find a ministry and relation that are its proper adjuncts. Barrett Wendell says in his "Principles" that we cannot but admire the skill with which a thing be done whether it be worth doing or not. His opinion is probably just if he limits the pronoun "we" to mean rhetoricians and the like. What does not have a kinship, a sympathy, a relation, an inspiration and an indissolubility with our lives ought not, and under healthy conditions could not have a place in them.

In 1941, in "The Noble Rider and the Sound of Words," Stevens noted some observations made by the French philosopher Charles Mauron, in his *Aesthetics and Psychology*. He also annotated his copy of Mauron's book, and there is an affinity of thought in those notes with the journal entry he had made some forty years earlier.

> A work of art is inactive . . . and constitutes a stimulus, which we enjoy for its own sake, since it entails no reaching beyond the enjoyment of the sensation it provokes. Thus the basis of the aesthetic emotion is the aesthetic attitude; contemplation without any idea of making use of the object of contemplation.
>
> Art sets out to express the human soul.
>
> Originality is an accentuation, through sensibility, of differences perceived.

The perception of differences is agreeable in itself.

The sensibility of the artist makes an original being of him, *un amoureux perpétuel* of the world that he contemplates and thereby enriches. He adds to the pleasures of the world his own.

Just as the artist is immobile before nature, so he is immobile before his own nature, at least enough so [as] to control it: not wholly merely to live his state of mind, nor wholly merely to pause and taste it; . . . and to accomplish this he must control his instincts.

The artist's task . . . to discover the possible work of art in the real world, then to extract it.

In his essay Stevens said of the poet's role that it was

to help people to live their lives. [The poet] has had to do with whatever the imagination and the senses have made of the world. He has, in fact, had to do with life except as the intellect has had to do with it and, as to that, no one is needed to tell us that poetry and philosophy are akin.

The next entry in the journal, again written on March 28, 1899, changes the mood:

I am uncomfortable in the spring of the year, and just as Charles Lamb spent the morning in anticipation of the genial evening, so I drag through March and April relying for my reward in May and June.

Could he have been in that same mood when he used the phrase, "April here and May to come," in "The Greenest Continent" (1936)?

Apparently after re-reading his journal later, he noted at the head of the next page: "On this 28th of September 1900 they all seem silly & immature; but I am unwilling to destroy them." He then drew a line through the first two sentences of the next entry, once more dated March 28.

I find that in the early part of this book I have written that I could never be a great poet except in mute feeling. This is a silly and immature observation. If my feelings or anybody's are so great that they would make great poetry, be sure that they are great poetry and that he who feels them is a great poet. Many of us deceive ourselves thus that we are glorious but mute. I doubt it. Glory peeps through the most trifling emotions; and so given great feelings and the glory attached to them will burst out of itself unaided and uncontrolled. Of course, in the first place, prosaic people do not have poetical feelings; but that is not part of the discussion. I am speaking of the fellows who feel sweet but small pains and curse the consequent ineffectiveness that retards the advance of good work.

The next entry was not written until almost two months later. During that interval a short story, "Part of His Education," appeared in an April issue of the *Advocate*, and Stevens became a member of the Signet Society, as we learn from a letter to him from his father.

> Just what the election to the *Signet signifies* I have no *sign*. It is *signi*ficant that your letter is a *signal* to *sign* another check that you may *sigh* no more. I suppose you thus win the privilege to wear a seal ring or a badge with the picture of a *Cygnet* on it—to distinguish you from commoner geese, or it may be you can con*sign* all studies de*signed* to cause re*signa*tion, to some as*sign* port where they will trouble you no more.
>
> You will know more about it when you have ridden the goat of initiation, and kneaded the dough enclosed.
>
> Keep hammering at your real work however my boy—for a fellow never knows what's in store—and time misspent now counts heavily.

No mention of the Signet Society appears in the journal, however.

May 21. Subject for a sketch: A crowd of children in a park dressed with pink, white, red, blue, in fact all colors of paper and flags for a holiday. Queen Mab and the faeries. Rain comes up and a drop falls on Queen Mab's cheek, they huddle in tears under trees which drip with the rain. Clouds clear. Rainbow. Sad procession home with light, pleasant good-heartedness of the sky as a contrast to their little, bedraggled selves.

May 23. The Scope of College Stories. How they begin "The wind *was* blowing against the building" etc. How they end "Well," she said with a smile, "suppose it was I."

Poetry and Manhood: Those who say poetry is now the peculiar province of women say so because ideas about poetry are effeminate. Homer, Dante, Shakespeare, Milton, Keats, Browning, much of Tennyson—they are your man-poets. Silly verse is always the work of silly men. Poetry itself is unchanged.

After a great poet has just died there are naturally no great successors because we have been listening rather than singing ourselves.

One more story, a very slight one entitled "The Higher Life," appeared in the *Advocate* before the year was over and Wallace returned to Pennsylvania for the summer, taking his journal with him.

Reading, Pa.

June 20.

There is one advantage in being here. Instead of the bad photographs of Tintoret and Reynolds or the reproductions of Hermes and Venus you have the real thing: green fields, woods etc.

[Ed] Livingood says that I would be surprised at the amount of learning possessed by the English poets. Not at all. But I doubt if he can explain the reason for their acquiring that learning. He thinks they did it as a part of their trade. On the contrary I think they used study as a contrast to poetry. The mind cannot always live in a "divine ether." The lark cannot always sing at heaven's gate. There must exist a place to spring from—a refuge from the heights, an anchorage of thought. Study gives this anchorage: study ties you down; and it is the occasional willful release from this voluntary bond that gives the soul its occasional overpowering sense of lyric freedom and effort. Study is the resting place—poetry, the adventure.

One ought not to hoard culture. It should be adapted and infused into society as a leaven. Liberality of education does not mean illiberality of its benefits.

Perhaps he was reading Dr. Johnson at the time; a note he made next to the "The Rambler" entry for July 9, 1751, seems appropriate to insert here:

The Harvard System keeps one closer to the aims of life and therefore to life itself. But in many other cases this is probably true. When one accomplishes a set task or finishes a prescribed course of studies the feeling is natural that one has finished the only worthy task and the one accepted course of studies. Freedom of choice gives liberality to learning.

The next entry in the journal is headed "Wily's, Berkeley, Pa."

July 7.

Came here yesterday morning. Cloudy and therefore somewhat uninteresting for a few hours, but I walked about the old place getting reacquainted. In the evening I walked slowly with a pipe up the hill to the West of the house toward the turnpike. The sunset was not very fine. I thought of a great many things such as that no one paints Nature's colors as well as Nature's self—this led on to a great deal more, all of which finally ended in literary applications. In the afternoon I had been reading R. L. Stevenson's "Providence & the Guitar" and on this walk I felt thoroughly how carefully the story had been written and how artificial it was. Leon Berthelini is a paper doll and entirely literary, partly illustrating the difference between literary creations and natural men. Out in the open air with plenty of time and space I felt how different literary emotions were from natural feelings. On the top of the hill I stood for about a quarter of an hour watching whatever color could break through the clouds, listening to the robins and other birds. I returned to the house almost as slowly as I had left it. And out in the corner of the flower-garden I met John Wily the owner of "Golddust" and a teamster who "never had a match." He talked and talked and talked. My back almost broke listening but he had had such a prosaic list of experiences which he told with such a perfect prose sincerity that I had to let him go on. "Oh Mighty!" was his favorite oath. For several winters he had sold a powder for the polishing of metals, tin cups and the like. He said that he could talk people to sleep in five hours! "Oh Golly! Them men was weaker th'n weak. My tongue was like the Ba'm of Gilead, it was like milk 'n honey." He then switched off to his abilities as a prophet. The sun had come out in the west and made the rain in the air glisten as it fell. We were talking under a lilac bush which was almost as high as a tree and so were keeping dry. He said that for the sun to shine when it was raining was regarded by the Germans as a sure sign that it would rain for three days following; but, he continued, the only signs that he himself regarded as infallible were the little dust whirlwinds from the south—those from the north might fail but from the south—Oh Mighty! After much more chatter we went into the office of the Mill and through the dirt and grime of the windows could see the fading of the last rose clouds—at least I could. I don't know whether the rest cared about them. The conversation turned to farm implements, so I lit my pipe and watched it grow dark. A little farmer's boy on my left was playing with a hound. I felt that I was making friends without half trying. I finally returned to the house, heard Sally play a few pieces which she admired: "The Shepherd Boy," by Wilson, Gottschalk's "Last Hope," "Heart's Desire" by somebody or other & Beethoven's "Sylphs." They were very pleasant. At ten I went to bed with thoughts of John still chattering in my head.

Those thoughts of John Wily resulted in a sketch that was published in the *Advocate* a year later, the first part of "Four Characters." Whether Stevens wrote it later on that year, or possibly the same evening as the journal entry, is not essential to know; it is interesting to see how he presented the material for publication, as opposed to his private notes:

As a horseman I never hed a match. My ol' horse, Gold Dust— eh? You remember her? Well, she *was* a horse. Never hed a match either—because I knew jes' how to treat her. Why, sir, I've been about horses ever since I was born. I remember jes' as well as not, as though 't was only the other day, how my ol' Gold Dust slipped once. Up she went an' down she came an' I lay in the gutter. Oh, Golly! I jumps up an' finds the blood pourin' out my forehead into my eyes, an' then I staggers to a tree an' sinks down on the curbstone. Oh, Golly! I set there and watched the men tryin' to get ol' Gold Dust to her feet. One of 'em gives her a kick; another says, "Oh," he says, "Get up, you damn horse." But ol' Gold Dust lies there on her side, her breath scattering the dust about her nostrils. By 'n by I jumps up an' gets on my knees in front of her and lifts her head in my hands an' says, "Ol' Gold Dust, don't you know me?" Oh, Golly, I plead with that horse. "Don't you know me, ol' Gold Dust?" I says. I patted him, oh, jes' like a little lamb. "Don't you know me?" I kept askin' an' askin'. An' my tongue was like the Ba'm of Gilead. You know in the winter when I can't do nothin' else I sell powder for polishin' medals, tin cups an' the like. Why, I can get a tin cup so bright—I did once. I went to Andy Wiggses' an' called his wife out on the porch. I asked her if she had an' ol' black tin cup. Oh, Mighty, how she looked! Then she laughed an' hunted one for me in a closet. Well, I polished an' polished an' held the cup up to her an' finally the sun struck it an' it shone like sliver. But Wiggses is Wiggses an' I had my trouble for my reward. My tongue's like the Ba'm of Gilead, but, Mighty! you can't sell anything to Wiggses. What! ol' Gold Dust? Oh, he's been dead ten years now, I s'pose. He died right there in the street that day. He never got up. Why once—"

A line has been drawn under the Wily entry before the journal continues.

July 7.

    8.00 a.m. Got up at six o'clock. After breakfast walked through the orchard and got the faint whiff of a sort of apple pungency in the air. It was like a vigorous wine. Then walked up the creek a short distance to the end of the island, looking at the shadows of the trees and at the banks in the surface of the water. The trunks of the trees shook with light reflected from the rippling water. At my back in a little wood I could hear the round, wood-like notes of a turtle-dove. From nearer, over my head, in fact, came more harsh and piercing notes of some wilder bird—probably a jay.

July 8.

    Yesterday forenoon and afternoon I made hay in the field North West of the house. Very warm especially unloading the stuff into the mow. I go home today to keep an appointment with a dentist. Should like to walk but there is quite a little rain.

July 17.

Returned after a week or more at Reading. The hay-making overheated my blood and caused quite a rash on my backside. In fact my blood was in a bad way. Am perfectly well again.

This morning it is cloudy and the whole of the summer so far seems to be unusually rainy. The chickens are at it; instead of the birds as I had wished; but any welcome is acceptable, just so it occurs in the open air. There is indeed a pretty little cheeping in the orchard to my left and I shall have to prize that.

This evening walked to turnpike and back. Standing on the bridge saw a fine rainbow: green, blue, yellow and pink: four distinct layers of pink. The sky cleared and was limpid and pure crossed by all the usual light white clouds and larger, more sombre, purple masses fringed with crimson edges. Smoked a pipe on step of mill, then went through garden with Sally in a half enchantment over the flowers. The distinction between perennial: everlasting peas and sweet peas is that the latter have a scent, frail and delicate. Larkspur is various and is to be known by the rabbithead-like corolla, if it be the corolla; taking the outer leaves as the calix—generally purple, or mixed purple and pink etc. Bergamot is a big husky flower or rather a weed with spicey smell. The leaf smells almost as good as the flower. Mignonette I must remember. It is a little, vigorous flower with a dry, old-fashioned goodness of smell. It blooms ["blooms" was originally "flowers," which has been crossed out] at the top of the stem although the rest of the stem is covered with little calixes which assist its busy, sturdy appearance. Snap-dragon, or as it is vulgarly known: the weed—"poor man's torment" is a close-knit, yellow, tumbled sort of thing which if looked at closely reproduces a man in the moon or rather the profile of a Flemish smoker. Coreopsis which I shall never remember is a miniature pink-eyed Susan. Petunias cover the garden almost with their white and scarlet faces. They smell very sweet; indeed, I have been arguing with the girls that they smell sweeter than honey-suckle; honey-suckle does probably possess more pure, simple sweetness; but petunias a deeper spice, almost I am sure, like the spice of carnations. Poppies are exquisite. The one I held in my hand was the color of a princess' cheek; although they are generally a fiercer red or scarlet. The least breath of wind shimmers over them and the impression of them is daffodylic. [This last sentence originally ended, "the impression of them is certainly comparable to that of Wordsworth's daffodils," but was revised.] It is impossible to say more—they are so splendid.

Besides these there were day lilies; blue and white; flame-lilies, a very old lily, differing from the tiger lily in not having spots, but being pure orange bursts; tall grasses of the Eulalia family etc. etc. A half-moon was in the middle of the sky as we left the garden and on the whole this has been a charming day.

July 18.

Walked over to Christopher Shearer's and had him show me his pictures. He said that after all nature was superior to art! Is this delayed conclusion not consistent with his belief that, when we are dead, we are gone? He does love nature, but from this point of view how much of it he must love. I said that the ideal was superior to fact since it was man creating & adding something to nature. He held however that facts were best since they were infinite while the ideal was rare. Now compare his hesitancy in putting nature above art, his materialistic religion and beliefs, and does it not seem as if he were unaware of anything divine, anything spiritual in either nature or himself? If this be so do his pictures possess humanity? Are they not so much mere paint: sky and trees and blank places holding a bird or two?

I almost forgot to add two or three little experiences that I had yesterday—that eventful day. Just as I was starting for the pike I saw two rabbits in the road and stopped to watch them—they cocked up their ears to listen but heard only the rare, bell-like, notes of some bird high up in an apple tree—they twitched their eyes at me and watched breathlessly, until I went on and left them undisturbed.

Later, when I had returned I saw a barn-swallow feeding its young. The brood were leaning on the edge of the nest which had been built under an eave of the barn and were waiting for the mother-bird. She was circling and skimming around the barn-yard for insects. When she found one, she would take a swift, reconnoitering wheel in front of the nest and on the next round settle down plunging the bug, or whatever it was, into the squeaking mouth of some unfed youngster. There was a squabble and twitter of unsatisfied pains from the rest and off went the mother for another bug.

In the afternoon I sat in the piano room reading Keats' "Endymion," and listening to the occasional showers on the foliage outside. The fronds of a fern were dangling over my knees and I felt lazy and content. Once as I looked up I saw a big, pure drop of rain slip from leaf to leaf of a clematis vine. The thought occurred to me that it was just such quick, unexpected, commonplace, specific things that poets and other observers jot down in their note-books. It was certainly a monstrous pleasure to be able to be specific about such a thing.

Shearer may be right about the infinity of facts—but how many facts are significant and how much of the ideal is insignificant?

The first paragraph of the next entry bears a very close resemblance to the second part of Stevens' "Four Characters." Here is that passage, as it appeared in the *Advocate.*

I was sitting on a fence at the edge of a clover field. There was not a single cloud in the sky and the whole atmosphere was very clear, bringing all the hilly perspectives into splendid prominence. The horizon was blue, rimmed, in the east, with a light pink mistiness; in the west, with a warm yellowish red that gradually died into thin whiteness. No star appeared until eight o'clock, and even then I could hardly make out the one I had probably been mistaking for Jupiter. Close at hand on a tall spray of blackberry bushes a robin was swinging in the wind, his throat pouring forth a song of ravishing beauty. While I was listening a middle-sized farmer came along and stopped at my side. His clothes were covered with splotches of clay from the field he had been ploughing. He was about to speak to me when suddenly he heard the robin who was quite lost in the ecstasy of his song. The farmer looked about until his eye caught sight of the bird. He stared at it wonderingly.
"Just listen to thet robin a'hollerin' over there," he said.

The journal entry, dated July 19, reads:

Last evening I lay in a field on the other side of the creek to the S.E. of the house and watched the sunset. There was not a single cloud in the sky and the whole atmosphere was very clear, bringing all the hilly perspectives into splendid prominence. The horizon was blue, rimmed, in the East, with a light pink mistiness; in the West, with a warm yellowish red that gradually died into thin whiteness. No star appeared in the sky until eight o'clock and even then I could hardly make out the one I have probably been mistaking for Jupiter. At half-past eight there were not yet half-a-dozen. I remember thinking that this must have been an old, Greek day, escaped, somehow, from the past. Certainly it was very perfect, and listening to the birds twittering and singing at the Northern Edge of the field I almost envied them their ability to ease their hearts so ravishingly at such a sight.
The moon was very fine. Coming over the field toward the bridge I turned to see it hanging in the dark east. I felt a thrill at the mystery of the thing and perhaps a little touch of fear. When home I began the third canto of "Endymion" which opens with O moon! and Cynthia! and that sort of thing. It was intoxicating. After glancing at the stars and that queen again from the garden I went to bed at

ten. The room was quite dark except for the window and its curtains which formed a big, silvery, uncertain square at my bed's foot.

July 21.

On the 19th I went with Livingood, the Savages, a Miss Benz from Lebanon, etc. on a fishing trip to Evansville. Miss Benz was very interesting to me because of her fine reserve and quietness—a quietness which held something. She was a typical Lee Smith in skirts, I think: gulping her literature from magazines and the latest novels. I told her that a good test of what was worth while was that she should distinguish between what she loved and what she merely liked. Yet it was despairing to feel one's powerlessness in the matter. I often doubt whether people ought to love the lasting. There must surely exist brains that need the excitement of "the latest" to keep them from sluggishness. Again I don't know but what Miss Benz listened to me because she was not used to an opinion different from her own in such things—at least fundamentally. I am going to lend her the "Heart of Man" and thus try to prove or rather illustrate that by literature is not meant merely old books still famous but books of any time that contain what is vital or feed what is vital; meaning by what is vital the best qualities of heart and brain.

Surely in this Stevens is echoing George Edward Woodberry, particularly his "New Defence of Poetry," from *Heart of Man*, which had just been published. There is a much later echo, too, in Stevens' "The Course of a Particular" (1950), of these lines from Woodberry's "defence":

The mind takes the particulars of the world of sense into itself, generalizes them, and frames therefrom a new particular, which does not exist in nature; it is, in fact, nature made perfect in an imagined instance, and so presented to the mind's eye, or to the eye of sense.

The journal entry of July 21 continues:

While fishing I saw a heron fly up into the trees on the opposite bank. Told Freeman about it last evening (July 20) and he remembered having seen a crane about ten years ago flying down the creek. It was blue and its long legs were dangling in the air to the length of at least a foot and a half. He was then quite young and says that he lost his breath for a moment at the sight.

Today I have been freshening up and storing myself with new [illegible word]: a half-hour in the garden, the sight of two immense white clouds in the field over the bridge and the notes of a catbird singing in the rain. Wednesday's chatter almost exhausted me, but a little more early morning strength and all-day loafing will soon give me new energy. Country sights both purge and fill up your fancy;

but it is impossible to go on since Owen sits at my elbow with a mouthful of smutty stories.

July 24.

Strong East Wind all day which invigorated the flowers. The tiger lilies were passionate with color and everything looked more vigorous and May-like. Have been dozing over De Quincy's "Essays on the Poets" and so far I find the one on Goldsmith to be remarkably well-done; indeed one of the best things I have ever seen on any poet (or prose-writer either for that). Have also been planning more poetry: I am full of bright threads—if I could only gather them together—but I'm afraid I'm almost too lazy.

July 26.

Last evening was haggard and depressing. The clouds broke in light-haired, blue-eyed spots over Irish Mountain but that was because the wind was about to change. This morning it is blowing a lively rate from the South-West. The rain (and it has poured down continually) has beaten down the golden glows, phlox, oats, etc. The sun, I think, will, in the end, make them all the more glorious.

The first day of one's life in the country is generally a day of wild enthusiasm. Freedom, beauty, sense of power etc. press one from all sides. In a short time, however, these vast and broad effects lose their novelty and one tires of the surroundings. This feeling of having exhausted the subject is in turn succeeded by the true and lasting source of country pleasure: the growth of small, specific observation. Weary of the deep horizon or green hill one finds immense satisfaction in studying the lyrics of song-sparrows, catbirds, wrens and the like. A valley choked with corn assumes a newer and more potent interest when one comes to notice the blade-like wind among the leaves; the same is true of flowers and birds in big grain-fields, of birds in the air, dashing toward the splendid clouds with a carol of joy, then suddenly wheeling and circling back to the clover and timothy in the most graceful of beauty lines. Orchards are enriched by the thought that they were almost prismatic in May; and by the sound of the rain upon their invisible leaves at midnight. Etcetera, etcetera: it is the getting below the delightful enough exterior into the constantly surprising interior that is the source of real love for the country and open air.

It is three nights since I have seen the stars.

Diaries are very futile. It is quite impossible for me to express any of the beauty I feel to half the degree I feel it; and yet it is a great pleasure to seize an impression and lock it up in words: you feel as if you had it safe forever. A diary is more or less the work of a man of clay whose hands are clumsy and in whose eyes there is no light.

July 31. Monday.

On Saturday Shearer, [Levi] Mengel and myself took an all day walk through Tuckerton, Temple, Pricetown, Blandon and cross-country back again. Our object was to visit the sand dunes near Pricetown which Shearer regarded as the shore of an early, inland sea. What we saw: boulders and the like, was very conclusive and I think this is one of Shearer's theories with which I agree. Most of the day however was taken up with conversations about gale-bugs or gale-flies, ichneumon bugs, tiger bugs, the argymous Cybele, mandibles, thoraxes of butterflies, birds: kingbirds, etc. etc. You felt in the two men an entire lack of poetic life, yet there was an air of strict science, an attentiveness to their surroundings which was a relief from my usual milk and honey. As we walked along Mengel would suddenly cry out "Oh! there goes a liptides Ursula" (or something of the sort), making a wild lunge in the air with his net, while Shearer at the very moment, with a senile shriek, would fly down the road after an "argymous Cybele." Without doubt, however, I learned more natural facts that day than in almost any other previous week.

Again, this entry was used, or at least his recollection of the day, for a short story that was published in the *Advocate* the following October, "Pursuit," which begins:

The clouds strayed lazily into the sky, like children into an open field, as we began our journey. Our nets tugged in the wind as we made amateur dabs after butterflies; and we had to be very careful to prevent their catching and entangling themselves in the thorns. It was delightful to be in the fields, waist deep in yarrow and the flowers of wild carrot, to creep up behind a pair of fine, black wings, to make a lunge with the net and then to behold those same black wings opening and closing contentedly against the face of some blossom or other a short distance away. We might have had a horde of the little clover and cabbage flies that kept flitting to and fro about our knees; but we were after prey, after booty, and had eyes only for what was bright and rare.

Again from the journal:

Sunday was spent at home in Reading. In the evening Livingood and I went to the Tower which we found almost deserted, the very cool wind keeping the mosquito-people away. We talked our usual range of topics from the sublime to the ridiculous. It was a splendid evening, the air being full of the smell of leaves; indeed all our surroundings seeming to have an extraordinary richness and body. The stars shone with a springtime keenness and, on our walk home from the Springs, occupied most of our attention.

Livingood is still struggling with ideals. He exposed his skin to the world last summer and found what a bitter sting lurked in the mildest air. Now that he is again protected he is trying to develop the citizen personality: he begins to yield to the expectations of the community, desiring more or less to be well-thought of, quenching his independence and getting into the highway. It seems strange that he should take all these things so seriously. I don't think he is quite free, yet, from the fascination of moods. He ought to have one definite and simple ethical rule which like a weather-cock could point every direction and yet be always uppermost. Moods ought not to wreck principles. He needs stability of desire. Personally I mean to work my best and with my might and accept whatever condition that brings me to. Such a principle strikes me as the only true sort of one, the real rockbottom.

John Wily, whom I saw some time ago, died of injuries last week and was buried on Saturday.

The flowers are about gone from the garden. I suppose there is a midsummer lapse in fine things but this rose on the window-sill is certainly Augustan enough.

Mid-summer is the time for prose. The life-long days are lazy and lack the pinch of frost that gives you eagerness and mental intrepidity. You doze—and what more does prose do. Roses unfold and droop sleepily etc. You become a mental aristocrat, not working-man.

Somehow what I do seems to increase in its artificiality. Those cynical years when I was about twelve subdued natural and easy flow of feelings. I still scoff too much, analyze too much and see, perhaps, too many sides of a thing—but not always the true sides. For instance I have been here at Wily's almost a month, yet never noticed the pathos of their condition. The memory of one day's visit brought tears to Livingood's eyes. I am too cold for that.

IMITATION OF SIDNEY:

To Stella. (Miss B?)

Unnumbered thoughts my brain a captive holds:
The thought of splendid pastures by the sea
Whereon brave knights enact their chivalrie
For ladies soft applause; the thought of cold,
Cold steps to towers dim that do enfold
Sweet maidens in their forceless chastitie;
Of snowy skies above a Northern lea
In their bright shining tenderly unrolled;

Of roses peeping dimly from the green;
Of shady nooks, all thick with dull festoon
To hide the love of lovers faintly seen
By little birds upon a pleasant tree;
Of meadows looking meekly to the moon—
Yet these do all take flight at thought of thee.

August 1.

Took a walk this morning Northward to the Stone Bridge, Lightfoot's, Maidencreek and back by Wily's bridge: almost a circle of signboards. Saw a number of large birds which were new to me; and even walked within five yards of a large, black crow before it hobbled away. Stopped at Lightfoot's to see whether Elwood was there. Was not. His sister, however, tried to welcome me in an extremely formal way that was very curious. It was only 9, but she asked me to stay for dinner. "I'd be very glad to have you, you know." Very dry sort of person. When I went she said "I'm very glad you came, but so sorry Elwood isn't here. Come again, however. Good-morning, Mr. S." An empty husk, an outline of heartiness—but interesting none the less.

Thought for Sonnet: Frost in a meadow. Is there no bird to sing despite this? No song of Love to outquench the thought of Death?

Thought for Sonnet: No lark doth sing in yon foreboding cloud etc. but it is growing dark and nothing can be heard but the last low notes of sleepless sleeping birds.

Thought for Sonnet: Oh, what soft wings will close above this place etc. (In the Garden) picture angels, roses, fair world etc. on last day.

Birds sing at edge of field at sunset—*thoughtlessly;* as I may have written above; with some development this might be made the seed of a song. Simple, earthly happiness; singing for delight in beauty, or more sympathy of beauty for beauty. A Full-hearted, thoughtless lilt.

Thought for Sonnet: Birds flying up from dark ground at evening: clover, deep grass, oats etc. to Circle & plunge beneath the golden clouds, in & about them, with golden spray on their wings like dew. Produce an imaginative flutter of color.

These images recur in the mature poetry. Note the closing lines of "Blanche McCarthy" (1915):

See how the absent moon waits in a glade
Of your dark self, and how the wings of stars,
Upward, from unimagined coverts, fly.

And these lines from part IV of "Sunday Morning" (1915):

> She says, "I am content when wakened birds,
> Before they fly, test the reality
> Of misty fields, by their sweet questionings;

as well as the closing lines of that poem:

> At evening, casual flocks of pigeons make
> Ambiguous undulations as they sink,
> Downward to darkness, on extended wings.

We find an "imaginative flutter of color" in the next journal entry, which also looks forward to the last section of "Four Characters."

> Wily's. Dusty peacock feathers, old grasses around the mirror. Cluster of gay Japanese lanterns from ceiling of sitting room. Marches for the piano. Honey from wax-plant. Luxurious color of phlox, dahlias, morning glories, petunias, tiger & flame lilies. Remember, as an incident, especially the "Giant of the Battles" Rose. Dust on the leaves, lilies of the valleys, fir-cones, cicada shells in cypress, dew on gossamers. Sunshine, rich grass—yet their own pinched, eerie faces; their minds tickled by the slightest feather; attempting to maintain, notwithstanding, a decent dignity. Mischievous Kate. Rose strikes the real note of despair, particularly in handing me the poems of John Wily, 1719 etc.—as though she, the last of her family, were saying "You see what we once were—well I and Kate & the rest are all that are left." There is too confounded much natural splendor here, however, to allow me to feel deeply the human destitution. You must read it between the lines—the lines of their faces. If my own family were to end—that is if I came from a long, & powerful family—if it were about to topple over—what a splendid place for ruins to be found in! Under a tangle of roses to find a musty bookcase! The roots of an oak grasping the ivory keys of a piano! A dead wall glistening with dew! *Morituri* to *Salutamus!* (Look up phrase) We who are about to die salute you! (Birds: catbird, robin, wren) song-sparrow.

Compare this and the previous entry with part VIII of "Notes Toward a Supreme Fiction" ("It Must Give Pleasure," 1942), where the "angel in his cloud, / . . . Leaps downward . . . / On his spredden wings, . . ."

> These external regions, what do we fill them with
> Except reflections, the escapades of death,
> Cinderella fulfilling herself beneath the roof?

and with the opening words of the next section, "Whistle aloud, too weedy wren."

Here in Berks there is possibly no weed more common than the ragweed. Chickweed ["Chickweed" has been crossed out and "(Vervain)" written above it.] is very common it is true but it lacks the diffusion and ubiquitousness of the ragweed. Plaintain or "pigs' ears" as it is called from its shape is very frequent in clusters—noticeably, I think, among stones, or in the little slopes that generally lead up to barn doors. In meadows wild carrot, yarrow (both white & somewhat aromatic) prevail; although it [is] difficult to claim for them an ascendancy over golden-rod, blue cornflowers, or the pink heads of milk-weeds. Occasionally you find strips of delightfully soft, fuzzy buffalo-clover; or, in fields, a careless strewing of delicate deer-grass which reminds you of timothy, if it does not actually resemble it. Along the sides of the roads are to be found black-berry bushes and their fellows, dewberry vines; a sauvagerie of polk, elderberries, huckleberries, Virginia creeper with its fine leaves and trifoliate poison ivy; these latter two of them intertwining over posts, or up the trunks of trees, like twin assassins.

Yesterday afternoon I lay in the orchard near the barn-yard gate tantalizing the barn-kitten which I have named "Petit Gris" from its size & color. It was like a plaything for a Cyclop but I tried to lighten the fury of its handling by chattering in my softest French, "N'ayez pas peur de moi, petit chat. Venez ici—sur ma jambe, ma main. Vous avez le bleu du ciel dans vos yeux—eh bien, jolie chose—n'ayez pas peur—montez—descendez—est-ce que vous pouvez atteindre cette pièce d'herbe—ah mon petit bleu, mon petit gris—soie de la coleur—songe d'une chose—jolie chose" etc etc keeping it up for a quarter of an hour at least, perhaps with countless mistakes in the French, but certainly with no flaw in the pleasure.

The feeling of piety is very dear to me. I would sacrifice a great deal to be a Saint Augustine but modernity is so Chicagoan, so plain, so unmeditative. I thoroughly believe that at this very moment I get none of my chief pleasures except from what is unsullied. The love of beauty excludes evil. A moral life is simply a pure conscience: a physical, mental and ethical source of pleasure. At the same time it is an inhuman life to lead. It is a form of narrowness so far as companionship is concerned. One *must* make concessions to others; but there is never a necessity of smutching inner purity. The only practical life of the world, as a man of the world, not as a University Professor, a Retired Farmer or Citizen, a Philanthropist, a Preacher, a Poet or the like, but as a bustling merchant, a money-making lawyer, a soldier, a politician is to be if unavoidable a pseudo-villain in the drama, a decent person in private life. We *must* come down, we *must* use tooth and nail, it is the law of nature: "the survival of the fittest"; providing we maintain at the same time self-respect, integrity and fairness. I

believe, as unhesitatingly as I believe anything, in the efficacy and
necessity of fact meeting fact—with a background of the ideal.

There is a good chance here to write a sketch containing color,
sound, & motion. The plants, the sun, the dam, the birds, the flowers,
trees, wind, cicadas, shadows, cropping fruit, contrast of stillnesses,
contrast of white house, lichens, looming phlox, dead leaves and grass
on ground in the green, sun making leaves transparent almost, air of
plenty, glitter of birds in air, brown and black blotched barks of
trees, Georgic distances, presence of possible romance (moon, stars)
etc. etc.

Just as I was writing the last two yellow jackets began to play
around my ankle. Wishing to get rid of them I jumped from my
chair and ran about 20 steps, accidentally crushing one of them under
my foot. As I turned to see what had become of them I saw the un-
injured one struggle with his wounded fellow and lift it heavily in
the air, flying to a place of safety in a tree.

From "Here in Berks" etc. was written outside the house in the
Dicentra Path.

The genus Dicentra includes the flowers known as "bleeding heart" and
"Dutchman's-breeches." Was he thinking of the latter when he used the
title "The Florist Wears Knee-Breeches" for a poem published in 1916?

> My flowers are reflected
> In your mind
> As you are reflected
> In your glass.
> When you look at them,
> There is nothing in your mind
> Except the reflections
> Of my flowers.
> But when I look at them
> I see only the reflections
> In your mind,
> And not my flowers.
> It is my desire
> To bring roses,
> And place them before you
> In a white dish.

The journal goes on:

I have christened that lumbering, 7.30, S. & L. freight "Hebe"
after the swift-footed messenger of the Gods. Oh, bitter thrust!

I'm completely satisfied that behind every physical fact there is
a divine force. Don't, therefore, look *at* facts, but *through* them.

In the sunset tonight I tried to get the value of the various colors. The sun was dimmed by a slight mistiness which was sensitive to the faintest colors and thus gave an unusual opportunity for observation. In this delicate net was caught up first of all a pure whiteness which gradually tinted to yellow, and then to heavy orange and thick, blazing gold; this grew light again and slowly turned to pink. The feathery deer-grass before me twinkled silvery in a little breeze, the ordinary blades of green-grass and wheat stubble glittered at their tips while the ragweed and clover were more dark and secret. The middle-distance remained stolid and indifferent. The horizon, on the contrary, was deepening its blue—a color to which the outermost clouds were already turning. The pink in the sky brightened into a momentary vermilion which slowly died again into rose-color edged with half-determined scarlet and purple. The rose-color faded, the purple turned into a fine, thin violet—and in a moment all the glow was gone.

My feelings tonight find vent in this phrase alone: Salut au Monde!

Aug. 3.

I must not forget to add that on Tuesday evening while the sunset clouds (in the West) were so bright and delicate, the sky over the house was pure, deep blue—something like the shade of an almost purple morning-glory. Into this fine, silent space a troop of chimney-swifts would come chattering and squeaking all manner of sounds and then with a sudden quietness dip noiselessly against the flaming West.

It would not have surprised me to see the Red Cross Knights pricking in Rothenberger's field or Una come jogging down the road to the Half-Way House.

Evening primroses: tall, yellow flowers that open at evening just as morning-glories open at day-break. Meadow-lilies: seem to be a stunted degeneration of tiger-lilies; somewhat redder; about 1½ inches in diameter; the petals close spirally. Passion-flowers are somewhat crude with an artificial appearance. This surprised my memory of them. Thorn-apples grow pink in autumn and are both edible and inedible.

Yesterday morning I took a walk straight away to the river. The water was shallow and transparent showing beds of iron and slate-colored rocks under the surface. Saw flickers and red-headed woodpeckers. Also a contrast of blue corn-flowers against red clover.

In the afternoon we had a mad-cap shower with a bit of hail. It had scarcely passed before a song-sparrow ventured to sing. I felt like applauding.

In the evening Rose, Kate and I took a drive to see their original family property granted to them by Wm. Penn. There was an old house on the place with curious shutters, front-door, exposed joists, huge fire-place, thin partitions. Also a bed in every room and a smell in every corner—these two latter being modern additions. We then called at Pearson's who are parchment-like, soft-eyed creatures. There I met Jeremiah Parvin whose heart is as small as a pea, but whose vanity is an overtowering cliff. We drove home under difficulties. Great sheets of lightning lit up the valleys about us but so blinded me that I could scarcely drive. Got home just in time to avoid a tremendous downpour in the midst of which the lightning struck close by. It sounded as though a steeple of some soft stuff had suddenly collapsed at my feet.

This morning all was bright and dazzling. Little water-jewels studded the cypress and flickered in the sun. Walking through the garden I started beads of rain rolling down the blades of grass which immediately flashed like faery swords in wild combat. Struck Rothenberger's hedge with my stick and knocked rainy sparks into the air. The splendor is almost too great: things seem a little over-dressed, a little overdone.

Vervain instead of chickweed.

Here three pages have been cut out before the next entry.

Aug. 5.
I return to Reading this morning. Took my last walk up the meadow last evening and heard all the birds over again; finding, as well, a jay's feather. Have just come from the garden which was starry with petunias and morning-glories. The dew made the grass white in spots; but on the whole the morning was rather common-place: this threatening to be a typical dog-day.

Three more pages remain in this first side of the first notebook that have not been written on. Reversing the direction, there are two scattered comments. On the back of the page carrying the entry for August 5, 1899, my father wrote: "Till lo! a little touch and youth was gone. Browning—Grammarian's Funeral." On the page above his July 17 discussion of flowers is written the word "coreopsis." The rest of the pages are blank.

Turning again to the second notebook, following the series of sonnets quoted earlier, four pages have been excised. The next page is not dated, but seems to continue the story of the summer of 1899, at a slight distance looking back.

Mengel on the contrary is a rare good fellow. He is unintentionally Bohemian—sloppy in person though a hard and painstaking worker. The three of us took a long walk in the middle of August, across fields etc. to Pricetown hills, to Blandon, to Berkeley, to Tuckerton and home. Their knowledge of natural things was very useful to me and I picked many grains from their wide fields of observation. The main object of the walk was to stand on the shore of what Shearer held to have been an inland sea. This we did convincingly. Shearer was full of reminiscences as we passed through places familiar to him while Mengel kept smoking and watching most of the day. Later Mengel and I visited the Pinnacle, the highest point of land in the county—up in the Northern End. The climb up the hill was very stiff—Mengel stopping midway to rest in a torrent of perspiration. The outlook from the top was not so huge as might have been owing to a sticky haze in the air. I killed a rattlesnake etc. We found foxes holes, holes in the rocks certainly made by strokes of lightning, feathers of blue-jays in great litters evidently clawed from the birds in fights with hawks ["hawks" was originally "crows," which has been crossed out], large pines with the limbs sparkling in the sunlight, and a slippery floor of pine-needles. On returning to the foot of the hill the farmer who was with us, as guide, found his wagon upside down in a creek and his horse, frightened by the flies, in a neighboring barn. Borrowing a chaise we bounced along to meet the 3.20 freight for home which pulled in about half-past five. While waiting for the thing, I saw an indigo bird and its mate, several scarlet tanagers and a host of robins. On the train the conductor agreeably passed around pears to the women aboard and on the whole we had quite a day of it.

Some time before this Fred Heilig, Luther Gable and I went to Evansville to fish down the Maidencreek. Before going to sleep in Huy's mill we climbed a field for the sunset. The Blue Mountains at our backs were blue indeed; the sky was very fine—with many turquoise spaces—but I was most interested in the field at my feet which was radiant with clover blossoms. In the distance facing us lay Reading at the bottom of a sky of smoke and dirt—certainly a nasty hollow and one we were glad to be free from. In the mill we slept on bags of grain—or rather tried to sleep. The affair seemed collapsing bit by bit, for there was a continual dropping of strange things at strange intervals which kept nipping our rest in its bud. We were up at five, stiff and cold. Once in the creek the sun soon warmed us up and we fished till seven in the evening. Walked home in our wet clothes and saw the second sunset of our outing—the sky being like a great dead ash with a little bright slip of the young moon near the horizon.

So and so the summer went. In early September we had some fine blue mornings with little clouds starting up at the edge of the sky like children venturing into an open field. Once I went up the Schuylkill to Ritz' lock and got a flimsy little boat which I rowed into a world of wild solitude and back again. The water was blue and the air was quiet except for the occasional shriek of some bird—almost fearful enough to upset my little craft.

Last week Livingood and I took a final tramp in the afternoon to Kuechler's. A rain had burnished the pines and brightened all the little purple flowers and goldenrod so common on the hills at this season. Coming home with a pint of claret in me the fields of wild white asters fairly swam about me and who can deny that I was Prosper le Gai in spirit if not in body?

About the 15th Livingood, Bard and I had a little dinner at the Springs, walking home over the moon and tree shadowed boulevard which Livy made howl with echoes of his Alpine yo-ho-yo-hos.

Also spent a number of evenings listening to the Spanish students —a little orchestra at Kline's saloon on Penn Street. One of them—Bistolfi—kept us there until after two in the morning with his fine talk. He said that a man met Life like a roaring lion in a desert—a figure of tremendous force. Casually called the table-full of us young fellows a cave of the fates—likewise a mighty strong thing to say off-hand. He was not only a rare bird but also a very rare man.

The last two afternoons before this I lay in a field near the Hospital and watched the wind in the goldenrod and wild-asters—letting it do my thinking for me.

Quite possibly that thinking led to this poem, which was published in the *Advocate* the following March over the pseudonym R. Jerries.

OUTSIDE THE HOSPITAL

See the blind and the lame at play,
    There on the summer lawn—
She with her graceless eyes of clay,
    Quick as a frightened fawn,
Running and tripping into his way
    Whose legs are gone.

How shall she 'scape him, where shall she fly,
    She who never sees?
Now he is near her, now she is by—
    Into his arms she flees.
Hear her gay laughter, hear her light cry
    Among the trees.

"Princess, my captive." "Master, my king."
    "Here is a garland bright."
"Red roses, I wonder, red with the Spring,
    Red with a reddish light?"
"Red roses, my princess, I ran to bring,
    And be your knight."

The journal entry concludes:

> And finally this afternoon, Sunday, I made my last visit to Wily's. A heavy South wind blew the sky full of a pageant of clouds which gave my walk a sense of great strength and speed. The girls were all at home and as delightful as ever. I stayed but a short time and when I went Kate stuffed a big cluster of roses under the band of my felt hat which I wore home like a garland—a coronal for the departing golden age. The three months have been kind to me. Certainly the memory of them will surpass any other that I have—the complete change of intellectual vestment has been like the exchange of a dusty road for a path through green and happy fields.

Above the page where that paragraph was written we find a later comment: "What silly, affected school-girl drivel this seems to me now. WS June 14/04."

IV

When my father returned to Harvard that fall, he dropped his journal temporarily, and the only glimpses we have into his thoughts are in the varied pieces that he published. We have already mentioned his story "Pursuit," which relates to his journal entry for July 31. It was followed in November by "The Revelation," a rather eerie story of a young man who takes a photograph of his sweetheart to be framed; after it is done and he opens the package, he finds a picture of himself. The same issue of the *Advocate* included a Stevens quatrain:

> Go not, young cloud, too boldly through the sky,
>   To meet the morning light;
> Go not too boldly through that dome on high—
>   For eastward lies the night.

Another story, "The Nymph," appeared in the December 6 *Advocate* over the pseudonym John Fiske Towne, at about the time we find my father's one midwinter journal entry; it is a sonnet with echoes of Keats and Santayana. (The heading indicates where it was sent for publication.)

Harvard Monthly—December 1899

TO THE MORN

> If this be night, break softly, blessed day.
> Oh, let the silent throat of every bird
> Swell tenderly in song, as though he heard
> Some brother singing deep within thy ray!
> Send but an unseen breeze aloft, away
> From darkness and dull earth, to be a word,
> A half-discovered sound: to make me gird
> Myself, and persevere this cheerless way.

But softly, softly, thou most blessed morn.
Mine eyes too long accustomed to the dark
May fail when thou in glorious heaven art born,
May fail against that far-entreated light
Catch but a glimmer of the distant lark
And drop, all blasted, at the sovereign sight.

Among other courses, my father was taking one that seems a continuation of a previous year's study of English literature, for it spanned the period from the publication of the *Lyrical Ballads* to the death of Tennyson; Stevens received an "A" for the first semester, but slipped to a "B" in the second. The only other "A" was for a course in the history of German literature, "with special study of the Classic Periods of the Twelfth and Eighteenth Centuries." He received an "A−" for "The Fine Arts of the Middle Ages and the Renaissance," and "B" for English composition and American history. Surprisingly, his lowest grade, "C+", was awarded for a course in French literature.

Early in the second semester, Stevens was elected president of *The Harvard Advocate;* one of his chores was to write most of the editorials that appeared there, and they cover the usual range of student interests, from athletic events to library facilities to plans for a fence around Harvard Yard. The first issue under his direction, dated March 10, 1900, included three Stevens editorials, a short story, "Hawkins of Cold Cape," and a poem, "Song."

Ah yes! beyond these barren walls
   Two hearts shall in a garden meet,
And while the latest robin calls,
   Her lips to his shall be made sweet.

And out above these gloomy tow'rs,
   The full moon tenderly shall rise
To cast its light upon the flow'rs,
   And find him looking in her eyes.

Two weeks later "Outside the Hospital" appeared, followed by a group of poems in the April 3 issue. The first of these "Street Songs" anticipates an image we find in "Le Monocle de Mon Oncle" (1918), at the opening of part XII:

A blue pigeon it is, that circles the blue sky,
On sidelong wing, around and round and round.
A white pigeon it is, that flutters to the ground,
Grown tired of flight.

The adolescent version:

THE PIGEONS

Over the houses and into the sky
    And into the dazzling light,
Long hosts of fluttering pigeons fly
    Out of the blackened night,
Over the houses and into the sky
    On glistening wings of white.

Over the city and into the blue
    From ledge and tower and dome,
They rise and turn and turn anew,
    And like fresh clouds they roam,
Over the city and into the blue
    And into their airy home.

We can also hear a reworking of his earlier "Quatrain" in the use of clouds and the dome. There were three more "Street Songs":

II. THE BEGGAR

Yet in this morn there is a darkest night,
Where no feet danced or sweet birds ever rise,
Where fancy is a thing that soothes—and lies,
And leads on with mirages of light.
I speak of her who sits within plain sight
Upon the steps of yon cathedral. Skies
Are naught to her; and life a lord that buys
And sells life, whether sad, or dark, or bright.

The carvings and beauty of the throne
Where she is sitting, she doth meanly use
To win you and appeal. All rag and bone
She asks with her dry, withered hand a dreg
Of the world's riches. If she doth abuse
The place, pass on. It is a place to beg.

III. STATUARY

The windy morn has set their feet to dancing—
    Young Dian and Apollo on the curb,
The pavement with their slender forms is glancing,
    No clatter doth their gaiety disturb.

No eyes are ever blind enough to shun them,
    Men wonder what their jubilance can be,
No passer-by but turns to look upon them—
    Then goes his way with all his fancy free.

IV. THE MINSTREL

The streets lead out into a mist
    Of daisies and of daffodils—
A world of green and amethyst,
    Of seas and of uplifted hills.

There bird-songs are not lost in eaves,
    Nor beaten down by cart and car,
But drifting sweetly through the leaves,
    They die upon the fields afar.

Nor is the wind a broken thing
    That faints within hot prison cells,
But rises on a silver wing
    From out among the heather bells.

Robert Buttel has made an interesting comparison between these verses and "Sunday Morning" in *Wallace Stevens: The Making of Harmonium,* calling them a "primitive version" of the latter, and pointing out many parallels despite the "great stylistic differences."

On May 1, 1900, the Class of 1901 Junior Dinner was held, and Wallace Stevens read an ode composed for the occasion. Some forty years later one of his classmates wrote to him:

> I remember when you wrote and read the most humorous poem I ever heard in my life. You drank a whole bottle of King William scotch just before spouting it at the class dinner, then, after reading it, you promptly passed out, and I had to take you home, and missed the rest of the dinner. When that poem was printed it did not have a humorous word in it, but was very fine indeed.

Unfortunately, all we have is the printed version.

I.

A night in May!
And the whole of us gathered into a room
To pack and bundle care away—
And not to remember that over the dark
The sea doth call—
Doth call from out an upward-rising day

For us to follow and to mark
How he doth stay
A patient workman by the city wall.
A night in May!
A night in May!

II.

A time will come to join him on the shore;
A time will come when other men who bore
Forth on his breast
To distant worlds will say,
"We long for rest,
Take ye the ships and labor on the deep."
Then this one night that we are living now
Will be forgot in the exultant leap
And bound of our aspiring prow.

III.

But not in May!
It is enough to hear young robins sing
To new companions
In the morn.
It is enough to feel our thoughts take wing
Into a happiness
Where none hath seen
A single, unenjoying, hopeless thing.
A life made keen
By its perfection!
All bright, all freshly glowing in the sun
That leads us into doing from what's done,
Without reflection.
Simply to gather and be one again,
To know old earth a mother,
To fill our cups and touch like men—
And be to each a brother!

IV.

A golden time and golden-shining hour
From out the cloudless weather
Is such an hour and time as this
That finds us here together
In May! in May!
And we are careless of the night;

We shall be ready for the day;
We shall behold the splendid sight.
We shall set sail for near or far.
With a shout into the light,
And a hail to the morning star.

As an example of one of Stevens' editorials, the first paragraph of "Local Color," in the May 10 issue, may be of interest.

So many of the stories submitted to us of late have had their scenes laid in and about the College, and so many of the names of characters have been those which every nine out of ten Bostonians bear, that a word in regard to local color may not be out of place. It is of course possible for an amusing event to take place in the Yard, and it is just as possible for the people concerned in it to be named Thayer or Hollis or Longfellow or Lowell. But because an event does take place in the Yard does not make it amusing, any more than a Thayer or Hollis makes it so. Nevertheless it seems to be a popular fallacy with a great many contributors that it is only necessary to stay within the shadow of dormitories to write an entertaining story or poem. Thus in a description of "The Yard in May" we find—

"The gazer in the polished glass
Reflecting from its mercury
     The sun god's face,
Impotent is its area.
All flaming, clear to demarcate,
     Its limit's trace.
To farers in thy greening lawn
Or idle strollers, passers swift,
     Thy beauty's lent:
They powerless thy glory feel;
In vain its sources, boundaries seek,
     Its curved extent.

"Above all name, great colors vast
Beyond the rainbow lucent shine
     And yet we name
A blackness tomb-like! Puny speech!
Imperial purple! Child's hair gold!
     O! petty game!
These nominate the living shade?
As well then red-gray designates
     Thy blades and clay.
Blood on a young crane's wounded wing:
A fiery kite beneath black clouds,
     Would better say."

The anonymous poet probably meant well by the Yard, but he can hardly be said to have expressed himself.

We can only wonder whether Stevens wrote the poem himself as an example; he did, after all, say that it was up to the editor to fill the *Advocate*'s pages, when commenting on his use of pseudonyms. He used "Kenneth Malone" in the same issue for a poem entitled "Night-Song."

> I stand upon the hills to-night
> And see the cold March moon
> Rise upward with his silver light
> And make a gentle noon.
>
> The fields are blowing with the breeze,
> The stars are in the sky,
> There is a humming through the trees,
> And one cloud passes by.
>
> I wonder if that is the sea,
> Rid of the sun's annoy,
> That sings a song all bold and free,
> Of glory and of joy.

Two weeks later he was "Carrol More," when publishing "Ballade of the Pink Parasol."

> I pray thee where is the old-time wig,
> And where is the lofty hat?
> Where is the maid on the road in her gig,
> And where is the fire-side cat?
> Never was sight more fair than that,
> Outshining, outreaching them all,
> There in the night where lovers sat—
> But where is the pink parasol?
>
> Where in the pack is the dark spadille
> With scent of lavender sweet,
> That never was held in the mad quadrille,
> And where are the slippered feet?
> Ah! we'd have given a pound to meet
> The card that wrought our fall
> The card none other of all could beat—
> But where is the pink parasol?
>
> Where is the roll of the old calash,
> And the jog of the light sedan?
> Whence Chloe's diamond brooch would flash
> And conquer poor peeping man.

> Answer me, where is the painted fan
>   And the candles bright on the wall;
> Where is the coat of yellow and tan—
>   But where is the pink parasol?
>
> Prince, these baubles are far away,
>   In the ruin of palace and hall,
> Made dark by the shadow of yesterday—
>   But where is the pink parasol?

In this poem Stevens' wit and talent for words is clear, to come to fruition in the poems of *Harmonium;* it seems a tremendous leap forward from the sentimentality of many of his earlier things, not only in its form but in its imagery. The short story in the same issue, "In the Dead of Night," which he signed with his own name, was not so convincing.

My father's days as an undergraduate at Harvard were drawing to a close. As a special student, we should remember that it had been planned from the beginning that he would spend only three years there, owing to the fact that his father was simultaneously educating three sons, and had two daughters coming along behind them. Yet, had Stevens decided to stay on for another year, it might not have been allowed, according to his friend and associate on the *Advocate* board, the poet Witter Bynner, who refers to my father by his Harvard nickname, Pete.

> It would seem to me interesting to preserve a brief account of the reason for Pete's leaving Harvard. In the Square at that time was a restaurant called Ramsden's or colloquially "Rammy's" where not only undergraduates but a few of the faculty would eat midnight buckwheat cakes. The favorite waitress there was a witty Irish-woman who seemed to me in those days almost elderly—her face wrinkled always with smiles and her spirit and repartee highly appreciated by customers. One night Pete had come in from Boston fairly lit and, announcing jovially that he was going to rape Maggie [Bynner later recalled that the correct name was "Kitty"], vaulted the counter, landing so heavily behind it that both of them fell to the floor. When she screamed with enjoyably dramatic terror, a member of the English Department who was present left his buckwheats and severely interfered. From him came a deplorable report to college authorities which led to Stevens' expulsion, which I think happened a year before his graduation.
>
> It was after this episode that Stevens, in saying good-by to Copey announced his intent of being a poet. I do not think this occasion has been as yet recorded by a witness but I happened to be there and think what happened was an interesting and pertinent exploit. None of us who were there were given any chance to testify in his behalf but I am sure that what we might have had to say would

have borne no weight against the word of a faculty member. Maggie, I am certain, bore no untoward testimony. Pete was one of her great favorites and I wish I could remember some of their banter.

The reaction of Charles Townsend Copeland (Copey), his English instructor, to my father is in a further comment by Bynner:

> I should say that before leaving Harvard, Pete considered writing as an avocation; but I remember Copey's asking him just before he left Cambridge what he was going to be and when the undergraduate answered, "A poet," Copey's exclaiming, "Jesus Christ!"

No matter what the truth about the story in the bar, it is an amusing anecdote and quite believable except for the fact that it did not result in expulsion. As to becoming a poet, Stevens once remarked, "When I got to New York I was not yet serious about poetry"; yet certainly he was serious about becoming a writer.

Before leaving Harvard, he spent an evening with George Santayana, and recorded the occasion on two blank pages at the back of his copy of Santayana's *Lucifer*.

> I dined with Santayana last night. He told me he had worked at *Lucifer* for ten years. Also, he regretted that the songs were not more lyrical, and that he had not been able to put more poetry side by side with the philosophy—but these things were not in him. I discussed the blank verse with him—and La Rose talked about some of the figures —all of which I have already forgotten—not having read the book through at the time. One thing he did say, however: He had intended to call the tragedy "The Temptation of Lucifer." He thought Lucifer *could* not be saved: he regarded L's last speech as the best, I think although I am not certain. Lucifer is the negative spirit—thus, he could see the beauty of love and of ideals, but could never participate in them etc. etc. Most of the songs in Act I are translations of the Homeric hymns. La Rose read a criticism in the *Nation* on his "Interpretation of Religion & Poetry." The criticism was decidedly unpleasant—and shallow. Santayana took it good-naturedly. Discussed the Emerson essay. Laughed at Emerson's habit of eating pie for breakfast etc. After dinner the three of us went to S.'s room. I tried to answer his "Answer to A Sonnet"—My sonnet went
>> Cathedrals are not built along the sea, etc.
> His answer was,
>> Then the wild winds through organ pipes descended
>> To utter what they meant eternally, etc.
> I said that the first suggestion of the organ-pipes came from the wind. He said that the wind was then a stimulus—the organ-pipe—a result etc. We both held our grounds. We smoked cigarettes, drank

whisky etc. until eleven when we broke up. I shall probably not see him again.

To learn more about occasions when Stevens and Santayana were together, one turns to some letters Stevens wrote many years later. In 1945 he said:

> I doubt if Santayana was any more isolated at Cambridge than he wished to be. While I did not take any of his courses and never heard him lecture, he invited me to come to see him a number of times and, in that way, I came to know him a little. I read several poems to him and he expressed his own view of the subject of them in a sonnet which he sent me, and which is in one of his books. This was forty years ago, when I was a boy and when he was not yet in mid-life. Obviously, his mind was full of the great projects of his future and, while some of these have been realized, it is possible to think that many have not. It would be easy to speak of his interest and sympathy; it might amuse you more to know that Sparklets were then something new and that Santayana liked to toy with them as he charged the water which he used to make a highball or two. They seemed to excite him. I always came away from my visits to him feeling that he made up in the most genuine way for many things that I needed. He was then still definitely a poet.

He put it another way to a different correspondent in 1949:

> I never took any of his courses and I don't believe that I ever heard him lecture. But I knew him quite well. That was almost fifty years ago when he was quite a different person from the decrepit old philosopher now living in a convent in Rome. A week or two ago he wrote a letter to a friend of mine who sent it to me to look at and in that letter he said: "I have always bowed, however sadly, to expediency or fate." For the last week or two I have been repeating that sentence. Santayana is not a philosopher in any austere sense.

It is obvious that Santayana had a lifelong influence on my father, despite his remark, in 1940, that "in him the religious and the philosophic are too dominant." He published "To An Old Philosopher in Rome" in 1952, the same year that he wrote, in September:

> I grieve to hear of the death of George Santayana in Rome. Fifty years ago, I knew him well, in Cambridge, where he often asked me to come and see him. This was before he had definitely decided not to be a poet. He had probably written as much poetry as prose at that time. It is difficult for a man whose whole life is thought to continue as a poet. The reason (like the law, which is only a form of the reason) is a jealous mistress. He seems to have gone to live at

the convent, in which he died, in his sixties, probably gave them all he had and asked them to keep him, body and soul.

The date of the inscription in *Lucifer* was May 27, 1900, and there is a quatrain in the June 2 issue of the *Advocate* that could have been dedicated to Santayana.

> He sought the music of the distant spheres
> By night, upon an empty plain, apart;
> Nor knew they hid their singing all the years
> Within the keeping of his human heart.

Before leaving Harvard, Stevens took up his journal again, making his entry on the page following the one where, the previous December, he had inscribed his sonnet "To the Morn."

June 2. 1900.

Summer time is returning again and with it comes the end of my college life. During the winter I have had a rather dull time of it. I meant to keep up my diary but was too lazy to make a start. Then, too, I shall be rather glad to forget many things that have happened. Nine months have been wasted. In the autumn I got drunk about every other night—and later, from March until May, and a good bit of May, I did nothing but loaf. Grandmother Stevens, my father's mother, died in September—that made a deep impression on me because I was very proud of her. I stopped over at Ivyland on my way back to Cambridge and got a last glimpse of her. She looked much as I had always known her. There was nothing unnatural in the little white parlor where she lay. Her face was calm and beautiful. Then at the Easter vacation I had a second though less personal loss. Kate Wily died of pneumonia. I don't know just how I felt about it. When I had come back to college I found the rose she had stuck in my hat still there. I did not dare to visit or to write to her sisters.

Today has been stifling. I have been working in the College library in preparation for the final examinations. The same birds are back in the garden—the same flowers; but somehow I do not have the affection for them that I used to have. To be sure they still delight me—but the delight is not the enchanting kind that I experienced last summer. I am conscious that when I leave Cambridge I shall leave all the surroundings that I have ever lived in—Reading, Berkeley, the mountains—and perhaps the clouds. I am going to New York, I think, to try my hand at journalism. If that does not pan out well, I am resolved to knock about the country—the world. Of course I am perfectly willing to do this—anxious, in fact. It seems to me to be the only way, directed as I am more or less strongly by the hopes and desires of my parents and myself, of realizing to the last degree any of the ambitions I have formed. I should be content to dream along to the end of my life—and opposing moralists be hanged. At the same time I should be quite as content to work and be practical—but I hate the conflict whether it "avails" or not. I want my powers to be put to their fullest use—to be exhausted when I am done with them. On the other hand I do not want to have to make a petty struggle for existence—physical or literary. I must try not to be a dilettante—half dream, half deed. I must be all dream or all deed. But enough of myself—even though this is my own diary of which I am the house, the inhabitant, the lock, and the key.

Certainly in this he was heeding his father, who had written to him a couple of years earlier (Nov. 1, 1898):

> Our young folks would of course all prefer to be born like English noblemen with Entailed estates, income guaranteed and in choosing a profession they would simply say—"How shall I amuse myself"—but young America understands that the question is—"*Starting with nothing, how shall I sustain myself and perhaps a wife and family—and send my boys to College and live* comfortably in my old age." Young fellows must all come to that question for unless they inherit money, marry money, find money, steal money or somebody presents it to them, they must *earn it* and earning it save it up for the time of need. How best can he earn a sufficiency! What talent does he possess which carefully nurtured will produce something which people want and therefore will pay for. This is the whole problem! and to Know Thyself!

His last journal entry written at Harvard is very brief:

> June 13. 1900.
> Warwick Green came up to the house this morning to say good-bye to me. We had a little chat then I started to pack my trunk etc. and he began to read notes for Santayana's Course in Philosophy: "Aesthetics."

Fortunately for us, he took his journal with him to New York and, for a while, kept it faithfully, so that we have a day-to-day record of this new phase in my father's life in the closing months of his twenty-first year.

> June 15.
> I came to New York yesterday. Stopped at the Astor House. At three in the afternoon I called at *Commercial-Advertiser* presented a letter from Copeland to Carl Hovey who introduced me to [Lincoln] Steffens a Californian, the city editor. Later called at *Evening Sun* and made an appointment for Monday next. At half-past six dined with Rodman Gilder and his "Aunt Julia"—a witty, old lady of some avoir-dupois and watery eyes who was disappointed because

the sherbet was pineapple instead of orange. After dinner hurried to the East River Park in Yorkville and wrote up a band concert for the *Advertiser*.

This morning I called to see Charles Scribner who was not at his office, and Arthur Goodrich of the Macmillan Company with whom I am to take lunch.

Goodrich took me to lunch at the Players Club—an interesting place where we saw celebrities. We sat on the verandah. Nearby was Reid the artist—I think it is Reid although now I see the word in black and white it may be Read. The walls of the house are covered with mementoes of the stage and actors. It is a near approach to Bohemia.

I called at Scribner's again and found Charles Scribner in his offices. He is a plain man with a keen face. He was pleasant to me and put my name down. Speaking of pleasantness, I must give the preference to Goodrich who although a stranger treated me like an old friend.

The house I am living in is a boarding-house kept by two unmarried French women. The elder, about thirty years of age, has a bosom a foot and a half thick. No wonder the French are amorous with such accommodation for lovers. The younger, about twenty-eight years of age, is of more moderate proportions. She has dark rings under her eyes. I have just slaughtered two bugs in a wall of my room. They were lice! Dinner next—wherever I can find it—with an aimless evening to follow.

Took dinner in a little restaurant—poached eggs, coffee and three crusts of bread—a week ago my belly was swagging with strawberries. Bought a couple of newspapers from a little fellow with blue eyes who was selling *Journals* and *Worlds* & who had to ransack the neighborhood for the ones I wanted. As I came back to my room the steps of the street for squares were covered with boarders etc. leaning on railings and picking their teeth. The end of the street was ablaze with a cloud of dust lit by the sun. All around me were tall office buildings closed up for the night. The curtains were drawn and the faces of the buildings looked hard and cruel and lifeless. This street of mine is a wonderful thing. Just now the voices of children manage to come through my window from out it, over the roofs and through the walls.

All New York, as I have seen it, is for sale—and I think the parts I have seen are the parts that make New York what it is. It is dominated by necessity. Everything has its price—from Vice to Virtue. I do not like it and unless I get some position that is unusually attractive I shall not stay. What is there to keep me, for example, in a place where all Beauty is on exhibition, all Power a tool of Selfishness, and all Generosity a source of Vanity? New York is a field of tireless and antagonistic interests—undoubtedly fascinating but horribly unreal. Everybody is looking at everybody else—a foolish crowd walking on mirrors. I am rather glad to be here for the short time that I intend to stay—it makes me appreciate the opposite of it all. Thank Heaven the winds are not generated in Yorkville, or the clouds manufactured in Harlem. What a price they would bring!

The carpet on the floor of my room is gray set off with pink roses. In the bath room is a rug with the figure of a peacock woven in it—blue and scarlet, and black, and green, and gold. And on the paper on my wall are designs of fleur-de-lis and forget-me-not. Flowers and birds enough of rags and paper—but no more. In this Eden, made spicey with the smoke of my pipe which hangs heavy in the ceiling, in this Paradise ringing with the bells of streetcars and the bustle of fellow boarders heard through the thin partitions, in this Elysium of Elysiums I now shall lay me down.

That entry seems like an "Anecdote of the Prince of Peacocks" that takes place in a "Gray Room": "The elysium lay / In a parlor of day." The journal continues:

I shall say my prayers up the chimney. That is their only chance of getting above the housetops.

I have just looked out of the window to see whether there were any stray tramps on the roof. I'Faith, there were stars in heaven.

June 16.
This morning I called at the Astor House for my mail and found a letter from my father. He called me a "brave fellow" for coming here. Great Scott! The streets are full of "brave fellows." He probably imagines me a sad-eyed, half-starved individual wandering about in search of Employment. As a matter of fact I went to bed at half-past nine last night, woke at six this morning, dozed until eight, took a cold bath, and went down stairs to breakfast. Then I made my call at the Astor House and later at the office of the *Evening Post*. The *Post* is run in an ideal manner—nine to three, and everybody a gentleman! I shall write them some special articles—That is necessary before any engagement is made.

I went down to the wharves along the North R. On one I found a rather pleasant, fat, red-faced, middle-sized old man surrounded by a half-dozen little Terrier dogs and a Newfoundland. I played with the dogs a quarter of an hour or more. Continued mousing about the wharves and saw hucksters, draymen and the like eating green beans and canned fruit for their luncheons. I found a ring of foreigners, in a park "shooting craps." They were having an exciting but good-natured time—making and losing ten-cent fortunes. I struck up Canal Street and saw an Italian family making its living. The husband was bent over an ice-cream freezer on the pavement—it was an invention of his own. It did not make my mouth water. In the doorway was his wife stitching at some piece of cloth. By her side was a little girl playing with a doll—an invention like the ice-cream freezer, but much dirtier. I stopped to eat a dozen clams for ten cents and got about half-way through the dozen.

I spent the afternoon in my room, having a rather sad time with my thoughts. Have been wondering whether I am going into the right thing after all. Is literature really a profession? Can you single it out, or must you let it decide in you for itself? I have determined upon one thing, and that is not to *try* to suit anybody except myself. If I fail then I shall have failed through myself and not through the imitation of what such and such a paper wants. To be candid I think the newspapers here are rank—excepting the *Post*, the *Tribune*, and perhaps one or two others. I got a curious glimpse of the *Post*'s dei ex machina this morning. In the room in which I sat was a book-case filled with "Familiar Quotations," "Gems of Poetry," "Phrase Books" etc. Perhaps this explains the French, for example, in this sentence from an editorial on "Macaulay's Diary" in tonight's issue: "We may add, also, that Sir G. O. Trevelyan had not learned the biographer's art of *tout dire*—that *secret de ennuyer*." New York is the greatest place to be Americanized in that I ever saw—or hope to see.

June 17. Sunday.

Last night I sat in an open square near the Washington Arch. A man passed me with his coat tightly buttoned, his hands in his trousers pockets, his head bent and his hat well pulled-down. His clothes were in rags. As he started to cross Fifth Avenue a 'bus drove by and he stopped to let it pass. On the top of the 'bus was a group of girls in neat Spring jackets and bonnets covered with cherries and roses.

This morning the church bells are ringing.

New York is the most egotistical place in the world.

I have spent the day experimenting on special articles. Have written two: "A Happy-Go-Lucky Irishman," "Wharves and the Sea." I shall take these to the *Evening Post* tomorrow and see what they think of them.

June 18.

Today I took my articles to the *Post*; and went in search of new material which I have just written up under the title "A Battery

Naples." Besides that I visited Trinity Church, saw some people praying there—a really impressive sight. I also visited the Cooper Union —a dirty hole, and the Astor Library, quite the opposite of the Union —a thing which more people would patronize if the Union did not exist; but then half the world is always particular about the best.

Yesterday I was taken ill after luncheon and stayed in bed—or practically so—until this morning when I felt better. *Trop de Cuisine Bourgeoise!*

June 19.

Encore de cuisine. I am beginning to hate the stinking restaurants that line the street and gush out clouds of vegetable incense as I pass. Today I bought a box of strawberries and ate them in my room for luncheon. Tomorrow I propose to have a pineapple; the next day, blackberries; the next, bananas etc. While I am on the subject of food I may add that I dine with Russell Loines at the Harvard Club tonight.

Re-wrote my "Wharves and the Sea" in an impersonal vein. Read Wordsworth and Thackeray and smoked several disagreeable pipes. It is disgusting to have to wait this way—minutes are hours, and hours worse than days. If the *Sun* does not have something for me next Monday I am afraid I shall back down and go to Reading for a while. But I am perfectly willing to expose myself to the chance of getting something to do.

Have just been to a barber's shop where they put four different kinds of oil on my face—not to mention a dab of vaseline in my hair and a spray of violet water up my nostrils. I feel like an "embalmèd sweet."

June 20.

Took re-written "Wharves etc." to the *Post.* Called on Simon Stern of Stern and Rushmore, Wall Street, who dashed off a pack of letters for me to the editors of *Munsey's,* N.Y. *Journal, World, Herald,* etc. He's in business up to the ears and doesn't waste any words. Took letter to *Munsey's*—it worked like a charm and I may get something after all. Also went out to Columbia College at Morningside Heights—a delightful place. The Seth Low library has a great deal of grandeur to it—its approach consists of terraces of granite stairs rising to a domical building with a porch of lofty columns. There are roses and evergreens planted here and there on adjacent terraces. Their scent filled the hot, motionless air that hung about the structure. Inside is a huge dome supported by encircling galleries and alcoves. From these, I could hear the song-sparrows singing in the foliage without.

June 22, 1900.

Yesterday I went over to Brooklyn to see the parochial school I attended when I visited my uncle Henry Strodach many years ago. My memory of it had gone through the customary rose-color process. It is unnecessary to say that the real was not the ideal. I found the place [St. Paul's Lutheran Church, at the corner of South Fifth and Rodney Streets], but hardly recognized it. The front of the church was covered with ivy—ineffectually. I went to the yard of the old school and found a little girl playing in it. She called to her mother who took me about the building. I asked her what had become of Strodach. She told me the whole sad story—though she said his death had taken place in Albany instead of Reading. [Strodach had committed suicide; he was the husband of my grandmother Stevens' (Kate's) sister.] I told her I was from Massachusetts etc. She introduced me to her husband, Hugo; and the two of them chattered away on

At this point about one-third of the journal page has been cut off; on the opposite side of the page, reversing the book, the last entry is the heading "December 31—1900"; it is difficult to tell which entry was elided, but presumably the latter. If so, however, why is it that, as we find it, the journal goes on after the cut seemingly without interruption?

the stairs where the girls of the school once cornered me and tried to borrow a pocket-knife—a ruse to find out whether I had one. They presented one to me shortly afterward on my birthday—one which went the way of all my knives. As I was leaving I caught a glimpse of the iron steps in the yard leading up to the door through which I had thrown kisses to the knife-presenting misses the day I took my leave. I wonder where they all are now. I have forgotten their names and even their faces though if I had kept my early letters I should find several from them with odd little designs thereon which I remember their writing to me after I had returned home. The old organ I used to drum upon was gone, too; and in its place was a piano wrapped in a dusty linen cover.

One can't help wondering whether this may not have been the scene for "Piano Practice at the Academy of the Holy Angels," which begins, "The time will come for these children, seated before their long black instruments, to strike the themes of love—" and includes the words, "Crispine, the blade." If "Crispin" is used by Stevens autobiographically, in "The Comedian as the Letter C," is it not possible to think of the "blade" as a "pocket-knife"?

Returning to the journal entry headed June 22, 1900, we learn:

In the afternoon I strolled up to Madison Square and sat in the garden, watching the fountain, and reading newspapers.

In the evening—more newspapers and a dip in [Robert Louis] Stevenson's "Letter To a Young Gentleman," "Christmas Sermon," and my old favorite "Silverado Squatters."

Today, at breakfast, I met the new land-lady of the house. Miss Vainé, the former one, has given way to a Mrs. Snyder, who is more suited to this tenement neighborhood.

The next entry in the journal is a poem which certainly seems a direct reflection of my father's life in the city at that point. But when we look back at his reference to reading Stevenson, and then take a look at the "Christmas Sermon," we find a good deal more: within the sermon Stevenson quotes a poem by William Ernest Henley (though he does not give its title, "I. M. Margaritae Sororis"), which begins

> A late lark twitters from the quiet skies;

and goes on to mention "the old, gray city," referring to London. Of the many revisions my father made in his journal poem, one of the few that is legible is the deletion of the word "lark's," which originally ended line seven; throughout, the tone provides one of the most direct echoes of his reading as well as of his life that can be found.

A WINDOW IN THE SLUMS

I think I hear beyond the walls
    The sound of late birds singing.
Ah! what a sadness those dim calls
    To city streets are bringing.

But who will from my window lean
    May hear, neath cloud belated,
Voices far sadder intervene [lark's]
    Sweet songs with longing weighted—

Gay children in their fancied towers
    Of London, singing light
Gainst heavier bars, more gay than in their flowers
    The birds of the upclosing night

And after stars their places fill
    And no bird greets the skies;
The voices of the children still
    Up to my window rise.

Revised.

June 26.

Scribbled away the day—rather the best way of doing it. This evening sat on step reading newspapers and watched the ivy dancing along the fronts of the houses opposite—that is all that does dance in this street. Poor, stifled boarders were leaning out of the windows for fresh air, proving what in less considerate days I thought a vulgar habit to be an instinct; but perhaps all instincts are nothing more than vulgar habits. Later I walked up Fifth Avenue for a little exercise. The janitors of the big houses were sweltering in area-ways; street-organs were rattling—a contrast to the bicycles that silently glided over the asphalt. I am afraid I shall melt in bed.

June 28.

Yesterday afternoon I went up on top of the *World* building in Park Row to get a look at the city. It had been sultry all day and here and there were masses of shadowy cloud. Suddenly a stroke of lightning struck a flag-staff on the building of the Tract Society a short distance off and knocked me down. I was up again in a minute, however, and did not waste much time getting down into the street.

This morning I went to the funeral of Stephen Crane at the Central Metropolitan Temple on Seventh Avenue near Fourteenth Street. The church is a small one and was about a third full. Most of the people were of the lower classes and had dropped in apparently to pass away the time. There was a sprinkling of men and women who looked literary, but they were a wretched, rag, tag, and bob-tail. I recognized John Kendrick Bangs. The whole thing was frightful. The prayers were perfunctory, the choir worse than perfunctory with the exception of its hymn "Nearer My God To Thee" which is the only appropriate hymn for funerals I ever heard. The address was absurd. The man kept me tittering from the time he began till the time he ended. He spoke of Gladstone & Goethe. Then—on the line of premature death—he dragged in Shelley; and speaking of the dead man's later work, he referred to Hawthorne. Finally came the Judgement day—all this with most delicate, sweet, and bursal gestures —when the earth and the sea shall give up their dead. A few of the figures to appear that day flashed through my head—and poor Crane looked ridiculous among them. But he lived a brave, aspiring, hard-working life. Certainly he deserved something better than this absolutely common-place, bare, silly service I have just come from. As the hearse rattled up the street over the cobbles, in the stifling heat of the sun, with not a single person paying the least attention to it and with only four or five carriages behind it at a distance I realized much

that I had doubtingly suspected before—There are few hero-wor-
shippers.

Therefore, few heroes.

It's interesting here to note that my father recognized John Kendrick
Bangs, one of the most popular writers of the day, whose *A House-Boat
on the Styx* led to several sequels. Among its references are the dispute
as to whether Bacon wrote the plays we know as Shakespeare's, and how
marvelous it is to have a duck for dinner. An exploration of the latter does
not provide any direct connection with my father's use of "A Duck for
Dinner" as a subtitle within "Owl's Clover," but reading both, one finds
some provocative analogies.

The next entry in the journal brings us up to date after a week's
hiatus.

> Fourth of July! but a commonplace one for me. I have been
> working on the New York *Tribune* almost a week. The *Tribune*
> had no sooner taken me than the *Evening Post* sent me a telegram,
> offering me a position. I was forced to decline it of course. I loaf
> about the office a great deal waiting for something to happen, and
> that is not especially profitable since I am paid according to the space
> I fill. Today I did not write a single line. But I planned much, read
> much, and thought much. A city is a splendid place for thinking. I
> have a sonnet in my head the last line of which is—
>
> And hear the bells of Trinity at night—
>
> bells which start ringing in my remotest fancies. In coming down to
> brick and stone I must be careful to remember the things worth
> remembering. I am going to get a set of Lowell's *Plato* as soon as I
> can afford it and use that as a sort of buoy. I still think New York a
> wretched place—with its infernal money-getting. Towards evening it
> rained and the showers washed the roofs and walls so that the city
> looked like a workingman who had just bathed. After dinner—
> shredded wheat, milk, batter cakes, chocolate—I went to office, then
> to Palisades (115th st. Harlem) and saw the sunset. I could not get
> rid of the lines—
>
> "outwinged in flight
> The pleasant region of the things I love."

Following this quotation from Santayana a sentence begins, "The region
was before me but" and the rest of the page has been cut off. The opposite
side of the page, when the journal is reversed, has an entry for Nov. 11,
1900, which has been interrupted. In the present direction, the journal
resumes on the next page with:

> At any rate I have regained my good spirits. I have not changed my
> address but expect to go over to West 9th st. within a few days.

Perish all sonnets! I have been working until 4 in the morning recently & have had plenty of time, therefore, to look over Stedman's "Victorian Anthology." There's precious little in the sonnet line there that's worth a laurel leaf. Sonnets have their place, without mentioning names; but they can also be found tremendously out of place: in real life where things are quick, unaccountable, responsive.

The other morning as I came home I walked up to Washington Square to take a look at the trees. The birds were just beginning to cheep & there was a little warm wind stirring among the leaves. I was surprised to find the large number of people who were sleeping on the grass and on the benches. One or two of them with collars turned up & hands in their pockets shuffled off through the sulphurous air like crows in rainy weather. The rest lay about in various states of collapse. There must have been a good many aching bones when the sun rose. The light was thin and bluishly misty; by the time I was in my room it had become more intense & was like a veil of thin gold.

I still patronize restaurants though I have been sick of them for a long time.

A month has passed since I have been in N. York & I have not yet written father for money. I am beginning to save already—perhaps a bad week will come & consume what I have laid up—still I have saved & the sense of miserliness in me is tickled.

Whatever else I may be doing I never fail to think of the country about Reading. During August I hope to run over & see all the roads & hills again. Besides, they do not seem real to me unless I am there. I can hardly believe that Wily's garden, for example, is as fine a thing as it was last summer. I am going up there, however, some day & shall see for myself. I miss my diary of last year, which is still in Cambridge. If it was here I could live over a few days at least. Now my flowers are all in milliner's windows & in tin-cans on fifth-story fire-escapes.

July 22. Sunday

Great Scott! it never occurred to me until this minute that the moon just ended is the one I called "that queen" last year. Neither sun nor moon is part of my world this year.

The impersonality of New York impresses me more and more every day. This afternoon I came across a charming set of church buildings—the buildings were not charming, but the ivy on their walls was—at Chelsea Square, taking up the whole square. Nobody could tell me what they were—except a maid in an area who told me she thought they were a seminary. There's impersonality for you!

One might note here that nine years later, when my parents married, they moved into an apartment directly across from General Theological Seminary in the heart of Chelsea; they lived there until they left New York in 1916. With all my father's personal reticence, it could be possible that he liked the neighborhood because of its "impersonality." The journal goes on:

> Another thing is the lack of locality! There are few places in the city —there is always something disintegrating, dislocating & nothing is distinct, defined—as Harvard for example is in Cambridge, the City Hall in Philadelphia, or the cathedrals, I imagine, in the towns of England & France. To this there are, of course, exceptions—as Lower Broadway & Upper Broadway, Wall St., Park Row, Brooklyn Bridge, & Central Park. But there is no air about Trinity, Fifth-ave., Union Sq., Madison Sq., etc. Madison Sq. approaches a locality but it is not definite etc., etc.
>
> I have been wondering today why I write so much about skies etc. I suppose it is because—Why does a mountaineer write about his Alps: or an astrologer about his magic?—

This last is reminiscent of Stevens' title "Botanist on Alp," used for two poems in 1934; the first one beginning, "Panoramas are not what they used to be." Surely, in his journal, he has been examining New York under his microscope.

> July 26.
> This has been a busy & therefore a profitable week. Tonight I received no assignment & so I am in my room. I almost said at home —God forbid! The proverbial apron-strings have a devil of a firm hold on me & as a result I am unhappy at such a distance from the apron. I wish a thousand times a day that I had a wife—which I never shall have, and more's the pity for I am certainly a domestic creature, par excellence. It is brutal to myself to live alone.

Here the next sentence has been erased, but is still partially legible. What remains appears to be "Especially when one knows whom one would"— followed logically by

> marry, if the thing was possible. I don't know—sometime I may marry after all. Of course I am too young now etc. as people go—but I begin to feel the vacuum that wives fill. This will probably make poor reading to a future bachelor. Wife's an old word—which does

not express what I mean—rather a delightful companion who would make a fuss over me.

July 20.

Made $21.65 this week.

Moved yesterday to my present address 37 West Ninth St. The room really belongs to an Italian—probably a very nice fellow. Oval gilt mirror on one wall, bureau with mirror on another, twenty or thirty pictures of actresses & a little set of shelves whereon I found a well-thumbed Dante in the original, Emerson's poems, somebody on the pleasures of solitude and one or two musical books. From my window I see something of the sky. There are high walls opposite covered with ivy. In the yard which is so much exposed clay—clean clay—a couple of mountain asters are growing. And in all this there dwell several birds who make a little music for me in the mornings.

Last night I went to the Harvard Club and in the *Harvard Monthly* for July I read an article by Daniel Gregory Mason on Philip Henry Savage. I did not know either of the men—although I used to be more or less familiar with Mason's face at college & of course heard a good deal of Savage, as all undergraduates do of successful graduates. Mason illustrates the effect of Harvard on a man's personality. The essay was written all through by a quaint & entertaining person. As a matter of good taste, it should have been written by nobody at all: it should have been absolutely impersonal. But Harvard feeds subjectivity, encourages an all consuming flame & that, in my mind, is an evil in so impersonal a world. Personality must be kept secret before the world. Between lovers and the like personality is well-enough; so with poets & old men etc. & conquerors & lambs etc.; but, for young men etc. it is most decidedly a well-enough to be left alone.

Savage had died in June 1899, and from my father's comments one gathers that he bore no relation to the Savages connected with my father's stay at the Wily's farm in Berkeley, Pa. And yet a copy of his posthumously published poems was sent to my father by Gertrude Savage [Mrs. Robert Staples] Collyer, in 1902; a further connection with the family may be obliquely referenced when my father notes, in 1908, "reading in the evenings to Robert Collyer." In 1900, we further note in the journal:

Savage was an admirable fellow. Mason calls his attempt at self-support "praiseworthy though quixotic!" This is absurd. Savage was like every other able-bodied man—he wanted to stand alone. Self-dependence is the greatest thing in the world for a young man & Savage knew it. I cannot talk about the subject, however, because

I know too little about it. But for one thing, Savage went into the shoe business & still kept an eye on sunsets & red-winged blackbirds —the summum bonum.

August 3.

Today I had a fascinating time. I received no assignments & from the point-of-view of money-making the day was a failure; from that of enjoying myself "a grand success." In the morning I read poetry & inwardly told the rest of the world to go to the devil (where I wish a good many of them really might go & stay). In the afternoon I wandered about—saw the Tombs, with Howe & Hummel's law offices right across the street; rode on the tail end of a dray until my rear was full of splinters & my entrails had changed places; and poked in & out among the wharves. I found a charming sailing-vessel—the "Elvira" of "Lisboa"—a Portuguese ship. She was a dandy—an old timer. Her hull was painted pink & blue and black; I forget how many masts she had; but there was a jungle of ropes overhead, in which were several sailors hanging like monkeys. The officers quarters were forward. The men were cooped up in the stern—a half-circle of filthy berths—excuse me! One fellow—the real thing—was dressed in pajamas of an explosive and screaming character. He said he talked a little English—but American was different. By the way, I had to ask a deck-hand where the quarters of the men were & not knowing the word for Quarters I used "*chambres*"—"*Où sont les chambres des matelots?*" which is execrable French—("*Les chambres où* etc.?"). The fellow snickered. The "*chambres,*" or rather this single "*chambre*" was more like a *salle à manger, à dormir, à baigner, à fumer, et à jouer les cartes* etc. It was an extraordinarily fine *mise en scène* for a "wee bit tale." I'm a wild polyglot tonight & no wonder! On deck were a number of chickens—several fighting cocks with which the sailors probably passed the evenings of unspeakable voyages. There was also a coop of pigeons—one a big beast that glistened as it strutted in the sun. If ever a ship opened a new world to me that one did. She sails for Freemantle, South Australia in about a week, to be gone for four months.

I also saw a fleet of canal-boats—a wilderness of domesticity. They lay like villagers and greenhorns in the water—the tide bounced them about like huge, clumsy logs. I could not help being a bit contemptuous. A dead cat lay under the rudder of one. Nearby was a little butterfly hunting sustenance. Silly jumble!

In the evening I went to the "Syrie Restaurant" on top of the Tract Society Building: 23rd floor. My first—or practically my first sunset of the summer. Everything deliciously pure & calm. Over

Brooklyn was a low, dark ridge like a mountain with deep crimson peaks—or like a wall over which one looked into the rose-gardens of Paradise. There were no other clouds visible. Looking toward the West I could see the river—like a shattered crystal. The sun simply went down—no colors—no delays—a simple progress. But the air was incomparably clear & revealing.

I begin to like New York & do like it hard. Reading seems childish & weak—but I like it, too—Boetia is Boetia especially when one is born in it. My liking for N. Y. & for R. are, however, quite different. I might spin any number of balanced sentences etc. around the difference—which amounts to this   that I saw Reading first.

I left Wily's today a year ago.

Among the poems I read this morning were thirty sonnets by David Gray, a young Scotchman who died of consumption December 3, 1861. The poems were called "In the Shadows" & were in the Bibelot. David Gray must have been a brave fellow, both rugged & melancholy. There are some things in these sonnets which almost bring tears to one's eyes—David Gray is in them. He's a new acquaintance & although probably a solitary person makes one love him & regret him. His verses occasionally have much beauty—though never any great degree of force—other than pathetic.

The poems of David Gray apparently made a great impression. Either he kept the book from the Italian's "bibelot," or he memorized the poem, for he quotes from Gray in a letter to my mother eleven years later:

Psychologically, the obscurity of twilight and of night shuts out the clear outline of visible things which is a thing that appeals to the intellect. The clear outline having been obliterated, the emotions replace the intellect and

> Lo! I behold an orb of silver brightly
> Grow from the fringe of sunset, like a dream
> From Thought's severe infinitude—

I swear, my dear Bo-Bo, that it's a great pleasure to be so poetical.

One's first thought would be that the three lines were my father's, but they are from Gray's sonnet beginning, "Lying awake at holy eventide," which closely resembles some of my father's undergraduate verses; perhaps the lines were so compatible that he assimilated them into his imagination as his own.

Returning to the journal, the next entry is brief:

I have settled down & am going to be "as lazy as I dare."

August 8.

Bargained for my room today—20.00 a month after September 1.

Pleasant little saloon at corner of 6th Ave. & 11th St. Went there last night for a beer and found a corking cat that curled up in my lap. A fellow of about 30 came in and saw me. He came up, sat down, chatted & drank & was genial until 12 o'clock. I was suspicious of him —something had happened to him—but he was extremely agreeable & I accepted him with no other introduction than Life's. He'd been around the Horn & was full of stories which he told unusually well, having once been a newspaper man in San Francisco. We—he rather —talked about shark's teeth, shark's timidity, the Magellan cloud (of stars), flying fish & their flight & sailors methods of catching them by means of a lighted sail at night etc. etc., calms, characters—he thought himself an awful ass—which he was not etc. He rolls his own cigarettes—thin, sweet-smelling wisps—& lives under the roof above a taxidermist's on 6th Ave.

August 23.

Made 24.50 last week.

The "Elvira" was formerly called the "Argonaut"—an English ship. She had not been to New York since '79 or '89 or some such date. '79 was the year in which I was born.

These last two weeks I have been working until 4 in the morning & am naturally tired of it all & impatient to be up and away and doing something that has some flash to it.

Hang it—a fellow must live with the world—& for it and in it.

Yesterday I saw a case of the delirium tremens at the foot of W. 10th St. (North River). A tall, husky Irishman struggled and squirmed—a snake himself. In spite of the horrible sight & example, a bystander picked up & emptied the drunkard's bottle.

Stevens' first summer in New York was coming to an end, and before it was over he returned to Reading for a brief vacation. One or more pages are missing from his journal after the previous entry, before one reaches the end of it, reading in the original direction. Reversing the book, it begins in the middle of a sentence written, it seems, late in August after the visit home:

naps at different places along the bank—& in Wily's meadow where I grumbled out something to a little squirrel in the limbs above me. Going home I crossed Dunkel's field which was full of clover, etc., & rising birds. I found the broken rail at the other end. Along the road the apples were beginning to look red & indeed everything was there as usual—excepting myself.

I walked over to Tuckerton & saw Levi Mengel & Christopher Shearer—both in their cottages, both happy, comfortable, content.

R.R. from Tuckerton—carried a bushel of potatoes into the smoking car for an old woman.

How bright & full of color the holly-hocks were!

Sept. 2.
The wind is blowing in the trees outside my window bringing me occasional gusts of chimes. The sky is already bright with the half-moon.

Dropped into St. Patrick's Cathedral this afternoon. Beautiful but cold. Gothic architecture.

September 10—4 A.M.
Have just returned from work. A most lovely night—The morning star—
How keen, how bright, how free from all despair—
So I have gone to seed. The city deliciously still. A few magic stars dropping through the sky—which startle and dazzle one. Amazing freshness & purity in the air.

What a wonderful hour this must be in gardens—on the hills & on the sea.

October 5.
Saw Richard Mansfield in *Henry V* tonight. Splendid spectacle—but oh the humor of it, as Bardolph used to say. Pistol a most delicious braggard as he comes swaggering into London among those "happy men" from France. That scene of welcome—with the flowers in the road—and the huge crowd of shouting people on

The journal entry breaks off here, at the bottom of a page; no excision is indicated before the next page begins:

I have been earning good wages of late—16.75, 26.50, 22.30 etc. —that's nothing *now*.

Expect to go home next week for three days & let that wind up my holidays for some time to come. I want to see father about the *Times;* I also want to see Livingood who has just come back from the West—where he did not prosper—and Frank Mohr fresh from the Philippines.

I do not expect to vote this election.

October 14.

I was home Wednesday & Thursday. Saw Livingood—still a sickly Hamlet. We went up to Kuechler's Wednesday afternoon & stayed through the evening. Magnificent moon came up over the hills. Stood in K's yard & apostrophized it. Livy very drunk. Coming down the hillsides we would turn to the moon through the trees and hold dialogues with it. Charming night.

In the morning I had called on Frank—Lieutenant Mohr. His den was filled with Filipino weapons, hats, etc.—a great variety of Oriental odds and ends. Frank is a first-class fellow & may come to N.Y. His trip took him around the world.

Thursday morning sat in a shaft of light in Livy's office—he read Milton's *Paradise Lost* to me.—The sun was better than the poetry—but both were heavenly things.

Thursday afternoon took a walk out Centre Ave. pike to Berkeley. Stopped at every tavern—for a beer, a cigar, and a poke at the bartenders. Livy & I thought it rather good fun to ask them about Mike Angelo, Butch Petrarch, Sammy Dante. We asked one fellow whether he had heard that John Keats had been run over, by a trolley car at Stony Creek in the morning. He said that he had not—he did not know Keats—but that he had heard of the family. Spirit of Adonais!

How much more vigorous was the *thought* of the old fellows than is that of any modern man.

Tuesday night Livy & I walked up the Boulevard. A delicate, blue night—more gorgeous, golden stars & the air as fresh and as pure as the air of the moon. I have a great affection for moonlight nights somehow—& could cry "moon, moon, moon" as fast as the world calls "thief" after a villain—What a treasure house of silver and gold they are—& how lovely the planets look in the heavens—Bah—mere words.

October 18.

I start today on a salary of $15.00 a week. This is considerably less than I have been earning on space—but I suppose I can get along. I have been promised an immediate raise if I do good work.

I have been walking in the Park of late in the mornings. The weather has been cool and clear and bright. The leaves begin to fall thickly & the wind is becoming audible. Somehow the Park is exquisitely musical—perhaps it is the music just "dying" from the harp of the muse under the head of Beethoven—near the terraces. The statue of Burns is unspeakably rotten.

Have been doing the art galleries & exhibitions.

Saw [William Jennings] Bryan the other day & heard him make 4 speeches in 3 hours.

It seems likely that he would have heard those speeches in his role as reporter for the New York *Tribune*, which carried a story on October 17, 1900, noting that "Mr. Bryan spoke last evening at Madison Square Garden, in the street outside the Garden, at Tammany Hall and at Cooper Union."

Oct. 21.

West street, along the North River, is the most interesting street in the whole city to me. I like to walk up and down and see the stevedores and longshoremen lounging about in the sun. They are always dressed in overalls and a blouse, with a cap on their heads, a pipe in their mouths & their hands in their pockets. They are either fine big-boned, husky fellows, or wretched decrepit wrecks. Then there is such a tremendous amount of business done in West street by the Jew with a few combs or cuff-buttons of cat's-eyes from Mexico to sell, through the hucksters, & fishmen, and grizzly oyster-openers, & ferry-keepers up to the men who run the steamship lines. The street is as cosmopolitan and republican as any in the world. It is the only one that leaves the memory full of pictures, of color and movement. Clattering trucks and drays, tinkling and bouncing horse-cars, hundreds of flags at mast-heads, glimpses of the water between piers, ticket-brokers & restaurant piled on restaurant.

The next entry has been crossed out with a large "X," but it is still legible, with my father's comment at the end. The eighth line was originally the same as the fourth line; each word has been separately lined out and the new line written beneath. The poem, with its echoes of Henley and Santayana, reminds me of "A spirit storming in blank walls," a line from "A Postcard from the Volcano" (1936).

SONNET

Build up the walls about me; close each door;
And fasten all the windows with your bars;
Still shall I walk abroad on Heaven's floor
And be companion to the singing stars.

Whether your prison be of greatest height
Or gloomier depth: it matters not. Though blind
I still shall look upon the burning light,
And see the flowers dancing in the wind.

Your walls will disappear; your doors will swing
Even as I command them. I shall fare
Either up hill or down, and I shall be
Beside the happy lark when he takes wing,
Striking sweet music from the empty air,
And pass immortal mornings by the sea.

Sorry I wrote it. Sorry I crossed it out.

October 26.

New York is so big that a battle might go on at one end, and poets meditate sonnets at another.

Mohr has been visiting me. He has the toothpick habit. Ugh.

Ate a big, juicy "bifstek" chez l'Hotel Martin, ce soir. Mais je ne parle pas au garçon; j'eus trop de peur.

November 10.

Been having a devil of a time—campaign finally over. Went home for election day, & voted the Democratic ticket—Bryan.

On November 2 (Friday) I heard W. Bourke Cockran speak in Brooklyn—an oration of profound convictions and magnetic beauty. They say he's bribed—perhaps he is—one never can tell. But he is certainly & all the same the most fluent, the most lofty and potent, and admirable speaker I have ever heard. His oration was printed in the Brooklyn *Eagle*—Nov. 3—*Sui vide*—

One can only wonder whether the unsigned account of Cockran's Brooklyn speech in the *Tribune*, headlined "Attempts to Prove that the Sultan of Sulu is President of the United States," was written by Stevens.

The journal continues on a more sombre note, still in the November 10 entries.

It is quite bleak outside. I enjoy it though—so long as it doesn't rain & isn't foggy.

Last night I saw Maude Adams as the Duke of Reichstadt in Rostand's *L'Aiglon*. The scene on the field of Wagram was too thrilling to thrill—the accusing voices in the wind (*id est*—wind-machine) must have had a fine effect on serious minds—they made me laugh. But it was all vastly entertaining as everything of the sort is bound to be in New York. There's something about Maude Adams that wrings a fellow's heart. Perhaps it is the pathos she inspires one to feel.

My desire to be off somewhere still exists, though no longer so exactingly. Summer is gone & the city is decidedly cozy and smart. Still I could enjoy mornings in Florida and afternoons and long nights in California—breathing fresh air and living at leisure—away from the endless chain to which I am fastened like a link—at constant strain. But Florida and California are limited regions & so my desire is limited. The calling is remote—there is not a voice in every bit of green or open space. May will be maddening when it comes. I keep asking myself—Is it possible that I am here? And what a silly & utterly trivial question it is. I hope to get to Paris next summer—and mean to if I have the money. Saving it will be difficult—with all the concerts and exhibitions, and plays we are to have—not to mention the butcher, baker, and candle-stick maker. But to fly! *Gli uccelli hanno le ali*—that's what they're [from this point on the rest of the entry has been crossed out, but is still legible] not here. Whenever I think of these things I can see, & do see, a bird somewhere in a mass of flowers and leaves, perched on a spray in dazzling light, and pouring out arpeggios of enchanting sound.

My work on the *Tribune* is dull as dull can be. I'm too lazy to attempt anything outside—& the fact that I work two days a week—Wednesday & Thursday—in Brooklyn spoils whatever laziness hasn't made on her own. Brooklyn is *the* most hideous—

The moon has not been bad of late. The stars are clear and golden and geometrical and whatever else they try to be. I rather like that idea of geometrical—it's so confoundedly new!

Sometimes I wish I wore no crown—that I trod on something thicker than air—that there were no robins, or peach dumplings, or violets in my world—that I was the proprietor of a patent medicine store—or manufactured pants for the trade—and that my name was Asa Snuff. But alas! the tormenting harmonies sweep around my hat, my bosom swells with "agonies and exultations"—and I pose.

I was speaking to a Tammany Hall man tonight. He had a re-markably comprehensive view of things—I remember his saying—
"Well, we are all human beings. Money is our object. Hence—"
Politics, I suppose.
After all, blink at it all we will, look at it from every point of view, coddle, coax, apologize, squirm or what one pleases we cannot deny that on the whole "money is our object." We all get down to that sooner or later. I won't cross this out either.

I heard another man today say—
"I've seen enough of life."
This idea of life in the abstract is a curious one & deserves some reflection.

How curious that forty-two years later he would write:

> Never suppose an inventing mind as source
> Of this idea nor for that mind compose
> A voluminous master folded in his fire . . .

in the first section of "Notes Toward a Supreme Fiction," subtitled "It Must Be Abstract." It did take "some reflection."

November 11.

Sunday morning. The sky is overcast and it looks as though we might have a flurry of snow. I love this snowy light. It is suggestive of evergreens and candles and open fires—a suggestiveness which charms the self-indulgent fancy. I should like to be stalking the hills under a crisp, blue sky—the fields white and shining below me—alone. And then I should like to go home after a cold, chilly, green and purple and pale red sunset and flirt with the spirits

The lower half of this page has been cut off. It is the reverse of the page ending "outwinged in flight / The pleasant region of the things I love," followed by, in reading from the torn segment, "The region was before me but . . ." where the July 4, 1900, entry has been interrupted. The apposition of July and November in the same "region" leads me to note my father's use of the title "The Region November," for a poem first published the year after he died:

> It is hard to hear the north wind again,
> And to watch the treetops, as they sway.
>
> They sway, deeply and loudly, in an effort,
> So much less than feeling, so much less than speech,
>
> Saying and saying, the way things say
> On the level of that which is not yet knowledge:
>
> A revelation not yet intended.
> It is like a critic of God, the world
>
> And human nature, pensively seated
> On the waste throne of his own wilderness.
>
> Deeplier, deeplier, loudlier, loudlier,
> The trees are swaying, swaying, swaying.

The next page of the journal begins in mid-sentence:

from a concert by Edward Strauss at the Metropolitan. I sat on the dizzy height of the upper gallery. When the people clapped, their hands from above appeared to simmer. The music was pleasant, airy, rather too cloying, full of little quirks & little quirks again, & cricket voices & jumps of sound & small melodies that took you to the ball-room & the court—and all decidedly in the manner & for the people of Anthony Watteau.

November 25.
Dull— Dull— Dull—

Friday a week (and more) ago I went to a Philharmonic re-hearsal at Carnegie Hall. *The* thing was Tschaikowsky's Concerto No. 1—B flat minor (op. 23) with Mme. Teresa Carreño at the piano. Fine—in spite of what the critics say.

Wrote up four dinners during the week—ate three of them.

Am waiting for Bernhardt. My ticket is for December 7.

December 7.
Have just returned from Bernhardt in *L'Aiglon*. I must write more—later.

Dec. 15.
Went to Boston yesterday—my day off. Cambridge did not seem what it used to be—but I was filled with animal spirits at being in it once again. Saw Saunders, Barker etc. Couple of bottles of St. Estephe at [unclear name, "Charlivari's"?]—a shiver through the streets & the midnight train. When I got here this morning the day was just breaking, and the sky was filled with veils of sweet vermeil.

Dec. 29.
Last night I saw Sarah Bernhardt in *Hamlet*. The critics have been jumping on her all week. Winter in the *Tribune* began his attack with "Alas! poor Hamlet." But it did not seem so bad to me. Bernhardt had a conception of the character; and this is a point of the first importance. I waited eagerly and curiously to hear her first speech—"A little more than kin, & less than kind." It was delivered in a level, unemotional, non-committal manner. Indeed, she seemed to be in a stupor up to—"Angels and ministers of grace defend us!" In this scene her character changed instantly—although her appear-ances remained pretty much the same as ever. So the play proceeded. I was struck with the intense abstraction of Hamlet's character. Bernhardt conveyed a suggestion of this abstraction, but nothing more. Her abstraction seemed more vacant than brooding. The scene with the ghost was thrilling—and the sense of vacancy disappeared when the actress cried
"O mon âme prophétique!"

From that moment on, Hamlet was cunningness itself.

I was shocked by Polonius. However talkative and childish he may be supposed to be, he ought not to be mistaken for a fussy, sap-headed, old ass; a silly, idiotic, utterly senseless, horrible guy. Hamlet's treatment of him was too rude for a prince, too indelicate for such a delicate nature. It occurs to me that Hamlet must have known that Polonius would report his madness to the King, and that he would thus be of the greatest assistance to carrying out his own scheme of feigned madness. In that case, Hamlet, if he were cunning, would not be quite so brutal personally as Bernhardt made him. Bernhardt's treatment of Polonius, in short, seems somewhat inconsistent.

Her treatment of Ophelia was much wiser. It is true that Hamlet speaks of Polonius vilely—but I think distantly, and with contemptuous dignity. His treatment of Ophelia is different; and Bernhardt made it so. There was a pathetic tenderness in Bernhardt's attitude, which warmed and deepened her character. At the grave, when she cried out—"Ophélie! Ophélie! Ophélie!"—one felt how profound her affection had been.

The scene, "La ruse d'Hamlet," in Act III showed Bernhardt's conception of cunning in clear light. The word "ruse" alone was almost enough for that. While Lucianus was pouring the poison into the Player King's ear, Hamlet crept up the King's dais and looked piercingly into the King's eyes [and] waited until Ophelia cried in alarm—

"The King rises"—

when he shrieked and clapped his hands with devilish ecstasy, crying—

"What! frighted with false fire!"

As he waved the lights in the King's face, when the latter was flying from the stage, he looked mad indeed—with victory and malignity. Altogether too harsh.

After that he saddened again and remained so.

In the *North American Review* for December there is an admirable criticism of Bernhardt's way of looking at the character. The writer suggests that Mme. B. portrays the character as it was conceived in Elizabethan days. The theory is attractive, and possibly true.

I got considerable satisfaction from following the play with the book. I noticed, as everyone else did, the skillful manner in which the "business" was introduced. It showed the resources of Mme. B's mind, and her skill and stagecraft.

Mme. B's concept may not be great, but it is interesting, and makes one think.

In 1943, in "The Figure of the Youth as Virile Poet," Stevens wrote:

> Long ago, Sarah Bernhardt was playing Hamlet. When she came
> to the soliloquy "To be or not to be," she half turned her back on
> the audience and slowly weaving one hand in a small circle above
> her head and regarding it, she said, with deliberation and as from the
> depths of a hallucination: *"D'être ou ne pas d'être, c'est là la
> question . . ."* and one followed her, lost in the intricate metamor-
> phosis of thoughts that passed through the mind with a gallantry, an
> accuracy of abundance, a crowding and pressing of direction, which,
> for thoughts that were both borrowed and confused, cancelled the
> borrowing and obliterated the confusion.

Despite her concept, it made a lasting impression. Returning to December
1900, we find:

> Walked along Riverside Drive this morning and got thoroughly
> aerated. Warm sun—cold air—clear sky—a magnificent day.

> Went home for a few hours on Xmas day. Talked with father—
> who is kept busy holding me in check. I've been wanting to go to
> Arizona or Mexico, but do not have any good reason for doing so. I
> am likely to remain here until Spring, at least. Europe is still on the
> other side of the ocean.

The next entry in the journal is dated "December 31—1900," but the
four or five lines following the date, at the bottom of the page, have been
cut off. (The opposite side of the page falls within the entry for June 22,
1900.) The next page, still obviously written on New Year's Eve, begins
within a sentence:

> my watch which runs along just as naturally as though it were telling
> off the old, regular, every-day minutes, instead of these solemn ones
> which make a fellow feel so confoundedly thoughtful. Well, it is
> some satisfaction to be still living in the nineteenth century—it's a
> rather cosy century & we've got used to it; but the change is coming
> —it must be pretty well on its way across the Atlantic by this time
> —and we will probably find some way of putting it to good use. The
> temptation to make resolutions is tremendous—but that's the one
> temptation I find easy to resist, and I do not intend to make any kind
> of attempt at turning over a new leaf. I had intended to go to St.
> Patrick's Cathedral to attend midnight mass; but I am now in my
> room & shall stay there. The church bells are ringing, the streets are
> filled with people—boys—girls—men—women—none of whom, most
> likely, will see the century out. But they are welcoming it heartily, if
> one is to judge by the noise they are making. I am carried away, and
> would like to kick or kiss something or somebody—What a nasty
> reflection at this moment! But time's scythe is not a magic wand, and

though the century changes, I still remain W.S. & can say *adieu!* to no part of me. So for the century so soon to go—*adieu! adieu!* & God rest her bones. I shall now crawl into my pyjamas & be meditative, if I can.

Quarter-of-twelve. The noise is rather confused & sounds like a horse-fly buzzing around the room. Ferries are tooting & chimes have broken out.

Horrid din—The Hour strikes—like roar of heavy express—or rolling of great mill—Chimes incoherent, Voices—Mass of sound— like strong wind through telegraph wires.
January 1—1901—Bon Jour.

Noise still great—noise within noise—noise—noise—noise—but it seems to be subsiding.

I was trying to say a prayer but could not.

Morning.
This morning it is cloudy though not gloomy. I ate a grapefruit in my room & then went down to the corner and had my boots blacked. In this way, I nurse an aristocratic feeling.

It is as quiet as a Sunday in the country.

Since I have left school & college, I have been surprised at the seasons, which seem to change much less abruptly and to be much less different than I had thought them. We're supposed to be in mid-winter now, but, except that I am not perspiring, I might as well be in midsummer.

Much later, in midsummer of the mid-1940's, one finds an echo of this youthful end and beginning, in the words "the last day of a certain year."

> Now in midsummer come and all fools slaughtered
> And spring's infuriations over and a long way
> To the first autumnal inhalations, young broods
> Are in the grass, the roses are heavy with a weight
> Of fragrance and the mind lays by its trouble.
>
> Now the mind lays by its trouble and considers.
> The fidgets of remembrance come to this.
> This is the last day of a certain year
> Beyond which there is nothing left of time.
> It comes to this and the imagination's life.

V

The twentieth century had begun. Wallace Stevens was twenty-one, had been living in New York for six months, and his journal continues:

> I have come to like New York heartily and sincerely. It is a fine thing to have your hands full every day—& N.Y. keeps them full. Then the interest of the town is strong. I have about made up my mind never to settle down in Reading.

But life in New York was lonely, even though he saw friends occasionally and, less frequently, returned to Reading. His career was not progressing well, and he was badly depressed at times, even to the point of suicide, according to William Carlos Williams, who noted:

> There is also the story of the down and out Stevens sitting on a park bench at the Battery watching the out tide and thinking to join it, as a corpse, on its way to the sea (he had been a failure as a reporter). As he sat there watching the debris floating past him he began to write—noting the various articles as they passed. He became excited as he wrote and ended by taking back to the *Tribune* (?) office an editorial or a "story" that has become famous—in a small way among the newspaper offices.
>
> But that finished him as a newspaper man. It may very well be that that moment was his beginning as a poet.

And Witter Byrner recollected, in 1958:

> I do not know whether Stevens' work as a reporter in New York in 1900 and 1901 was connected with his literary ambition or was for financial reasons. In any event, it was a very good offset to the fastidious instruction we had been receiving at Cambridge. When I saw him after my graduation in 1902, he was at law school. . . . He was living in a small room to himself. My memory would say that it was a hall bedroom.

My father's first comment on "the Law" appears in his next journal entry.

January 31, 1901.

I have been interested by the sentences passed on the four men in the Bosscheiter murder case in Paterson, N.J. Three of them received (!) 30 years, one 15. The imagination cannot project itself forward as far as to conceive the future lives of these men. But what a terrible avenger the Law is. It seems as though the sense of Justice which dictated such sentences was not human. The mere length of time is a ghastly thing to contemplate. Jonah must have written the Law, where it is so terrible as this. A Judge ought to tremble when he executes it.

Again, we cannot prove that Stevens wrote the account of the trial which had appeared in the *Tribune* the day before, but the opening paragraph helps to put his journal entry into perspective:

The four murderers of Jennie Bosscheiter were sentenced to the extreme penalty of the law by Judge Dixon this morning in the Court of Oyer and Terminer. His voice trembled with emotion as he described the enormity of the crime and the manner in which it had been committed. The courtroom was crowded, among the spectators being the mother and the brothers of the murdered girl. Mrs. Bosscheiter sat at the end of a seat, and her skirts were brushed by the four men as they were led in and out of the courtroom.

Oddly enough, Williams does not refer to "the Bosscheiter case" in *Paterson*.

I have determined to go to England this summer, if nothing unexpected happens. I already have the price of the passage one way —and a little more.

February 6.

Father was in town two days ago. I took luncheon with him at the Astor House—baked shad, asparagus etc. We remarked that we looked well.

It is cold as the deuce this morning. No doubt of the season & midsummer is damned far off.

By the way, I have moved to No. 124 East 24th St. Am in a hall bedroom, as they say, and rather like it.

Feb. 7.

Last night I was skipping about the Upper Bay on tugs trying to find out about a meeting on the bark *Astral.*

This afternoon I took a walk from the house up to Central Park and through it. I got to the Park after sunset, although the Western horizon was still bright with its cold yellow. The drives were white with snow and at times the air was quite full of the cheering sound of sleigh-bells. I hurried through the Mall or Grand Alley or whatever it is; went down those mighty stairs to the fountain; followed a path around the lake, and came to a tower surrounded with a sort of parapet. The park was deserted yet I felt royal in my empty palace. A dozen or more stars were shining. Leaving the tower and parapets I wandered about in a maze of paths some of which led to an invisible cave. By this time it was dark and I stumbled about over little bridges that creaked under my step, up hills, and through trees. An owl hooted. I stopped and suddenly felt the mysterious spirit of nature—a very mysterious spirit, one I thought never to have met with again. I breathed in the air and shook off the lethargy that has controlled me for so long a time. But my Ariel-owl stopped hooting & the spirit slipped away and left me looking with amusement at the extremely unmysterious and not at all spiritual hotels and apartment houses that were lined up like elegant factories on the West side of the Park. I crossed to Eighth Ave., and in a short time returned to the house.

February 20. Wednesday.

On Monday night I went to the Garrick Theatre, having finished my work early, and saw Ethel Barrymore as Mme. Trentoni in "Captain Jinks of the Horse Marines" by Clyde Fitch. I was charmed. Hang me if I don't write a play myself. I am quite excited about it and have already arranged the plot. It is to be called

OLIVIA:

A Romantic Comedy

IN FOUR ACTS.

The plot so far amounts to this—

I. (A Room.) Olivia Rainbow, an American, is visiting France with her brother Harry. She goes to Dijon or some other place (which will not be decided until I have examined Baedeker & the maps) to spend a few days in the chateau of the Duke of Bellemer, a friend of Harry's. There she encounters, besides the Duke, three Frenchmen who fall madly in love with her. She is very vivacious & perhaps inclined to flirt & so she appears to encourage each of the three. (One of the three is a poet—or a dreamer—the other two have not yet been given characters.) Their conduct plainly shows that they are in love—the Duke's does not.

II. (A Wood.) Olivia is driving through a wood near the chateau in company with the Countess or something of something else, a sister to the Duke. The side of the carriage is seen in the scenes to the right. The three Frenchmen come from the left and salute the passing carriage—begging Olivia and the Countess to alight. It appears that the meeting had been arranged by the Countess who is rather fatuous & has been amused by the appeals of the three. She explains to Olivia who, light-heartedly, agrees that whichever of the three shall knock a leaf or a flower or something off her shoulder (?) shall have the privilege of at least one rendezvous with her where he may speak for himself. She mentions the place & time of such rendezvous, etc. In the duels that follow canes are used. The three retire—They are to come up one by one & are not to know the result of each other's contest. The first knocks off the flower; the second also; the poet fails—Olivia jabs and pokes him with her cane while she is holding him off & makes him ridiculous. He is tall, dignified, wears a frock coat etc. The three separate—the first two in bliss—the poet in consternation.

III. (A Garden.) (In Act II I may arrange that the rendezvous is made privately with the first two & that the Countess who adores the poet pities him & puts him "on.") The scene is romantic—foliage, flowers etc. Olivia and her maid are talking together. Harry and the Countess (whom he is making love to) pass over the scene and disappear. A step is heard. The maid hides herself. The Duke comes on & mistaking Olivia for the Countess takes her off—she thinking it is one of the two who had appointed with her. The maid reappears. The first of the two comes on and states his case. He goes off. A number of laughing gossipers come on & say things etc. then exeunt. The maid comes out again—the second of the two comes on—states his case and goes off. The maid in consternation. The Duke runs on horribly cut up—has been saying things to Olivia which he meant to say to the Countess alone. Goes off. Olivia comes on in a merry mood—finds that the two have come & gone & sits down, dismissing the maid. Enter the poet—who poetizes etc.—exit Poet. Enter Countess & reenter gossipers.

IV. (A Room.) Scene same as in Act I. Olivia and the Duke. (The dénouement is not yet settled but it will be much like this.) Then Harry with the first two. The Countess with the Poet. Olivia explains that the first two have not kept their appointments etc. but that they can have the maid or something of that sort. The poet is out of the question because he did not knock off the flower. Olivia accepts the Duke & the Countess accepts Harry.

February 21. 1901.

I saw a good villain yesterday at ship-runs. He was courteous but slouchy. His clothes loose—coat buttoned, soft hat with high crown pulled down to ears—carried a cane—good mustache—raised his eyebrows when he spoke—spoke timidly & cautiously—nervous as though he needed a drink—carried a cane—listless—great possibilities if made desperate—swallows insults.

Siegel tells me that Ethel Barrymore took grapes—I mean luncheon—in this house one day last summer. Oh Heavens!

Feb. 22.

Last night I saw Ethel Barrymore in "Captain Jinks" again. Beautiful angel.

Feb. 28.

Saw Ethel Barrymore in "Captain Jinks" again tonight. She's charming in the last act in that white and green dress with the roses on it. It pays a fellow to see an ardor through. I'm interested in studying the play now—chiefly because it is, as the newspapers say, so fragile. Its very fragility is an advantage to me since it makes the mechanism simple & the means of running it plain.

Today I finished the first rough draught or sketch of "Olivia" in extenso. I have developed the plot etc. but I do not think it quite long enough yet for an evening's entertainment. Heaven save me from being dull.

March 11. 1901.

The streets are blue with mist this morning.

Went home last Thursday for a few hours—first time since Xmas. Reading looked the acme of dullness & I was glad, therefore, to get back to this electric town which I adore. I had a good long talk with the old man in which he did most of the talking. One's ideas don't get much of a chance under such conditions. However he's a wise man. We talked about the law which he has been urging me to take up. I hesitated—because this literary life, as it is called, is the one I always had as an ideal & I am not quite ready to give it up because it has not been all that I wanted it to be. The other day, after returning to New York, I called on John Phillips of McClure, Phillips and had a talk about the publishing business. P. is philosophical and serious & yet, I think, a person of no imagination—or little. He told me that the business was chiefly clerical—unpleasant fact— & that I could hardly expect to live on my wages—etc. etc. I was considerably jarred by the time he got through. The mirage I had fancied disappeared in the desert—where I invariably land. However, I've made a market for Mss—if it's at all worth while!

I've been giving "Olivia" a rest for a short time—so as to be able to inspect it as it should be inspected, before I start it.

The mist outside has grown visibly thicker since I wrote the above. The season is changing.

As the season changed, my father gave more thought to changing his career. It may be noteworthy that, many years later, in "Auroras of Autumn"—a poem filled with parental images, especially of "the father"—Stevens uses the phrase "The season changes" in part II, which opens, "Farewell to an idea. . . ." Is it possible that he was thinking back to 1901?

March 12.
To illustrate the change that has come over me I may mention that last night I saw from an elevated train a group of girls making flowers in a dirty factory near Bleecker St. I hardly gave it a thought. Last summer the pathos of it would have bathed me in tears.

I recently wrote to father suggesting that I should resign from the Tribune & spend my time in writing. This morning I heard from him &, of course, found my suggestion torn to pieces. If I only had enough money to support myself I am afraid some of his tearing would be in vain. But he seems always to have reason on his side, confound him.

Again, in "Auroras of Autumn" we find that the father "measures the velocities of change."

March 14.
Having a glorious time today. Just dropped in as I passed the house. Ran through Madison St. & Pitt St. and the whole East Side almost & then down through Tompkins Square to Stuyvesant Square (where I stepped into St. George's & sat down for a short time—how inspiring the man St. George is!). Then to [illegible word] Scheffel Hall in 17th St. where I had a Pilsener—a thundering good saloon—through Grammercy Park & its airs. Really the walk did me good—I was like Dante passing from star to star & f. world to world.

Haven't smoked since Friday—5 days—I feel a thousand times better, but long for a cigarette.

I've just come from seeing a two-headed Hebrew child—Horrible sight. The first head is all right—the 2nd protrudes from it—there is, of course, only one face. The mother looks dreadfully. She told me that the doctor had told her that an operation would be

necessary. She asked him if the child would be alive after the operation. He said it would not. If that is not murder, what is?

The remaining pages in this second notebook are blank, the only later
entry being the already noted comment, of June 1904, on an entry originally made in the summer of 1900. When Stevens stopped working as a
reporter cannot be precisely determined, nor do we know where he spent
the summer of 1901, though it was not in England as he had planned. Most
likely he spent some time in Reading and in conversation with his father,
for on October 1, 1901, he entered New York Law School. From his
application for admission to the bar of the State of New York, dated May
11, 1904, we learn that he was on vacation from the law school from June
12 to June 23, 1902, and then began his clerkship in the office of W. G.
Peckham. Within a month he had been invited by Peckham to visit his
summer home in the Adirondacks, and we learn more of that visit (somewhat obliquely) from a letter my father wrote to Richard Eberhart in
1950, after the poets had been together in Cambridge.

> After leaving you, I walked through Hilliard Street, the name of
> which seemed to be familiar, until it came out on Cambridge Com-
> mon by Radcliffe. At the point where it comes out Radcliffe is on the
> left. At the right there is an old dwelling where one of the most
> attractive girls in Cambridge used to live: Sybil Gage. If your wife is
> a native of Cambridge, she may have heard of Sybil Gage, although
> I am speaking of a time long before your wife was born. Her father
> was a friend of W. G. Peckham, a New York Lawyer, in whose
> office I used to work at one time, and the two of them, and some
> others, were, I believe, the founders of the Harvard Advocate. But
> my principal interest in Mr. Gage, who was dead when I lived in
> Cambridge, was the fact that he was the founder of Sybil. A few
> years after I had left Cambridge I was a guest at Peckham's place in
> the Adirondacks and who should turn up but this angel; so that
> instead of being a street that I had never heard of Hilliard Street
> turns out to be a street that I passed every day.

The Eberharts suggested that Sybil's married name might be Holbrook,
but I recently learned that she had become Sybil Weddle and moved to
California. My informant described her "as a gracious, highly intelligent
woman, much interested in literature. She was especially fond of poetry."

He went on to say:

> Sybil told me that she and her family used to go up to the
> Adirondacks in the summer, and that there she met Wallace Stevens.
> What there was between them she didn't say, though from your
> father's letter to Richard Eberhart it is obvious that he was smitten
> with Sybil. She told me that she had been studying Froebel and
> Pestalozzi, and was enthusiastic about them. She had been telling

Wallace Stevens about them, and what great contributions they had made to children's education. According to Sybil, your father was a bit skeptical about the two men, and wrote her the enclosed poem, both to kid her about her enthusiasm, and to pay her a very pretty compliment.

TO MISS GAGE

Froebel be hanged! And Pestalozzi—pooh!
No weazened Pedagogy can aspire
To thrill these thousands—through and through—
Or touch their thin souls with immortal fire.

Only in such as you the spirit gleams
With the rich beauty that compassions give:
Children no science—but a world of dreams
Where fearful futures of the Real live.

                                        —WS

Knowing my father's fondness for a real Sibyl adds a dimension to his use of that word in "The Sail of Ulysses" (1954):

What is the shape of the sibyl? Not,
For a change, the englistered woman, seated
In colorings harmonious, dewed and dashed
By them:

Despite the fact that "All that glisters is not gold," we must remember that my father referred to Sybil Gage as an "angel."

The poem "To Miss Gage" is dated July 1902. It was shortly after my father's return from the Adirondacks that he began to keep a third notebook, headed "Wallace Stevens: Journal. 1902." It does not refer to the lady, however.

Saturday, August 9. 1902.

Oh, Mon Dieu, how my spirits sink when I am alone here in my room! Tired of everything that is old, too poor to pay for what's new—tired of reading, tired of tobacco, tired of walking about town; and longing only to have friends with me, or to be somewhere with them: nauseated by this terrible imprisonment. Yes: I might put a light face on it and say it is merely a depression rising from lack of exercise, but from my present point of view I see nothing but years of lack of exercise before me. And then this terrible self-contempla-tion! Tomorrow if the sun shines I shall go wayfaring all day long. I *must* find a home in the country—a place to live in, not only to *be* in.

To relieve my dreary feelings after writing the above I scribbled several letters and started for a smoke in the Square. I was thinking how easily my thoughts were flowing while I smoked, like the tunes that used to spring from the flutes of tobacco-less shepherds; and I had scarcely finished the figure when I felt queasy and bum—my stomach disagreed with the tobacco. But perhaps an Arcadian flute is better after all than a metropolitan corn-cob.

Sunday. August 10.

I've had a handsome day of it and am contented again. Left the house after breakfast and went by ferry and trolley to Hackensack over in Jersey. From H. I walked 5½ miles on the Spring Valley road, then 4 miles to Ridgewood, then another mile to Hokokus [*sic*] and back towards town 7 miles more to Paterson: 17½ in all, a good day's jaunt at this time of the year. Came from Paterson to Hoboken by trolley and then home. In the early part of the day I saw some very respectable country which, as usual, set me contemplating. I love to walk along with a slight wind playing in the trees about me and think over a thousand and one odds and ends. Last night I spent an hour in the dark transept of St. Patrick's Cathedral where I go now and then in my more lonely moods. An old argument with me is that the true religious force in the world is not the church but the world itself: the mysterious callings of Nature and our responses. What incessant murmurs fill that ever-laboring, tireless church! But today in my walk I thought that after all there is no conflict of forces but rather a contrast. In the cathedral I felt one presence; on the highway I felt another. Two different deities presented themselves; and though I have only cloudy visions of either, yet I now feel the distinction between them. The priest in me worshipped one God at one shrine; the poet another God at another shrine. The priest worshipped Mercy and Love; the poet, Beauty and Might. In the shadows of the church I could hear the prayers of men and women; in the shadows of the trees nothing human mingled with Divinity. As I sat dreaming with the Congregation I felt how the glittering altar worked on my senses stimulating and consoling them; and as I went tramping through the fields and woods I beheld every leaf and blade of grass revealing or rather betokening the Invisible.

A look into "The Comedian as the Letter C" discloses:

> He knelt in the cathedral with the rest,
> This connoisseur of elemental fate,
> Aware of exquisite thought.

In 1953, in a letter to Renato Poggioli, Stevens wrote, in reference to that poem (which Poggioli was translating into Italian):

There is another point about the poem to which I should like to call attention and that is that it is what may be called an anti-mythological poem. The central figure is an every-day man who lives a life without the slightest adventure except that he lives it in a poetic atmosphere as we all do.

The bottom two lines of the page in the journal where the "cathedral" entry was written plus the entire following page have been cut out.

Sunday, August 17.

Left the office on Saturday at noon for a long walk in the country from which I have just returned. Went to East Orange by train; there I was to have met a friend, who failed to keep his engagement. After waiting an hour I started alone, going through the Oranges to Eagle Rock, where I had the first remarkable view of what turned out to be a very viewy tour. From Eagle Rock I ambled along past the Montclair golf course, by Verona Lake (an excursiony place) towards Pine Brook. A carpenter gave me a lift as I was about to step into the Passaic Valley. Told me of a good place for hunting: Chester. Said that Rockefeller who keeps the inn there told him—no: all this was related to me later by another individual. The carpenter having a good horse and the air being rather fresh, between all three I found the drive invigorating. Plodded along after I had alighted, sniffing with exhilaration the evening air and rhapsodizing on I have forgotten what natural beauties. Chap in a gig pulled me about three miles & talked the price of cabbage, milk etc. He aptly called the valley we were passing through—the Rockaway, a region of "dry knobs and old pond-holes." Said he had recently found a quail's nest with *twenty-five* eggs in it—another with fifteen. He left me where the road split and bounced on his way to Montville. Night had fallen by this time; but was bright and companionable with a large moon. Reached Boonton, my destination, shortly after eight, where I secured lodgings at the Mansion House, grubbed, strolled to a public reading-room and read Bacon's essay "On Friendship," returned to the hotel and turned in. The bar below me buzzed long after I was weary of it. Up—and down to breakfast at eight with glorious weather awaiting me. Astonished by the magnificent view from the village street—and by the price for breakfast (which I hastened to forget). Turned out of my way to climb a hill called the *Torn*, though an ancient Irish farmer told me he had so much as heard it called the Rattlesnake—geography is in a feeble condition up that way. Well, I was immensely pleased by the views from the top of this hill, whence

I could look all about the Northern region of the state. By all odds, one of the most beautiful scenes within a Christian distance of New York. Lay down on a rock and took a sunbath for a half-hour. Returned to Boonton in a leisurely way and then struck out for Butler —nine miles away. *Magnificent* walk—Boonton Lake from the upper middle looking down is a perfect thing of its kind. Brook Valley opens up green hills and blue distances and is altogether lovely. Reached the outskirts of Butler about one o'clock and lunched forthwith on well water and milk biscuits. Thence I pulled out for Paterson, about ten miles off, which I reached shortly after five. The road between the two points is a splendid affair and must make marvellous driving. Near Pompton I saw the grave of General William Colfax, Captain of Washington's Guard, and of Hester Schuyler, his wife. From these two have descended a notable family. The burying ground is as simple as it could well be. The Pompton Valley is fairly neat, and as I wound through it, I found much to delight me. Came across some wild cactus. Napped for a half-hour on a cool hilltop. While dozing I heard and recognized a dozen wood sounds and was undisturbed; once, however, I heard the crackle that a man makes in moving and was on the alert at once. Why? What is the reason for this instinctive guard against our kind? Weiss nicht. Took trolley at Paterson (Haledon) and rode to Passaic. I detest the inhabitants of this neighborhood, who are still savages, so took the train at Passaic for Jersey City. Scarcely seated when one of the above-mentioned inhabitants came along, placed a little girl beside me, who was all elbows, and then sank down herself. Three in one seat! My God, I took flight. Crossing the meadows, the rushes were green and the sky pink. City overhung with smoke, which the moon struggled to silver.

My walk covered about forty miles all in all. The story about the Chester Rockefeller was told me at Breakfast in Boonton. R. told the feller whoever the devil he was that he would try to keep a good hotel: try to make an honest living or else go out and work. A poor story unless looked at in the right light. I have bathed now, and duly journalized, and am ready for bed.

August 18.
The heart opens on high ground. I am thinking of some of the hill-tops I stood upon—the blue sky stretching vastly to the low horizon—the clouds seeming to mount step by step—the little world at my feet. The one I napped on was specially delightful. I lay under a group of dark cedars near that strange wind-sown cactus with its red blossom. The sun glittered among the boughs. As I looked straight ahead from under my eyelids—nothing but clouds and clouds.

A momentary pause, here, to note the opening lines of "Of the Surface of Things" (1919):

> In my room, the world is beyond my understanding;
> But when I walk I see that it consists of three or four hills
> and a cloud.

The same image recurs thirty years later, in "An Ordinary Evening in New Haven":

> It may be that they mingle, clouds and men, in the air
>
> Or street or about the corners of a man,
> Who sits thinking in the corners of a room.

As the journal continues, we find an augury of the lines, "Such floods of white / Came bursting from the clouds," from "The Sense of the Sleight-of-Hand Man" (1939).

> Near Boonton Lake, saw a field of buckwheat in flower. The white expanse rose to a hill over which clouds were coming—carrying out a pretty composition. The white of the flowers was not so pure as of the clouds.

> August 24.
> Walked from Point Lookout (which I reached by trolley and train and boat from Mineola) on the South Shore to Long Beach today: a very short walk perfect in itself but contemptible to get to and to come away from. I am not at home by the sea; my fancy is not at all marine, so to speak; when I sit on the shore and listen to the waves they only suggest wind in treetops. A single *coup d'œil* is enough to see all, as a rule. The sea is loveliest far in the abstract when the imagination can feed upon the idea of it. The thing itself is dirty, wobbly and wet. But today, while all that I have just said was true as ever, towards evening I saw lights on heaven and earth that never were seen before. The white beach (covered with beach-fleas etc.) ran along behind and before me. The declining sun threw my shadow a frightful length on the sand. The clouds began to become confused and dissolve into a golden mist into which the sea ran purple, blue, violet. The sun went down lighting the underworld and gilding a few clouds in this one. The West filled with a blue city of mist etc. Turning to the East I saw that a storm was creeping up, and suddenly then I caught sight of two rainbows swinging down. Walking over the beach under this lowering sky was like stepping into a cavern. Two women—one dressed in yellow, one in purple moving along the white sand—relieved the severity of the prospect.

Stevens, looking at the sea, then writes about it "as one improvises, on the piano." And clearly he improvised on his journal, and particularly on this entry and those immediately preceding and following it, for the rest of his life, whether consciously or not. These passages are surely seminal, and there is, in particular, a very direct connection with a much-later work, "The Poem That Took the Place of a Mountain" (1952):

There it was, word for word,
The poem that took the place of a mountain.

He breathed its oxygen,
Even when the book lay turned in the dust of his table.

It reminded him how he had needed
A place to go to in his own direction,

How he had recomposed the pines,
Shifted the rocks and picked his way among clouds,

For the outlook that would be right,
Where he would be complete in an unexplained completion:

The exact rock where his inexactnesses
Would discover, at last, the view toward which they had edged,

Where he could lie and, gazing down at the sea,
Recognize his unique and solitary home.

September 4.
    Last Sunday I walked from Englewood, New Jersey, to Nyack, New York—say fifteen miles. The Alpine Road, or rather the Boulevard, as it is called, along the Palisades is very attractive. The woods resounded with locusts. Killed a fair-sized blacksnake that darted at me in its agonies. Crossed from Nyack to Tarrytown on a ferry; then trolleyed to White Plains—seven miles; walked along the old Post road until a fellow driving from Kensico took me to Mt. Vernon behind a smart little mare. Came home by train.
    The next day, Labor day, being a holiday, I spent some six hours on the sand and on the high seas at Manhattan Beach. Very gay time dreaming in the sun.

    I have smoked only two cigars this week and my mind is like a drop of dew as a result. Today while thinking over organic laws etc. the idea of the German "Organismus" crept into my thoughts—and as I was lunching on Frankfurters & sauerkraut, I felt quite the philosopher. Wonderfully scientific & clear idea—this *organismus* one. Yes: and if I were a materialist I might value it. But only last night I was lamenting that the fairies were things of the past. The organismus is truck—give me the fairies, the Cloud-Gatherer, the Prince of Peace, the Mirror of Virtue—and a pleasant road to think of them on, and a starry night to be with them.

September 8.

From Undercliff to Piermont—was my route yesterday—accompanied by Dana and Barton. Some ludicrous adventures with shy country girls on the road. Met a Doctor Leitner at P. whose name I record as that of one who loves his fellow-men. Slept in a bad bed in a sort of rat-hole & steamed back to town this morning.

September 15.

Suddenly it has become Autumn. The hollows at twilight are like charming caves—mists float in the air—the heat of the sun is that bracing Septembery heat straight from the star without any gusts from the earth. I was in the woods yesterday (never mind where I walked). The fact is I have discovered a solitude—with all the modern conveniences. It is on the Palisades—about opposite Yonkers, reachable by cutting in from the Alpine road at the proper place. Silver ropes of spiders' weaving stretched over the road, showing that my retreat had had no recent visitors. There was no litter of broken bottles or crushed egg-shells on the brown needles—but a little brook tinkled under a ledge into a deep ravine—*deep* en vérité—; two thrushes fidgeted on the logs and in the boughs; stalks of golden rod burned in the shadows like flambeaux in my temple; I thought I heard a robin's strain. Oh! I can fancy myself at my ease there. How often I shall stretch out under those evergreens listening to the showers of wind around me—and to that little tinkling bit of water dripping down among those huge rocks and black crevices! It is really very undisturbed there.

I was saying it had become autumn. The sumach leaves are scarlet, and there are other weaklings that have turned in these chill nights. Yet the world is still green. Witness: that mighty promontory bathed in the light of the next to latest declining sun.

Item: At noon I lay on a rock taking a bake. Was startled upon gazing into the heavens to find them swarming with birds whirling about at an immense height. Think they were crows.

October 1. 1902.

Ran home a week ago. Found Livingood just back from one of his flights, Heilig just from Europe, Lee Smith in England. Weather stupefied me. Yet a trip of the kind is a benefit: here I can polish myself with dreams, exert myself in hard work, live in a fine, false way; there dreaming is an effort in itself and hard work is merely meritorious—not instructive, and the way of the world is neither fine nor false. Fate carves its images there in a tedious fashion, and neither beautifully nor well. And the very wings of Time hang limp in the still air. Alas! it did nothing but rain. Once I got a few miles into the country. I sat on a stone wall facing a pool of rain-water in a field of green wheat watching a few plover feed near by. The sun shone for a short time on the pool. The wind covered the pool with reflections of gold. Far off the hills lay blue in the mist. Again I visited the Wilys who (with their angels) grow more and more pathetic. More, I visited Kuechler on his hill-top and found him still and pale—his beautiful beard spread over his bosom, the gleam of an invisible sword darting about him. Called on Miss Lewis and found her to be without manners: that is without any more than I have myself. I have

Here two pages of the journal are missing. It resumes:

I can almost see Dan Cupid smoking Egyptian cheroots and saying "Oh, Fudge!"

October 8.

It is true, doubtless, as some one was saying to me today, that, though women are vain, men are vainer. I was told that if a woman met a man with an atrocious nose and said to him, "What fine lines your face has!" he would cry "Nonsense!"—and be found admiring his abominable proboscis in a mirror shortly after, wondering that he had never before noticed that the lines *were* fine. Yes: that is probably true. An unattractive woman can draw almost any man to her by discreet flattery; but when a man flatters a woman the woman doesn't feel any the kindlier toward the man but takes his praise as quite true & winds up by cutting him—as not quite good enough for so fair a creature. Flattery mollifies a man; elevates a woman. Voila!

Yet a man can be flattered against his better sense. He may *know* he's rotten, and yet be persuaded that nothing is sweeter than he is.

October 13.

Apollo & I tripped it through rainy woods yesterday afternoon. I raced to beat him to the top of one hill before he could get down another—and I won. The thing happened thus: heavy with Sunday dinner I rode to Englewood, then walked to Tenafly & there resolved to climb a certain familiar mount before the sun had set. I had to run up my hill, but got there in time to see a damp Sunday roll over the Western mists & disappear in a dim flame. I crossed my hill into a favorite solitude. The rains had swollen my tinkling stream into a thundering cascade that filled the trees with a sweet sound. Overhead the moon shone from a strange azure of its own creating. Spirits seemed everywhere—stalking in the infernal forest. The wet sides of leaves glittered like plates of steel; nightbirds made thin noises; tree-frogs seemed conspiring; an owl chilled the clammy silence. But pooh! I discovered egg-shells—sure sign of a man & his wife & a child or two, loafing in my temple. How fine, though, was the mystery of everything except the damned egg-shells! How deep & voluble the shadows! How perfect the quiet! Came

The bottom two-thirds of this page have been cut off before the journal resumes:

the roads are strewn with purple oak leaves, brown chestnut leaves, and the golden and scarlet leaves of maples. I doubt if there is any keener delight in the world than, after being penned up for a week, to get into the woods on such a day—every pound of flesh vibrates with new strength, every nerve seems to be drinking at some refreshing spring. And after one has got home, how delicious to slip into an easy chair & to feel the blood actually leaping in one's pulses, a wild fire, so to speak, burning in one's cheeks.

November 14.

 Stayed over last Sunday with the Peckhams at Westfield. Pleasant time. Horseback with Mr. P. Paul & Ruth Peckham in the over the hills & through brown woods [sic]. Walking with Ruth P. in the afternoon. The P's part of Jersey is quite like New England—strange and Northern.

November 23.

 It has been a long, long time getting cold—hot, misty, damp nights. Last Sunday I saw a bee perched on a clover blossom unconscious that it was the middle of November. But today the wind be zipping chill, the clouds are heaped up in long Novembery lines, & the weather is more comme il faut. Expect to take a walk later in the day—been held up so far by a friend.

The next page (on the reverse of which is part of an entry written in August 1904) has been cut out. The journal resumes a month later.

Dec. 29. 1902. Reading, Pa.

 A favorite walk yesterday—via Leinbach's tavern, Epler's Church, Stout's Ferry, & so on home—almost a circle. Country white with snow—a hundred novel lights and airs—sky as blue and tender as Mid-May. Very cold yet I could feel the sun on my back as I went out. Heard Bob White & saw his tracks—often, saw a squirrel, several crows ('round corn shocks), hawks (near farms) & several wild ducks unless I'm mistaken. Icicles on eaves, dogs under stoves, wind-pumps creaking.

In that entry we get an intimation of the significance of the hawk in part
XXIV of "The Man with the Blue Guitar" (1937):

> A poem like a missal found
> In the mud, a missal for that young man,
>
> That scholar hungriest for that book,
> The very book, or, less, a page
>
> Or, at the least, a phrase, that phrase,
> A hawk of life, that latined phrase:
>
> To know; a missal for brooding-sight.
> To meet that hawk's eye and to flinch
>
> Not at the eye but at the joy of it.
> I play. But this is what I think.

Stevens gave his own explanation in 1953:

> A hawk of life means one of those phrases that grips in its talons
> some aspect of life that it took a hawk's eye to see. To call a phrase
> a hawk of life is itself an example.

Another page has been cut out of the journal here (again, the reverse
falls within the August 1904 entry), before we come to his New Year's
resolutions for 1903.

> What I have resolved to do next year so far as possible is this:
> to drink water & to abstain from wet-goods—not that I booze but
> that I love temperance & that the smallest liqueur is intemperant.
> Ask Colin. And in the second place, to smoke wisely. And in the third
> place, to write something every night—be it no more than a line to
> sing to or a page to read—there's gold there for the digging: j'en suis
> sur. And lastly, not to go to bed before twelve candles of day gutter
> in their sockets & the breeze of morning blows; for sleep only means
> red-cheeks and red-cheeks are not the fit adornments of Caesar.

If he wrote "something every night," it was not in his journal. The
first entry for 1903 is dated:

March 1.
    Went to Trinity Church

Though the following page has been cut out, the next page seems to complete the same sentence:

> this morning and heard a parson, whom I take to have been Dr.
> Morgan Dix, preach an exceptionally beautiful sermon on the powers
> and principalities of heaven. It was old-fashioned—no boasting or

bragging of new thought, but a lament that in this world the good are polluted and the pure, ruined. Angels have visited the earth and there are angels all about us now—and roaring lions. There was not one single blessed word of cant or conventionality—rather it was Dr. Primrose's good heart flowing in Oliver Goldsmith's words. I feel quite simplified and content.

Went walking this afternoon—same old route—same superb air—same lofty views—same windy trees and springy roads—same electric sun; and I, the same; thank my angel for that, for I have become quite topsy-turvy during these two months of rainy Sundays—a bit disgusting at times. Beyond Undercliff I met with an encampment of gypsies—I shall expect soon to be meeting Christians in Broadway and philanthropists among the lawyers. Speak to me, spirit of George Borrow!

March 11. Wednesday.

Heard Chief Justice Alton B. Parker speak in Earl Hall, Columbia University, on his court, the Court of Appeals, this afternoon. Remarks chiefly historical and anecdotal. Parker very handsome, very strong, very much of a man. Impressed me as a man of great morality & of lofty determination & of kindness of heart. Is in his prime. He was wonderfully encouraging and cheering and agreeable. Something of the country-boy about him—it struck me. He has lived away from cynics & dreamers. He seemed to think that the chief function of the court of appeals is to expand the law.

April 5 or 6. Sunday.

Started early this morning and walked until sun-set. Decidedly cold in the morning—the roadsides. . .-bling with frost and in the

The bottom third of this page has been cut off, including the word or words at the beginning of the line after "roadsides," as indicated by the elision above. (On the reverse, still the August 1904 entry.) Once again the journal resumes within a sentence:

a long and precise horizon. As I passed through Madison Square I remarked that the cold had killed the pansies over-night. In the country, however, the hardier wild-flowers were bright in their sunny-nooks: the Spring-flowers, and a kind of white heliotrope or a thing with a

Here two-thirds of the page has been cut off; the entry resumes mid-sentence:

during the week took flight; the witches of "salesse" straddled their brooms and whirled away through

Once more an interruption (still in the August 1904 entry on the reverse), as three-quarters of the page has been cut off; and once again the next page opens within a sentence:

> on a salary in some law office and to work as hard as I can work until I can get enough business of my own to hang out a shingle. The mere prospect of having to support myself on a very slender purse has brought before my mind rather vivid views of the actual facts of existence in the world. There are astonishingly few people who live in anything like comfort; and there are thousands who live on the verge of starvation. The old Biblical injunctions to make the earth fertile and to earn one's bread in the sweat of one's brow are one's first instructions. True, it [is] not necessary to start from the soil; but starting with nothing whatever—to make a fortune—is not wholly inspiring after a fellow has spent more or less time lolling about. It is decidedly wrong to start *there* with one's tastes fully developed & to have to forego all satisfaction of them for a vague number of years. This is quite different from beginning as other men do. It is more like being up already & working down to a certain point. Another phase of the thing is that when one has lived for twenty-five years with every reasonable wish granted & among the highest associations—starting at the bottom suddenly reveals millions of fellow-men struggling at the same point, of whom one previously had only an extremely vague conception. There was a time when I walked downtown in the morning almost oblivious of the thousands and thousands of people I passed; now I look at them with extraordinary interest as companions in the same fight that I am about to join. At first, I was overwhelmed

Here we find further excisions: one or more pages are missing. (In this case, it is impossible to tell whether the reverse was an entry in July or in August of 1904.) The next page is headed

> June 7.
>   I'm sure of my law degree. One week more and the drowning out process begins. It feels like entering the hospital for an operation. Nevertheless, I'm not so gloomy as I might be.

Three-quarters of that page has been cut off; the next begins

> a *taste for style* in everything, a taste for the brilliant, the graceful, & that common-place the beautiful. Moral qualities are masculine; whimsicalities are feminine. That seems hardly just but I think it is exact.

The bottom two-thirds of that page has been cut off (the reverse has an entry dated July 7, 1904), as has the following page (where the reverse falls within an entry for May or June 1904). The next is dated

July 5.

Spent the Fourth with the Peckhams at Westfield. Upon my soul, the mosquitoes were the worst I ever met with. The air and the earth were full of them. Today I am covered with their damnable

And again the bottom two-thirds of the page has been cut off (the reverse falling within an entry dated May 23, 1904).

It is the last excision for some time to come, and the journal goes on uninterrupted for most of the summer of 1903. Because I inherited the journals via my mother, I suspect that the excisions noted may have been made by her after my father's death, if she found personal references she did not wish preserved. On the other hand it is quite possible that my father edited the journal himself, knowing my mother's regard for privacy. At any rate, it was during the summer of 1904, when their courtship began, that drastic "cutting" occurs.

On June 10, 1903, Wallace Stevens graduated from New York Law School and resumed his clerkship in W. G. Peckham's office. We know little of his routine while he was a student, but it must have been hard work, and fairly depressing at times. At any rate, he seems always to have been glad to escape the city.

July 12. Sunday.

Have just returned from Manhattan Beach, where I spent the day bathing in the icy water and loafing on the hot sand. Philosophized on the fact that some children (evidently X-ray photographs personified) should have the intelligence they showed, and the names they bore. With my face buried in the sand, I heard the legions of men and women about me as if they were passing in airy clouds. But the sounds were not lamentations or avowals—but "Why there's Eddie—Hello, Ed.—Women's colleges—No, I'm from Louisville—There they go—Isn't the water extraordinarily cold."

July 26.

Another day at Manhattan. Water warm, air cold. Saw "a pretty pair of legs," as George Moore would say. But mostly my face was buried in the sand & my thoughts were busy making wise saws such as, A cynic is the name the torpid give a wise man, Abstractions bear only a spirit aloft, and so on. Felt rather domesticated & friendly to people. Came home for tea & after a Bock Panatela crawled up to bed, where I was soon rescuing a drowning beauty etc. Alas! I couldn't fall asleep. And so when the clock struck ten I jumped out of bed— and now, damme, I'll read till my eyelids drop of their own weight.

I've just been reading my journal. A month or two ago I was looking forward to a cigarless, punchless weary life. *En effet*, since then I have smoked Villar y Villars & Cazadores, dined at Mouquin's on French artichokes & new corn etc. with a flood of drinks from crême de cassis melée, through Burgundy, Chablis etc. to sloe gin with Mexican cigars & French cigaroots. I have lunched daily on—Heaven's knows what not (I recall a delicious calf's heart cooked whole & served with peas—pig that I am) & on Tuesday, I start for British Columbia to camp & hunt until September in the Canadian Rockies, *Quem Deus vult*—

This Mexican cigar life has its drawbacks. The faces one sees through its smoke are not the faces of St. Paul or St. Francis or of Mary or Ruth. At this table sits a Saturday night fop, at that is an unaccountable fellow with a pampered looking belly, at another is a charming looking girl in tremendous spirits smiling & chattering, at another is a coarse animal & its mate. One talks. It is gossip. Then it is Durham Cathedral. Then it is Bar-le-duc jelly and Gervais cheese. Then it is gossip again. The orchestra comes in & plays—How deathly tired one is by midnight!

There are three fires burning now. One, the moon, lights mountainous camels moving, without bells, to the wide North; another, the twilight, lights the pine tops and the flaring patches of snow; the last one, the camp-fire, shines on Mr. Peckham in an enormous woolen shirt, on Hosea (Mr. Hosey) warming his hands, on Tommy baking beans—or rather a stew of beans, bugs, dirt and twigs. The lamp is lit, too, & no doubt we shall soon have a reading by the boss. The trout that Tommy caught now swims in inland seas.

Wednesday, August—.

The beggar world is in the mail this morning.

I am using a stump for a lectern or rather scriptern, while Hosea & Tommy turn jack pines into benches and a table. A moment ago while trying to cross the river on a log, the log slipped beneath me and I sat in the water—this retires another pair of breeches with appurtenances to the clothes pole. However, the haymaker is out and (haymaker is Woods-ese for sun) so no doubt I shall soon be in shape again. There was a fine January light on the glacier and snow-fields this morning and the river dashed through the beams like running fire. My camels have turned to purple clouds. Oatmeal, beans and corn-pone soaked in huile d'olive made our rather fastidious breakfast.

Thursday, August 6.

Yesterday afternoon Tommy and I climbed one of the hills opposite the Kootenay glacier. Plenty of moose signs, but old; bear nibblings; and some fresh goat tracks. We got up about 9,000 to 9,500 feet. Huckleberries and strawberries kept the dust out of our throats. We caught glimpses of magnificent snowy summits; also of the distant neighborhood of the Vermilion Pass faintly blue and white like a gate into the Sun. Plunged down hill until we came to rubbish formed by snow-slides over which we had to pick our way with rare neatness. Worked down into the upper gulches of the Kootenay, threw a tree over the roaring water—and so through the woods to camp. Bathed & waited for the others to come in. Locke has found a wonderfully promising spot and is going to it tonight. As miners we are entitled to venison & mean to have it.

The good weather has brought out the insects. The mosquitoes are abominable during the day—yet not so abominable as they are in Jersey. The big, black bull-dog flies buzz through the tent like demons. They make excellent bait for trout. The ground swarms with ants. But these and everything else—except our horseflesh— stretch out at night and remain quiet. Wrapped in my white Hudson Bay blanket, I look like a loaf of bread by the fire. W.G.P. sits up with his lamp translating Heine aloud endlessly; or else retelling his eternal cycle of stories. By and by, the Eastern star glitters over a hill-top and we crawl down into our boots & fall into a chilly snooze.

Friday. August 7.

The mountains last night seemed to be posing for the Detroit Photographic Company.

We are having fine luck with trout and grouse. Hosey came in this morning without having seen anything over night. W.G.P. took a douse the other day. Today he complains of ulcerated teeth, face pains and neuralgia. We eat with our fingers entirely now.

A bird flew into one of the pines this morning. W.G.P. called it a moose hawk; Hosey said it was a venison-hawk; Tommy held out for Whiskey-jack. Whiskey-jack it is, then.

On the page above the previous paragraph (the reverse of an entry for March 31, 1904), Stevens has drawn a long-tailed bird, with rather long legs, and labeled it "Whiskey-jack."

There are certain areas of spruce and fir in the forests that take on the appearance of everglades. They are filled with a brownish gloom, still, mysterious. Here the city heart would emit a lyric cry if a bird sang. But we have no music here. The wells of song would freeze overnight.

Lying in one's tent, looking out at the sky, one's thoughts revert to New York: to the trains stopping at the L stations, to the sinuous females, to the male rubbish, to the clerks and stenographers and conductors and Jews, to my friend the footman in front of Wanamakers, to Miss Dunning's steak, to Siegel and his cigars.

Here come the ants—heads, feet and bellies.

Saturday, August 8.

Today Hosey shot a yearling doe and we are having venison fried in olive oil tonight. Last night we had, besides stewed grouse, a shortcake made out of bannock and wild strawberries. A long string of trout are being kept cool in the river for breakfast. The grouse are thick. I shot a cock this morning. Or was it Tommy who shot it? We both fired. Yesterday I bummed around camp all day, taking sunbaths and fighting mosquitoes and dipping into the *Lettres Spirituelles* of [Jacques] Bossuet—a real summer's day. Today I walked twenty-five miles & more: to Well's Ranch & back. The distant mountains there slip off into a thousand diaphanous shades of ether.

Monday, August 10.

Sunday we stayed in camp except W.G.P. who went out on the horse in the afternoon.

Today Hosey & I visited the sources of the Kootenay. We followed an execrable trail made by Pedley a trapper (who with several others dropped in on us on Sunday afternoon). We were rather well up by noon & stopped for lunch catching about a dozen trout in a mountain lake & roasting them on willow sticks. Hambone could not have been sweeter. By four o'clock we had mounted several thousand feet. Hosey went a peak higher than I did & made my hair stand on end with his climbing. I could look Westward and see infinite snowy summits—the Selkirks, I think. Below us were two or three wonderfully clear lakes. While Hosey was on his summit a storm crossed the valley & the thunder was soon clapping about our ears. We descended in a heavy rain, each leaf putting a spoonful of icy water down our necks—each tree a bucketful. Home in time to bathe & change clothes before dark. Tommy had hot venison broth waiting for us—and more wild strawberry shortcake. Tonight it is gusty & there's a chill in the wind. Tommy, Hosey & W.G.P. are playing Pedro, as usual & I am waiting to turn in.

Tuesday.

Small adventures. Saw the mountains near the Vermilion Pass hooded in the gray of their rocks like deathly nuns. Saw bluebirds in the burnt woods. Porcupines in the bottoms. Picked up kid on the trail near the lick (where Hosey & W.G.P. spent the night) & rode him home watching, meanwhile, a sunset. Lost kid overnight to my consternation. Up at five—after a most majestic night—& watched the sunlight quench the belated moon. Found kid a short way down the river & started out to pack Hosey & W.G.P. back to camp. Met Hosey on the trail, the dew dripping from the brim of his hat. Saw a dove in a tree. Waited three hours for W.G.P. who went home by another route—damn his boots. Living chiefly on broiled venison steaks.

The peaks to the South shelve off into the heavens. Snow & cloud become confused. And the blue distances merge mountain and sky into one.

> At the entrance to the
> Vermilion Pass about Forty
> or Fifty Miles in the Kootenay

August 17. Tuesday.

The game being somewhat scarce on the Kootenay we followed the trail through Well's & Boyce's ranches and the burnt timber and across patches of wild strawberry and saskatoon and after infinite trouble caused by W.G.P. have set up a magnificent camp just ouside the gigantic Vermilion. Two Englishmen with a large pack camped with us last night. I took a drop with them and being fagged by a reconnoitre over the hills went to bed shortly after eight o'clock with the stars, & the twilight, and the guides playing Pedro, and the clink-clink of the horses' bells to make me drowsy. It has been a wonderfully clear and cold morning. The sun shines in on us at last and today we should have a hunt worth while.

Last Thursday I rode out to Leanchoil for provisions which I freighted from Palliser after midnight. Friday it rained & I read *Kidnapped* and *King Solomon's Mines* & smoked & fed furiously: at Nixon's. Saturday Jack N. & I started in, Sunday we moved, yesterday we settled, today—

Wednesday. 18 August.

Scarcely a cloud in the sky yesterday. Bob and I set a bear-trap on a likely hill in the morning, smearing the hill-sides with black New Orleans. In the afternoon I swam and laundered a bit. Went fishing about sundown and got a huge trout on the hook, but the hook snapped & no doubt 'Sieur Trout, like Tommy, is now sulking with the toothache. The rocky range to the right of the pass was yellow and pink & purple. The stars were shining in a multitude.

This morning I was up at five o'clock—fishing in the rain. Caught two small trout. The sky has cleared now & it's going to be a hot & mosquitoey day. Hosey & Bob are starting on a two-days hunt.

Friday, August 20.

Hosey returned from his hunt with a big black bear to his credit. The beast has been skinned & Bob & I used half of his hind quarters to bait traps with today up the Vermilion. Last night Bob caught my big trout & this afternoon Tommy caught another—both between four and five pounds—terrors. It is raining now, after two perfect days; Hosey is bathing, W.P.G. is hunting. Tommy is tinkering a paw and Bob & I are in the tent smoking.

Sunday, August 23rd (date unreliable).

Yesterday I visited the nearest bear-trap with Bob, the bush being much too wet to do more. Read Heinrich Zschokke's *Tales*— charming things, the rest of the day until after dinner when Bob & I watched for deer until eight & after, on a dark hill-side. This morning I found one of my boots half-filled with the night's rain. We have snuggled together in the tent to rest a bit until the weather clears. Fresh snow on the mountains.

Tuesday, August 25. (*sic*)

Hosey and I have just returned from a two days' goat hunt. Hosey fired four shots in as many seconds at one, hitting him with the first and last plunks; but the beast managed to limp away to an inaccessible place. Hosey searched for two hours on terrifically dangerous ground but could not follow the blood over the slippery gulches. I waited for him on a nearby peak in the midst of a snow-storm—shivering with the wet and cold. Spent a warm but sleepless night in the Pass—without cover. At four we started to examine the mountains to the right of the Pass, that is: the little Pass. Enormous views, good climbing, goat tracks etc. Found a bear's den in a cliff (where I had to go on hands and knees & pull myself along with plants) also a hedge-hog's hole filled with dung. Home early in the afternoon, bath & now for a nap.

Saturday, presumably.

Wednesday, Hosey & I went down the Valley on the right bank & came back on the left. Found a good deer country. On Thursday I loafed. On Friday Bob and I went down to the junction of the Vermilion & the Kootenay along the ridge. Found ideal hunting grounds at the Forks with lots of old Indian tepees, Broad beaches & good meadows. Plenty of signs of game. Hosey shot another deer on Friday morning. W.G.P. was so mad that he wouldn't let a hair of it be brought to camp. However after a night of quarrelling Hosey & I are to bring it in this morning. W.G.P. now goes round saying that Hosey's habit of putting his knife in his mouth & then in the other fellow's butter is enough to make the sore jade wince; & Hosey quietly remarks that W.G.P. is a poor damned lunatic. Roule, Tambour d'Arcole et [illegible word—"couvre"?]—. The sky turns green of nights; the new moon swings down below the hills; the campfire sputters; W.G.P. asks whether I am awake & reads me a line or two from Heine; his Dutch lamp flickers—Adieu.

Quasi-Sunday.

Tommy & I have been picking huckleberries. W.G.P. shot a lynx *in a trap!* Hosey's off fishing.

Last day of August.

Hosey came back with a big mess of trout. The place looked like a fishmarket until Tommy put the f. in the river. This morning, it is cloudless & cool. Tommy had to use a can-opener to get through the ice; and the logs at the ford were covered with iridescent sparkles of frost. Bob is going to look into his traps in the Pass; W.G.P. has started off on his affectionate kid; Hosey & I linger in camp undetermined.

Tuesday, September 1, 1903.

Hosey & I brought in two willow grouse & a hatful of splendid huckleberries yesterday afternoon. We propose, if the weather looks well & if Hosey finds his horse, to spend the next two days on the Gibraltar to the left of the Big Pass. After that, I shall loaf pretty much until we go out. I explored pretty well—& the hunting is so bloody difficult that all one's energy is spent in getting through burnt timber patches, willow swamps, slash etc. & not in watching or following game. I think we are all getting rather keen to go out. When you stay in camp, you roast to death all day & freeze to death all night. We have a huge amount of venison, trout, grouse etc. on hand & the chipmunks nibbling at the stores cause us no anxiety.

The twilights grow more short; the stars more in a multitude & immensely bright. The calling moon of the moose is rounding out. I look in the fire at evening & conjure up a hand to hold; W.G.P. transforms the logs & flames into griffons & monkeys. The season cools.

Thursday.

Hosey & I have had the best two days of the whole trip, I think. We started about two o'clock on Tuesday afternoon with the mare of Hosey's for the foot of our Gibraltar. Near Lake No. 2 we started several grouse & both of us rushed after them into the bush. The mare followed. On trying to chase her back she gave us a devil of a chase; first up-hill & then downward on the trail towards camp. Hosey nipped her. Further up along the trail I shot a partridge; & near the first trap, beyond the dead-fall, pumped a bullet into a porcupine's belly (stupid beast). We camped in some tall timber on a foot-hill. The moon covered all the hills with a violet haze & looked through our trees in a strangely distant way. I was awake practically all night. At daybreak, & after I had watched the progress of innumerable stars, Hosey started with the teapot in search of water. We were off about six in a great sweat. The slope we ascended seemed inter-minable & we had barely reached the last [illegible word] of rocks when Hosey caught sight of a lion. We chased it over the summit but without getting a shot. A moment later I caught sight of a splendid goat watching us from the top of a higher ridge. We crept along as well as we could & finally got within reach. But we were by that time in a shaky position & the goat was a good distance below. I aimed but was afraid to shoot off my gun, since I had all I could do to keep my balance—not to speak of banging away with a 45–90. Then Hosey took a hand & fired four shots, whereupon the goat gambolled away like a lamb in May. I caught him trying to get up hill & struck near him. This was our last shot. [On the page above this Stevens has drawn a diagram showing the position of the goat in relation to Hosey and himself, and a note: "If Hosey had gone to B & cut off the goat's escape up A & if I had gone via D to C, we might have had a better chance. We both went to B & the goat went to C & down to E & we had to fire down a precipice & missed."] It being bitter cold we decided to come down. I had been walking on snow and quite àpropos. The air suddenly darkened & we had a ripping little storm. The trail down hill was the most terrible I have ever travelled. At no time could one have fallen more than ten feet, but it was a difficult thing not to fall ten feet every minute. I thought I had broken my left knee-cap after one jolt; but beyond weakening & stiffening the leg no harm was done. I left a good part of my shoes on the way. Well, we reached our starting point, had some venison & prunes & cold tea & started for camp. The confounded mare had slipped her noose & so we had to carry our blankets home strapped over our rifles. We've had a happy time!

The upper slopes of the mountains are radiant with red & blue wildflowers & the rocks are covered with lichens—yellow, orange, red, brown & green.

At this point about eight pages have been torn out of the journal, and one blank page remains before the notebook reverses in direction. Centered on the back of the blank page Stevens has written:

THE B. G N.

Our business is not with the breeches and periwigs,
with the hoops and patches, but with the divine hearts
of men, and the passions which agitate them.
THACKERAY, *Catherine*. Ch. X.

There are remnants of the missing pages; following those the account of the trip continues, seemingly without interruption.

At five o'clock this morning, the sky was cloudless, there was not a breath of air stirring, the ground was white with frost, there were two inches of ice in the pail & my sponge was frozen solid as a rock.

Friday.
Hosey and I (toujours!) shot a black-tail deer this morning. And not above the timber-line either. W.G.P. (who has left camp—be damned to him) thinks that all the game is lurking in the clouds. This one was in lowland. We had set out to collect some traps & had gone but a mile, if that, from camp, when Hosey pulled up his horse & excitedly whispered, "There's a big buck." I hopped around his

horse's flanks & sure enough there was a big deer broadside in the trail. We took aim instantly but the animal ducked into the bush, without our getting a shot. I followed a short distance & then returned. Barely were we underway, when Hosey cried out, "There he is again" and leaned forward over his horse's neck to shoot. He couldn't get his shot, however. While he was aiming, I thought I saw a chance & fired, whereupon the deer wheeled & disappeared. A minute later to our immense surprise, he turned up a third time. I held Hosey's horse & let him go forward. He caught sight of the animal's big ears wagging within range, levelled his gun & cried out like a calf. Whereat the deer, being both startled & puzzled, stood up—a magnificent shot. Hosey hit him through the shoulders. He then crashed into some timber, with Hosey & I both after him. We came up to him just as he fell. I fired into his brisket splitting his heart. That ended him. We found it to be a magnificent dry doe. Well, we picked up the traps. On the way, I hit a partridge in the body, my heavy bullet leaving nothing but feathers to tell the tale. The horse raised hell when it came to packing the deer home on him. We got him loaded notwithstanding & he stepped out for camp in a wonderfully gingerly way, casting constant frightened glances back at his burden. By the time we reached camp, he was almost in a panic; I was standing on one side of him, loosening a knot, when he gave a devil of a kick at the deer's ears, which were flapping between his thighs. The kick landed flat on the right hand pocket of my breeches—a pocket full of matches. The matches took fire & burnt out the bottom of the pocket. The leg is sore a bit, but otherwise no harm was done. We had planned a moose hunt for tonight. But Hosey says it is a sin to have a half-ton of meat in camp all at the same time.

Sunday.

It has rained steadily for twenty-four hours. The clouds parted long enough this morning for us to see that the tops of the mountains were covered with snow, which promises a fine sight when the sun shines again. The clouds are low & thick. Camp-life is infinitely dull—we are all busy with some small thing or other merely to occupy our time—all of us have taken a turn at chopping wood. Hosey has been singing "We're only waiting here below"; Tommy is half-dead with tooth-ache (teeth-ache, says Hosey) & I am just a wee, wee bored.

September 18, 1903.   New York

Well, I'm home again—busted. Yet I am in such high spirits that the mere fact of having only 70 cents—no it's 40 now—to my name, doesn't worry me, that is to say not much. We grew weary of waiting for Nixon, and so, packing our stuff on Hosey's "Dolly," we got as far as Boyce's ranch where we met Bob. He told us that Jack was on his way after us & shortly thereafter Jack came rushing up with all the impedimenta we had abandoned bobbing about on his horses' backs & Pinky, the Englishman, as rear guard. We camped at Boyce's overnight, I in great torment, for the rats kept up a diabolical skampering which made Pinky, from his bed on the floor, whimper and miaow like a cat. The next two days we plodded through the mud to Leanchoil. Hosey & I walked from there to Palliser & from there rode in a freight to Golden. Here we stopped at the usual Queen's Hotel, bathing in new tubs to our heart's content. From Golden we went to Field, picking up Bob and the traps on the way. At Field we stopped at a rather ordinary hotel—drowning the bar-room. It was beastly cold in the dark little hole, but we managed to be cheerful. Here we caught the Imperial Limited on which we came East through icy mountains, prairies of snow, & then the pleasant warm lakes & fields of Ontario. I got home yesterday & started in at the office directly. It is ten days ago since we left camp.

October 20.

It is a pleasant life enough that I lead. After the day's work I climb up these stairs into the distant company of strange yet friendly windows burning over the roofs. I read a few hours, catch glimpses of my neighbors in their nightgowns, watch their lights disappear and then am swallowed up in the huge velvet October night. On Sunday I stretched my cramped legs—doing my twenty-five miles with immense good cheer. Fetched home a peck of apples in my green bag. The wind pounded through the trees all the day long. At twilight I picked my way to the edge of the Palisades & stretched out on my belly on one of the dizzy bosses. Overhead in the *clair de crépuscule* lay a bright star. I've grown such a hearty Puritan & revel in such coarse good health that I felt scarcely the slightest twinge of sentiment. But tonight I've been polite to a friend—have guzzled *vin ordinaire* & puffed a Villar y Villar and opened my dusty tobacco-jar—and my nerves, as a consequence, are a bit uneasy; so that the thought of that soft star comes on me most benignly. Tomorrow, however, I shall reassume the scrutiny of things as they are. Fielding, in *Amelia*, rightly observes that our wants are largely those of education and habit, not of nature. My poverty keeps me down to the natural ones; and it is astonishing how the tongue loses a taste for tobacco; how the paunch accommodates itself to the lack of fire-water. Indeed, sound shoes, a pair of breeches, a clean shirt and a coat, with an occasional stout meal, sees one along quite well enough. Only, at the same time, one must have ambition and energy or one grows melancholy. Ambition and energy keep a man young. Oh, treasure! Philosophy, non-resistance, "sweetness and light" leave a man pitiably crippled and aged, though pure withal.

December 2.

Occasionally there is a shout in the street. People always run and shout so when it has been snowing. And on looking out of my window I find that the town is covered with a white mask. Moonlight and snow—which corner do I turn to enter Paradise?

Apparently he did not find the corner to turn, for his first entry in 1904 indicates that he had not found Paradise.

February 7.

These last two months have been utterly useless to me. Pleasant enough day by day but horrible to see in retrospect. What a duffer I am! I live as much without energy as if I were an old man with a bank account. I don't even dare to make new resolutions—they are so damned disappointing. I have my golden haze—& that's all. That's all that's worth while, too; but, odds boddikins, I have my way to make—& disdain a good many ways of making it, at that. My pleasures seem illegitimate because they are pleasures. Here am I, a descendant of the Dutch, at the age of twenty-five, without a cent to my name, in a huge town, knowing a half-dozen men & no women. God bless us, what a lark!

February 14. Sunday.

Whatever I was going to write when I turned to this page has escaped me. I'm in the Black Hole again, without knowing any of my neighbors. The very animal in me cries out for a lair. I want to see somebody, hear somebody speak to me, look at somebody, speak to somebody in turn. I want companions. I want more than my work, than the nods of acquaintances, than this little room. I do *not* want my dreams—my castles, my haunts, my *nuits blanches*, my companies of good friends. Yet I dare not say what I do want. It is such a simple thing. I'm like that fool poet in *Candida*. Horrors!

As Marchbanks says in Act II of Shaw's *Candida:* "That is what all poets do: they talk to themselves out loud; and the world overhears them. But it's horribly lonely not to hear someone else talk sometimes."

February 24.

Spring is coming. One smells it in the air—faintly.

The rest of that page is blank. It is possible that something had been written on it and erased, but the markings that remain are so faint it is impossible to be sure. The following page has a sketch of "Spruce trees to right of camp," with "Mountains facing the camp," that my father drew above the page where his entry of August 18, 1903, began.

March 7. 1904.

Another Hamlet—Forbes Robertson's. By no means, an old story. The tendency seems to be to thicken the clouds about this character—but here they were all blown away. There was very little shadow, *no* melancholy; rather delay than irresolution. I don't know that it pleased me. Robertson raises no stage illusion; he is incorrigibly sane, cold, indeed almost familiar & commonplace. But I believe he was a man. Gertrude Elliott's Ophelia was hard & lacked grace. The Polonius I cannot agree with. The actor [Guy Lane] looked too vigorous (like Dowie in fact) so that his garrulity was inconsistent. The whole thoroughly English & unemotional.

March 8.

Tonight, I saw Ben Greet's company in "Twelfth Night" at Daly's—very satisfactory (to be cold-blooded about it); very charming (to be candid). Nothing is so agreeable to an exacting gallery-god, such as I am, than pleasing minutiae. One cannot very well fly to Illyria, a half-hour after dinner, if the scenes are shabby; or if one catches glimpses of the stage-carpenter, and so on. Tonight, these details were admirably managed and the footlights were no barrier to the company of Sir Toby Belch & of Sir Andrew Aguecheek (a sleezy spindle-shanks in flame-colored hose). Some of the poetry, too, floated up to me. One of the finest comedies I have ever seen, as Pepys might well say.

March 11.

Last night, for example, Charles Dana and I drank half and half at the Old Grapevine till past midnight, after which I walked slowly home.

March 13.

Walking is my only refuge from tobacco & food; so today I put on an old suit of clothes & covered about twenty miles or more—to Palisades and back. Felt horrible when I started: heavy, plethoric, not an idea in my head & accusing myself for having let the past week go by so vainly. I must instantly become a harder taskmaster to myself. This is all simple enough when one is free on a good road; but somehow it becomes next to impossible in town

Here about eight words have been crossed out (the first four may be "dear, damned, it is"; the last four are illegible) before the entry goes on:

during the week. It enrages me to see my sleek figure & fat face and to think how I have lost ambition & energy. I haven't a spark of any kind left in me—no will,—nothing. And the worst of it is that if I make new resolutions, I do it with my tongue in my cheek. Well, while I was thinking pleasant things like this, I saw two bluebirds, gathered some willow catkins, munched birch buds and otherwise noted the advent of Spring. A most beautiful day in the woods, but there was no spirit in me to feel any elation. The sky was silver, the trees were touched with blue shadows, the melting snow gleamed on the emerging rocks. Yet feeling that I had done no good, of late, I felt quite as though I carried the burden of some undefined sin—and that feeling deadened me to all others. I bought a cake at Fort Lee & ate it contritely; though twenty devils were at each of my ears suggesting methods of spending the evening more politely. I enjoyed the cake, at all events.

March 17.

As You Like It. Certainly no dearth of Shakespeare this winter. Ben Greet's company again. I thought the play delightful up to the appearance of Phebe and Silvius in the Fourth Act. The dialogue here was tedious, the play dragged, the whole illusion of the theatre escaped (or, one might say, invaded Arden). These two characters ought by all means to be cut absolutely. Some details were not so good (such as the person representing Hymen) but, on the whole, the thing is very agreeable. Jacques' (Ben Greet) "All the world's a stage" was admirable. Jacques had a decidedly Holbeinish get-up. Greet plays his parts in a droll way, I think. Imagine last week's Sir Andrew Aguecheek as this week's Orlando. Olivia's garden a capital scene. For one thing, a play like this should breathe forth rich airs from time past. If it is quaint, it is antique; it is curious. When the curtain rises, it should be like the opening of a casement through which should stream sweet & lively odors. Some of that delicate perfume tonight suggested something artificial. It showed the difference between a bouquet still wet with dew and a garland of wax.

March 31.

In the reeking basement of Cooper Union, with its innumerable pillars, and low ceiling, I listened to Tschaikowsky's Sixth Symphony tonight, this time played by the Russian Symphony Society. The adagio is certainly a very noble bit of music. There is a theme in it (I recall it well) that is as languorously despairing as any in the world. It falls on one like a calm—profound and ravishing. Leo Schulz played Rubinstein's Melody in F and gave as an *encore* another Rubinstein. My very flesh was melting under the influence of this *encore* when a bed-bug made its escape from some neighboring Jew and passed by way of my left hand up my sleeve. I made a dab at it but I doubt whether I knocked it off. Imagine my state of mind! Well, they played an overture by Glinka (in the Russian novels the soldiers are always whistling something of G's); and a phantaisie by Musorgski, whoever the devil he was. The audience was made up largely of Jews, some with suspiciously long hair. I remarked one fellow with a bristling, black pompadour wearing carnations. A sentimental-looking German stood behind me; and a fat Greek wearing glasses sat in front of me. A lady on my right said to the gentleman with her "*Vous sentez de l'air?*" He replied, "*Non, mais je sens votre mouchoir.*" I was unable to distinguish it myself.

April 4. 1904.

Extraordinarily brilliant day. A day for violet and vermilion, for yellow and white—and everything of silk. *Au contraire*, people looked like the very devil. Men who'd been taking a drop of the Astor House Monongahela now and then through the winter, or else had been calling in at Proctor's for an olive or a fishball before starting up town, looked like blotchy, bloodless, yes, and bloated—toads; and many a good honest woman had a snout like a swine. And this on a day when the rainbows danced in the basin in Union Square! Spring is something of a Circe, after all. It takes a lot of good blood to show on a day like this. Everybody's clothes looked intolerably old and beggarly. The streets were vile with dust. Personally, I felt quite up to the mark; yesterday, I walked a score of miles sloughing off a pound at every mile (it seemed). There were any number of blue birds afield—even the horizons, after a time, seemed like blue wings flitting down the round sides of the world. Saw a fiery robin & I know not what other birds; & noticed the first clucking of the wood-frogs, which sounded like the creaking of Flora's wain. The creatures seemed to be choking & no wonder; for some of the ponds were still filled with slush & rotten ice. Item: any fool could have found pussy willow in abundance. Some of the berry bushes had turned purple & there were plenty of green boughs of something or other. Spring comes this way, trait by trait, like a stage sunrise, *bien calculé*. Once, when I stopped to drink, my eye fell on a green point which in a week will be a weedy skunk cabbage. The cedars glittered in the dismal woods. At the terminus of my walk, to call it so, I went to the edge of the Palisades, that having been my route, & lay on my belly on the top of one of the cliffs. This is something of an adventure for a man subject to being dizzy. Even a gull, some distance below me seemed to be conscious that it was flying high. But it was infinitely agreeable to listen to the shore so far below & to mark a catamaran of bricks sailing by & to see a wily shad-fisher feeding excelsior to his goats. More, I watched the sun as it came from behind patches of cloud light up certain hills, while the others lay in shadow. Explored a gorge, where there was still more or less snow—and quite a gorge, too! Stood on a hill. From a hill that overlooks a proper valley other hills look like very decent waves or like clouds or like great ships. No doubt, if it had been a bit nearer sunset, the particular hills I gazed at so long would have been very much like the steps to the Throne. And Blake's angels would have been there with their "Holy, Holy, Holy."

Noting the reference to Blake's "A Vision of the Last Judgment," this entry adds to our understanding of Stevens' "Not Ideas About the Thing but the Thing Itself" (1954), as we note the last lines:

> That scrawny cry—it was
> A chorister whose c preceded the choir.
> It was part of the colossal sun,
>
> Surrounded by its choral rings,
> Still far away. It was like
> A new knowledge of reality.

April 9.

Strange phantasmagoria! Bynner, the old *Advocate* poet, dropped in on me last night & I went with him to the Café Francis in West 35th Street where we sat & smoked & talked & drank St. Estéphe until after midnight. An inexplicable fellow—the manners of a girl, the divination, flattery & sympathy of a woman, the morbidness & reverie of a poet, the fire and enthusiasm & ingenuousness of a young man. He has gathered his own impressions & odd ones they are. Has he passed safely through the sentimental, sketchy stage?

April 11. 1904.

Yesterday I saw a butterfly, a worm and a dormer window of iridescent glass (in Gothic Coylesville). Tonight I feel like studying & by some odd perverseness the house is like a mild Pandemonium—Schmidt is whining and groaning over a Sudermann tragödie & Sayre is tinkling on his mandolin.

April 18.

Mon luth! Mon luth! Walked from Undercliff to Fort Montgomery yesterday, just failing of West Point. A good 42 miles. Up at four with the help of an alarm clock. Had breakfast at Schwarzwalds (sausage & buckwheats) and then started. The Fifth Avenue hotel was covered with a strange astral light & looked very much like Rousseau's (?) painting of Fontainebleu. Managed to get across the river by seven and from that time until half-past six at night, I walked without stopping longer than a minute or two at a time. How clean & precise the lines of the world are early in the morning! The light is perfect—absolute—one sees the bark of trees high up on the hills, the seams of rocks, the color & compass of things. Seven, too, seems to be a fine hour for dogs. They were nosing about all along the first stretches of road. One or two were stretched out on porches dozing away comfortably, ideally at their ease. The sun blazes wonderfully then, too. The mere roofs are like pools of fire. From the Palisades, I looked down on the Hudson, which glimmered incessantly. In the distance, the Sound shot up a flare. There was a ship below me & I made note of the whole business in a sketch on a scrap of paper, which I copy. Will it help me remember the thing?

I heard a dry murmur in the reeds (may I never forget it); and I observed a robin sitting on a stone. For all that, there were hundreds of robins. And some of them, with other birds, made "sweet moan." Yes: seven is the hour for birds, as well as for dogs and the sun. Near Tompkins' Cove I made a map of the river which, like the sketch of the *Mary Ann* above, I copy here for memory's sake.

The sketch appears in the journal with "ye sounde" written beside it. The map is accompanied by the following: "*Notes on ye above Mappe of ye Hudson R.* At this point, ye distance was as blue as ye eyes of a Norsk virgin. & Here lies Stony Point, where ye battle was fought. A damned queer place for a battle." The entry continues:

God! What a thing blue is! It is one of the few things left that bring tears to my eyes (or almost). It pulls at the heart with an irresistible sadness. It seems as if it were the dusk of the lost Pleiades, as if it were a twilight where any moment the fairies might light their lamps. 'Faith, that point about the fairies is only too true. It has set my bladder rattling, as witness:
Time. Any absolutely cloudless day.
Place etc. On a high hill. Stevens stands on the alert and his large ear picks out these sounds twenty miles away.—
Persons. One of the fairies singing to his harp:

> Be thou my hood
> Bright columbine
> And thou my staff
> O, green, green vine
>
> I would pursue
> The beam that brings
> So sweet a hope
> Of sweeter things

And rest me there
On its soft star,
To hear it chime—
Songs from afar.

Well, such was the effect of Tompkins' Cove. The road from
there on amply justified the cry of regret I seemed to overhear from
the dim horizons. It ran along, up and down, to and fro, around, and
back again. Therefore I took to the railroad tracks, heading for a
misty cove that lay up the river. In its shadow, I found a station &,
deciding not to push on, I lay flat on my back on the platform &
waited for the train. I made a sketch of the cove, but suppress the
drawing.—One word more. I thought, on the train, how utterly we
have forsaken the Earth, in the sense of excluding it from our
thoughts. There are but few who consider its physical hugeness, its
rough enormity. It is still a disparate monstrosity, full of solitudes &
barrens & wilds. It still dwarfs & terrifies & crushes. The rivers still
roar, the mountains still crash, the winds still shatter. Man is an
affair of cities. His gardens & orchards & fields are mere scrapings.
Somehow, however, he has managed to shut out the face of the giant
from his windows. But the giant is there, nevertheless. And it is a
proper question, whether or not the Lilliputians have tied him down.
There are his huge legs, Africa & South America, still, apparently,
free; and the rest of him is pretty tough and unhandy. But, as I say,
we do not think of this. There was a girl on the train with a face like
the under-side of a moonfish. *Her* talk was of dances & men. For her,
Sahara had no sand; Brazil, no mud.

Among Stevens' many uses of the "giant," another instance in which he is
given limbs is found in "A Primitive Like an Orb" (1948):

Here, then, is an abstraction given head,
A giant on the horizon, given arms,
A massive body and long legs, stretched out,
A definition with an illustration, not
Too exactly labelled. . .

Richard Ellmann has also related the previous entry to "Imagination as
Value," wherein Stevens says, "the great poems of heaven and hell have
been written and the great poem of the earth remains to be written."

April 20.
    Alas, I am a wreck again tonight. And dead, dead broke. I &
Zubetkin dined together fancily, & we drank deliciously & then we

did a very, very improper thing. We were so drunk we had our photographs taken.

Tonight I have 10 pennies, owe three weeks board & feel like a pup.

The day of the sun is like the day of a king. It is a promenade in the morning, a sitting on the throne at noon, a pageant in the evening.

Or, perhaps, as Stevens says in "Questions Are Remarks" (1949): "It is his own array, / His own pageant and procession and display. . ."

May 23. Monday.

Charles Dana & I took the Patten Line "up the picturesque Shrewsbury" last Saturday afternoon & stayed in the neighborhood until last evening. From Pleasure Bay we took the trolley to Asbury. Strange country—filled with the crudest display of architecture in the world, I should think, and, at this season of the year, quite deserted. We found a saloon in a cellar within a very short time & then wandered to the beach where we joshed two servants for an hour or more. The night was too lovely to waste in bed, so after filling the ladies with soda, we returned to the boardwalk. At the end of it, we crawled under a pier & thus reached Bradley Beach. There, the sea beat at our feet & the Milky Way etc. etc. etc. The sand sparkled electrically near the surf under our shoes as we gathered wood. We soon had a fire & a circle of light & for a while we ate corned beef from a can & drank whiskey from a bottle. When the fire fell in, we lay on our backs & watched the stars, Charles sporting chestnuts. Ere long the sun rose like the side of a house & we dozed off—The rest of the trip was made up of sitting on piers, drinking root beer, smoking stinkers, riding in trolleys & then down "the picturesque Shrewsbury" (again). The crowd on the boat was quite as picturesque as anything else. Sirloin & cucumbers at Smith & Mc-Nell's & then home again.

The rest of this page, about two-thirds, has been cut off, and the following page has been excised. The next page begins in the middle of a sentence, and it is difficult to tell when it was written; the entry following it is dated in July. What remains here is:

set down here what a beast I think him—nerves, vanity & money.

It is impossible to tell to whom he was referring, but certainly it was not Witter Bynner, to whom my father had written on an unspecified Thursday in May:

My bar exams are on June 7 & until then I intend to apply myself most conscientiously to grinding. Therefore our congeniality must *ex necessitate* be a thing apart from "drink" (as you call it—hideously). In fact, I detest rum, & never intended that, if we were to see much of one another, there should be much liquor spilled. It is a tiresome thing. My idea of life is a fine evening, an orchestra & a crowd *at a distance*, a medium dinner, a glass of something cool & at the same time wholesome, & a soft, full Panatela. If that is congenial to you, we can surely arrange it after June 7—unless I flunk. In the meantime we must be without much ceremony, although eager enough.

In connection with passing the examinations for the bar my father filed an affidavit on May 11 that outlined his qualifications to become a lawyer. It states that he had lived at 124 East 24th St. in Manhattan for at least the previous six months, that he had been certified as a law student on November 19, 1901, that he had attended "as a student in good and regular standing" the New York Law School for the required term of "two school years of not less than eight months each," and that his attendance ended on June 5, 1903. The affidavit also includes the dates of his vacation periods while serving his clerkship under W. G. Peckham:

> to wit, the periods beginning on June 12th, 1902 and ending on June 23rd 1902; beginning on September 23, 1902 and ending on October 1st, 1902; beginning on June 5th, 1903 and ending on June 10th, 1903; beginning on July 29th, 1903, and ending on September 17th, 1903; . . .

the latter "vacation" being the one spent in the Canadian Rockies.

VII

When my father was admitted to the bar, on June 29, 1904, he was home in Reading on an extended visit. Both of his brothers were practicing law in Reading, and it is possible that Wallace consulted his father about doing the same, although he obviously decided against it and returned to New York late in the summer. During this visit, however, he met a young lady in Reading and fell in love with her; she would become his wife, and my mother.

Elsie Viola Kachel was born in Reading on June 5, 1886, making her seven years younger than Wallace Stevens. Her parents had been married only a few months before her birth and her father, Howard Irving Kachel, died the next year. Her mother, née Ida Bright Smith, did not remarry until Elsie was eight; owing to the brevity of the first marriage, there were apparently a good many questions (and some aspersions cast) about my mother's legitimacy. All her life, at least during the time I knew her, she suffered from a persecution complex which undoubtedly originated during her childhood, and which I was unable to understand for a long time. Certainly she was "different," when compared with my friends' mothers; for example, the first time I called her "Mommy," as I had heard my playmates address their mothers, I was told never to use that word to her again: it sounded like "Mummy," which indicated to her that I thought of her as an Egyptian mummy, a dead body wrapped in rags. We did not get on well together until after my father's death. Part of his legacy to me was to carry on the devotion he had for her; and as I began to understand, I also "grew up."

When Elsie's mother married Lehman Wilkes Moll, in 1894, Elsie became known as "Moll," instead of "Kachel," although she was never formally adopted by her stepfather. And she insisted to her friends that her name was "Kachel," though as the years went by she apparently became used to "Moll": all of my father's love letters to her came in envelopes addressed to Elsie Moll. She left high school during her first year, owing to financial pressures on the family and, as she told me, because her eyes were so bad she couldn't see the blackboard. Her parents either didn't believe that her eyesight was bad or, more likely, couldn't afford the glasses she needed. But her eyesight did not affect her skill at playing the piano; when she left school she went to work in a department store, selling sheet music by playing the pieces in the store, and she also earned money by giving lessons at home. I have never known whether she had any formal training or whether she taught herself to play; she had a sure, light touch, and during the time that I studied piano (from someone else) as a child she often corrected my practice (though if I argued, "My teacher said . . ." she did not persist). She played well enough to accompany singers at recitals and to give recitals of her own, at least during her early years in Hartford, Connecticut, where she was a member of the Musical Club. She did not stop playing until arthritis stiffened her fingers.

It's odd, but "stiff" was the word one of her contemporaries used to describe her; Claire Tragle Bauer told me in an interview that when she had first seen my mother, she noticed her walking down the street, "very stiff, straight and stiff, like a gendarme almost." She was very beautiful, but shy and uncomfortable if she became the center of attention; she was very self-conscious. By the time she met Claire, early in this century, Elsie was living with her family at 231 South Thirteenth Street in Reading, well on the "wrong" side of the tracks, which run through Reading at Seventh St. Tenth Street was "beyond the pale," and "nice girls" didn't venture to that part of town. Nevertheless, Elsie and Claire became friends, and it was through Claire that my parents met at a party, when a group of her male acquaintances in town asked whether they might bring along a friend from New York, who was "a very fine poet."

As we have noted, there are quite a few excisions in the journal for the summer of 1904. Following his last entry in May, the next is headed "Reading, Pa.," and is dated July 7: "Been home for several weeks. Swimming most of the time at the"—and here about two-thirds of a page has been cut off, before the entry goes on:

> chief occupation & having him at the table our greatest trial.
> Have been walking to Wily's, to Shearer's, to O'Reilly's, to Speises's etc. etc.

where again two-thirds of a page has been cut off, and one or more pages following that excised. The next full journal page indicates that Wallace and Elsie had met, and that my father had been "smitten."

> August 6.
> Dear me, that warm mouth counts too; and that ravishing hand; and that golden head trying to hide in my waistcoat somewhere; and those blue eyes looking at me sweetly though without intent.

In Gomorrah, I forgot the whirring of the locust. The sound is everywhere in the trees today. It starts low & then rises until just before it stops. And it sounds, perfectly, like a field-noise at harvest.

A day or two ago I walked up the Tulpehocken to Van Reed's. It was the most matutinal morning this year. It was actually blue and the air had a sparkle to it and the birds cut and rushed, and I walked in delight. From Van Reed's I ascended the "colline" to the right & thence I went over the fields and through the woods to Leesport. Near Leesport I dropped in on the Wily's who are now living at Huy's, Mrs. Wily's old home. Both this house & the one at Howard Grove were built in 1817. But this one—! Yet the Wily's seem not to mind the change greatly. At Tuckerton, Levi Mengel gave me a quart of old-fashioned meade, some checker-cake & a cigar.

On the day following, Thursday, I went through the Gettysthal (sic)—it might even be Goettesthal. It's a mild defile running N. & S. in the hills between Temple & the Pricetown road. I found it ferny & dreadfully damp but worth some pains. Returned via Heckman's hotel, the old Clymer furnace etc. In the afternoon canoed & swam.

The rest of that page has been cut off.

How he bundles us all to bed at the same time! What infinite wisdom there is in three meals a day, and four seasons a year!

A pool on a quiet estuary is a perfect image of peace. It invokes meditation—even on a train.

Again, the rest of the page has been cut off. The next page begins, mysteriously,

human abiding place.

August 18.
    Tonight, I am still faintly homesick,—remembering home & thinking of it, as if it were—Dash the hurdy-gurdies. At least half-a-dozen have rattled up the street—they distract me utterly. Yet I was just recalling Lou Heizmann's pianola. And for recollection's sake let me take note of sleeping on the steps at O'Reilly's Gap, of that quiet *sentier* through the woods on the nearest ridge, of H's piazza & Bull Durham cigarettes.

Here about one-third of a page has been cut off, and the next one begins:

cloud in the East, of Mrs. Wily's showing me her books, of that idle drive [illegible word—"single"?] Lance, of that ossified morning at the Tower,—[about five words have been crossed out heavily here and are illegible] of the bitterness of Greater Reading cigars—the ragginess rather—, of [illegible name, beginning with "S"] & Nolans & John Kutz at the Club (damn 'em), of Elsie & I taking a peep into Christ Cathedral, of the odor of sachet that she exhaled, of the spirituality she suggested [two words have been crossed out here and are illegible] Is there nothing else? I want every little thing— there's that bug-killing performance with Katherine Loose who is to spend the winter in Florence. I see Bob Hoff paying Nine ($9.00) Dollars—it *was* mine—as pew-rent to a white-haired man in a cool, cellar-ish room at Trinity. S'help me, I almost forgot reading Heine with Miss [illegible name, beginning with "B"] at the home of the author of "Olla Podrida." She wrote to me saying that she liked those Hebrew songs when played on my bassoon. With what amused disgust I used to read the *Times*, sitting at breakfast in my pyjamas! Then I must think occasionally of the cherries I ate, of the strawberries, of the little cobs of sweet-corn, of the first sweet apples—

> Pas derrièr chez mon père,
> Vole, mon coeur, vole!
> Pas derrièr chez mon père
> Li-ya-t-un pommier doux—

of the canteloupes & sweet potatoes & that one massive huckleberry pudding—and the ice-cream. Also, of the cigars I smoked late at night on the steps & in my room, & of memorizing several hundred lines of Maud & of the incomparable regularity of life. Alas! I have reserved nothing by way of climax (unless it be the red moon casting its light

The following page has been excised. The next one goes on, seemingly uninterrupted,

on Levi Mengel's eleven cigars). Well, these things are all mere marionettes for my fancy at most. They need no climax where they play. I have built them here & now a little stage set round with tapers. Let them drop in & out as they will.

There is another "stage set round with tapers" in Stevens' "Carlos Among the Candles" (1917), which, as he commented in 1935, "was one of the plays that had to do with the effect of changing light on the emotions."

To return to the journal:

August 23rd. Tuesday.

On Sunday Billy Barton & I rode to Wharton (Port Oram) in Jersey and from there walked through the huge government powder depot at Picaniny (sic) over a difficult ridge and along a checkerberry-covered road & up hill & across flats to Green Pond, a singularly beautiful place, where we had grub. The last stage of the road was most novel. The foliage looked like the foliage in an arboretum—but I am too languid to be descriptive. From G. P. we climbed over the G. P. mountains into the Longwood valley, down which we went to some hole in the ground & then by a roundabout way to Nolen's Point on Lake Hopatcong. Here we sat on the piazza of the villa eating biscuits and wringing out our handkerchiefs & lazily watching the lake. To disappoint the hotel-keepers, we hunted up a camp (Camp Six) and slept in dirty cots under a circus tent. It was frightfully chilly in the morning, but Barton managed to swim a bit. The dew fell like rain.

The rest of the page, about one-third, and the following page have been excised. The next page begins within a sentence:

the sun in a dirty place—a dead fish lying in the sun in a dirty place and that has lain there for a week. One or two things made a fine flutter—*mais seulement ça.* We were robbed at Englewood by a druggist. Feeling a trifle hungry in the evening I ate some corn-beef hash, ice-cream, bananas and biscuits. That suggestive menu seems inclined to set my bowels bubbling biliously. But as I propose to select my own victuals during the week it may not be so bad. I shall soon beat Mrs. Rorer:

Breakfast
Force
Frogs
&
Fritters

Lunch
Peas
Pigeons
&
Pie

Dinner
Clams
Cocoa
&
Cake

Late Lunch
Beer
Bretzels
&
Belly-ache

September 12.
     The fact of the matter is:

> *Breakfast*
> Force
>
> *Lunch*
> One coffee roll and hot rice-pudding
>
> *Dinner*
> Onion Soup
> Sweet-bread croquettes
> Stuffed Tomatoes   Cucumber Salad
> Musk-melon

I challenge Mrs. R.

September 13.
     Another letter from Elsie. I could write to her every night—but she will answer only once a week, and then four pages are all I get. Lord! how I study them—those four pages—& turn them into a volume. Tonight, I have been re-

The rest of this page, about two-thirds, has been cut off.

September 26.
     [Arthur] Clous & I ought to get on well together. His bad points are much better than bad points usually are. He can dispose of only one idea at a time—& he does before he takes up another. Thus if he were about to say "Good Morning!" and you interrupted him and talked steadily about a thousand things for an hour, he would calmly go ahead with his stupid "Good Morning" when you concluded. This is irritating. His ideas strike me as being all very elementary. But once you understand a man it is very easy to make life pleasant for him. (An amiable, egotistical theory.)

October 23rd.
     Living a strange, insane kind of life. Working savagely; but have been so desperately poor at times as not to be able to buy sufficient food—and sometimes not any. Last night, however, I went to Smith & McNell's and had steak & pumpkin pie & then walked home under the full moon up Broadway. Felt as weak as a tired child and went to bed at half-past eight dropping off at once. Slept splendidly until half-past nine this Sunday morning, when I went out & got breakfast. It is a gorgeous day & I am only debating which of many roads I shall follow.

October 30.

Didn't dress until half-past two today. Had breakfast (Force and grapes) in the room and then pulled a sofa into the sunlight and lay there smoking and reading Elsie's letters and thinking of her. Finally A. C. & I went up town to an exhibition of water-colors and then walked around the Reservoir and through the Park.

Nov. 7.

Last week was the first since Elsie and I began writing to one another that I have not had a letter from her. Everything hangs in suspense as a result. I say to myself that I am sure to hear from her in the morning and I convince myself that if I do not I shall feel abominably cut up; and no doubt I shall. I think I shall have to use the tactics approved of by the novelists—feigning indifference & the like. But then I'm going home for Thanksgiving which is only a short time away & I think my real feelings will explode all fake ones then. Our letters seem to have wrought changes. It will be like two new persons facing one another. Will it be *two* happy ones?

The next two pages have been excised, and the journal continues within an undated entry, presumably written after Thanksgiving in Reading.

In other respects, my visit was like many others. The family, to be candid, insuperably dull. The country incomparably duller. Spent more or less time with the dentist & now sport two gaudy gold teeth, as a consequence, with more to follow at Xmas. On Sunday morning, I started on a bit of a walk. It had been snowing slightly and, far off, the fields were white. Beyond these stood the little blue hills, very pale in the light, very delicate. Went through the Göttesthal which as usual was decidedly muddy. Yet Reading is my *"fons Bandusiae, splendidor vitro"* and while I muddy it yet I bring my lamb duly

> Child of the race that butt & rear
> Not less, alas! his life-blood clear
> Shall tinge thy cold wave crystalline
> O babbling Spring!

There are no further entries in this third notebook, although many pages remain blank that could have been used. There is no record of the Christmas season in 1904, and we do not know whether my father stayed in New York or went home to Reading. If he did, his visit was brief, for the fourth and final journal opens with the new year in the city.

January 1. 1905.

The current doesn't flow much more rapidly or through very strange countries. But we shall see. Up at noon today. Loafed until

three when Arthur and I went to the exhibition of the National
Academy of Design. Walked in the Park afterwards—the air soft with
Duft. Dull crowd.

January 15.

Walked all afternoon along the river. A little snow, a little ice &
a [three words have been crossed out here and are illegible] lot of
coldness. Feel in remarkable trim. But with the thermometer close
to zero—

Jan. 20.

A journal's a bore at times.

February 5. Sunday Night.

Went to Clinton Hall tonight with Arthur Clous & dined *comme
il faut.* Drank Chianti and apricot brandy & then went to Calvary,
where we were both rather drunk. Came home singing hymns.—Dull
life of it! Office and theatre and perpetual cold weather.

March 5.

Work, concerts, letters from Elsie, books, jaunts around town—
these are what I seem to live for. I feel that Spring is in the ground,
seething. But there is still plenty of snow and ice and I continue to
wear a sweater (& sometimes) mocassins in bed.

April 10.

I fear that the habit of journalizing has left me. Still one doesn't
care to write a story all of one thing and my own history nowadays
would make rather a monotonous Odyssey at best. Yet how irresis-
tibly one changes—in details. Tonight, there was a long twilight and
after dinner I took a stroll as I am wont to do in summer-time. I
could not realize that it was I that was walking there. The boy self
wears as many different costumes as an actor and only midway in the
opening act is quite unrecognizable. Now and then something happens
to me, some old habit comes up, some mood, some scene (both of the
sun, and of the moon) returns, and I return with it. But more often
my days are mere blots on the calendar. There is nothing new in the
Spring for me, or so it seems; and yet my spirits are high enough: I
do not write this in melancholy. I feel a nervous desire for work.
That is all that is left. Long ago, I gave up trying to make friends
here, or trying really to enjoy myself. *C'est impossible.* I dream more
or less—often of Elsie. [Here seven words have been crossed out and
are illegible.] But I actually plan more—making one day fit another
and keeping ends together. I feel a little inclined toward deviltry
now and then, but *only* a little. I have money in pocket but not in

bank & I pay most of my bills promptly & all of them eventually. Still my hands are empty—& that much idolized source of pathetic martyrdom, *mon pauvre coeur!* How scandalous it is not to regret "the silver seas!" I thought yesterday that four and twenty blue-birds baked in a pie might make me a modest breakfast—because one must have blue-birds one way or another (even if one only says silly & affected things about them). Sometimes, just before I go to sleep, I fancy myself on a green mountain—Southward, I think. It's simply green, the grass,—no trees, just an enormous, continental ridge. And I have windows there—(John Bland & I drink lager & porter at the Old Grape Vine for three hours here—no more of the green mountain tonight.)

I am reminded here of the subtitle "The Greenest Continent," which Stevens used in "Owl's Clover," where "The statue . . . belongs / To April here and May to come."

April 11.

I think I'll start a gallery of comparative humanity. First—this morning I saw a girl wearing a waist with alternate pink and white stripes an inch wide. In the evening at a Beethoven recital by Eugen d'Albert I saw two women, not sitting together either, each with the "Sämmttiche Sonaten von Ludwig von Beethoven" on their knees. One had no chin. The other had a large red nose and carried some smelling salts in a bottle concealed in a piece of paper. D'Albert was rotten—terrible tempo & loud pedal all the time. I didn't know any of the numbers except "3 b"—*rondo a capriccio* (opus 129 according to the program); and that was almost unrecognizable. Walked from the office to Carnegie & had dinner there—regular table d'hote of the kind one gets everywhere. Sickening. Delightful air. It blew up my coat sleeves & made me feel as if I'd like to take off my shirt. I'm going to come down from the green mountain tonight and imagine a warm sea booming on a tropical coast.

April 12.

Had three square meals today—did a lot of work—& tonight I feel like carousing—not with wine and so on, but with good fellows. I believe I could hold up my end of an argument.

I have caroused. Not wildly—yet my nerves are absolutely at rest. It is only ten o'clock—a walk, four glasses of [here the word "whiskey" has been crossed out] rum! ["rum" has been underlined twice], three cigars—now for a page of Paul Bourget.

One of the things that Claire Bauer told me about my mother was that my father used to call her his "Princess of *lointaine*," and he uses that phrase in his next journal entry.

April 27.

Went home for Easter—rather I went to see Elsie. My word, she seemed *une vrai princess lointaine*. On Easter afternoon we walked over the ridge north of O'Reilly's gap. Found arbutus, cowslips, violets and so on. I was in the seventh heaven, I think, although I kept no count of them. We descended the great hill above Rosedale with the sun full in our faces.

By this time Wallace was deeply in love, but apparently all was not going well in the courtship and succeeding journal entries indicate a certain depression and dissatisfaction; none of the letters between my parents have survived from this period, except in excerpts that my mother copied out and saved.

April 30.

I am in an odd state of mind today. It is Sunday. I feel a loathing (large & vague!), for things as they are; and this is the result of a pretty thorough disillusionment. Yet this is an ordinary mood with me in town in the Spring time. I say to myself that there is nothing good in the world except physical well-being. All the rest is philosophical compromise. Last Sunday, at home, I took communion. It was from the worn, the sentimental, the diseased, the priggish and the ignorant that "Gloria in excelsis!" came. Love is consolation, Nature is consolation, Friendship, Work, Phantasy are all consolation. [The last sentence, about seven words, of this entry has been crossed out and is illegible.]

Surely the April entries hold many premonitions of "Sunday Morning," which, to the best of my knowledge, was not written until ten years later: "April's green endures."

If I were to have my will I should live with many spirits, wandering by
                    caverns measureless to man,
          Down to a sunless sea.
I should live with Mary Stuart, Marie Antoinette, George Sand, Carlyle, Sappho, Lincoln, Plato, Hawthorne, Goethe and the like. I am too languid even to name them.

May 8, 1905.

The Spring in a way is a bad quarter of a year for me, because I am always in a tempest of discontent then. For two weeks I have been in a frightful mood. Sunday before last I rushed home from church in the evening and memorized Shakespeare's "Tired with all these, for restful death I cry." And I wished it had been a thousand times as long and a thousand times more bitter. Today, too, I could have been seen on Broadway with my head down and my hands behind my back destroying everything and everybody. I shan't go into it. It's simply New York and a bad liver combined, I suppose, for I *am* capable of excessive delight. But man is not a noble animal and it isn't often that his cup runneth over.

The rest of this page, about one-third, and the following page, have been excised; the next page begins at the end of a sentence:

to sleep. Tomorrow, I move to East Orange.

31 Halsted-Street
East Orange, New-Jersey

May 15.
   Here I am.

May 23.
   Not much to describe—simply a nice cheerful house and room, excellent rations & much greenness. There's a bell ringing in a tower—that's something new—and old; and there are many such things.

May 30—Memorial Day.
   Nice day.

June 18. Sunday.
   What a business! Been drinking gin & courting the moon. That's done for now & I shall be decent until autumn. Still deeply in love!

July 2.
   This is a wet Sunday morning. It is not yet half-past seven, so that under the circumstances I am still in bed. What a blessing it is to wake up and to be able to listen to the moving of the trees.

A week later my father found himself moving again, this time around the country. For the first time since his trip with Peckham to the Rockies, he traveled outside his familiar orbit, which, centered now in New York City, extended to Boston on the northeast, and Philadelphia and Reading to the southwest. His travels must have been job-related, because of his financial situation, but no details are available. His first business trip was a quick one:

July 16. Reading, Pa.
   Home for a two weeks loaf. A week ago I left New York for the West. Found Chicago—cheap; Kansas City—a mere imitation of civilization; Kansas—glorious; and when I got to Colorado I could

have kissed the very ground. Went down to Raton, New Mexico and did a bit of business. Then went to Clayton, New Mexico, and did more. When the work was over, I went out onto the prairie & lay full in the sun looking at the sky stretching above Texas, which was at my foot. An interesting world in some ways—a good place for airy solitude. Returned to Colorado & went via Pueblo to Colorado Springs, which is as nice as any Eastern suburban town except that the streets being so wide are without proper shade. Thence I went through Nebraska & Iowa (which is a superb state) & on to Niagara Falls & to New York & home. The best thing I saw was a lightning storm on the prairie. I leaned out of the smoking-room window and watched the incessant forks darting down to the horizon. Now & then great clouds would flare & the ground would flash with yellow shadows.

The geography he traversed put him near, if not in, Oklahoma and, in his reference to "a lightning storm," perhaps the background for "Earthy Anecdote" where

> Every time the bucks went clattering
> Over Oklahoma
> A firecat bristled in the way.

The next entry begins within a sentence, preceded by an excised page, and we cannot be sure whether it was written in Reading or after Stevens returned to New York. Certainly the territory described is Berks County, Pennsylvania, or nearby.

the hotel there. We drove right and left and got to Strausstown at four o'clock (circa). Here we had ham and eggs (I and Livingood had the same thing there about four years ago) cakes & jelly—I write this merely for auld lang syne! It is like remembering pigeons on a roof, or chickens feeding around a cow at twilight, or the courses of rain-water down a slope. We left Strausstown about five o'clock. The sun came out for the first time during the day. Every barn was a castle; every rooster, Chanticleer. The hills—the Blue Mountains—were white with misty light. I was as happy as a lark in a cloud of gold, and I pulled Elsie close to me—oh, it *was* our day. When we came to that stretch of the road near Womelsdorf where the trees have fine leaves (so Elsie describes locust trees) it was deep twilight.

My father's poem "Contrary Theses (II)" was first published in 1942. It may be wrong to make a personal connection between the poem, with its references to locust trees, and this journal entry; nevertheless, remembering that my mother's talent was for playing the piano, it seems pertinent to quote the closing line of the fifth stanza, and the first line of the sixth:

> The leaves were falling like notes from a piano.

> The abstract was suddenly there and gone again.

The same undated entry, after a break, goes on:

Once, during the week, I visited Ephrata. Old von Neida recognized me—same whiskers, same glasses, same U. S. Ma-a-i-i-l voice, but I think a considerably enlarged complaisance. His register is no longer bulky. Had I been more watery, I should have wept; for there was an ancient smell there, that I knew well. I rather think it must be the soap. And there were many names and initials crying loudly from the walls. On the seat of one of the summer houses I found "W.2." done in wood—& I remembered what a monster of difficulty the letter "2" used to be to me—& my knife. Memory is too much of a pyre. I think human bones may be among my ashes.

As for the rest, as one says at eighty,—mother is sick, father is sick, John is sick, the house is a wreck, everybody's gone to the devil. Sometimes I care immensely. This morning I don't care a damn.

August 2.   East Orange

Shall I blot out the rest? It is almost blotted out already and that without the least assistance on my part. It was so dull that it affected me like an elegant phase of paralysis. It always rains when I'm home—if I wait. Well, it rained almost constantly the second week. It wasn't funny. It wasn't maddening. It was stupid.

Let me see, we went up to the Tower twice, & we climbed the Boulevard. From the Tower I saw the Milky Way; from the Boulevard, I saw a lot of mist and sun. It was like sticking one's nose into the Jovian atelier.

One afternoon I walked up the Tulpehocken to the Red Bridge and found Mrs. Smirk in her willow barouche under a purple parasol. What an immortal ascendancy the Smirks enjoy—and all the rest. I cringe by nature before them. I am not envious but I am consumed with vain longing. If these fellows *are* butchers' sons how *do* they *do* it?

Item. Went out to height of land this side of Ontelaunee—the safe end of the hellish Shalterian dip. The wretched fence there was not made to sit on or to lean against. But I got a certain long range look and watched a cloud about as big as Lancaster County.

August 7. Monday.

On Saturday, I made a midsummer tour of New York. Walked from the office up to 91st Street and back again to the ferry—I cannot just now recapture the vicious, dark mind I had—but it was my New York gloom, the creature of rainy Sundays and hideous miscellanea. On Sunday—yesterday—I spent the morning loafing with *Jane Eyre*. In the afternoon, I walked into a near-by valley. Drenched by heavy rain. The ground steamed visibly after the rain and I saw many white shoes & stockings that will go no more to the [illegible word] (the secrecy of a dress is a god-send to more than one woman). There were two millers beating against my screen a moment ago. There are all sorts of noises in the trees & grass tonight—the most summery thing in the world. At the end of the week, I move from 31 Halsted-Street to 24 Halsted-Place.

Three days later my father *was* on the move again, but toward the south and not merely within East Orange. Again, it must have been a business trip; and it took him to parts of the United States that he had not seen before, including a possible site for an anecdote.

En tour.—August 10.

Going South—rather I have been for some little time. Am now in what, to judge from signs, is "S. W. Va." The water now flows to the Gulf. Baltimore was all hideous tunnel. At Washington I had time to go up to Pennsylvania Avenue and admire the electric lights. (Warm jolly train.) We are approaching Tennessee—green, hilly, sunny-cloudy place.

Was it then that Stevens first conceived a poem published in 1919?

> I placed a jar in Tennessee,
> And round it was, upon a hill.
> It made the slovenly wilderness
> Surround that hill.
>
> The wilderness rose up to it,
> And sprawled around, no longer wild.
> The jar was round upon the ground
> And tall and of a port in air.
>
> It took dominion everywhere.
> The jar was gray and bare.
> It did not give of bird or bush,
> Like nothing else in Tennessee.

He was there again in 1918, and perhaps the "Anecdote of the Jar" comes, by way of my father's imagination, from both visits; as he wrote to my mother on the later trip, "I have always been of two minds about Tennessee." Ambiguity at its best?

Returning to 1905:

August 11.

    Got through red Tennessee, and Alabama too, and this morning I saw a golden sun-rise over the Mississippi pine-tops. Am now at Covington, Louisiana—excessively hot. Have a little robin's blue suit so as to look more *comme il faut*. Café Roubion. My room: wooden walls, matting, great bridal canopy over the bed, fire-place full of cigarette stumps and spider webs. Here's what I've seen—women chopping wood, wash drying on fences (the memory must bring tears to the eyes of absent Tennesseeans), bare-legs: black, white, and yellow, Greek temples, rotten melons in a creek, women generally with men's hats on, ox-carts, everybody sitting down, mule on kitchen door-step, Talbot, Bishop of Central Pennsylvania, sleeping with his mouth open, boys at Morristown selling grapes, melons, fried chicken, po' white trash leaning against things, rain, ale while it was foamy, cotton, river cane, woods like creeks

Whatever the reason for these early business trips of my father's, the area round Covington and Folsom, Louisiana, is still cattle ranch territory today, and it is possible that his practice of law had led him into such areas as bonding herds, or at least investigating cases where cattle never reached their destined market. When he joined the Hartford Accident & Indemnity Company in 1916, his first, and major, role was with one of that company's affiliates: he became a director of the Hartford Livestock Company. He must, therefore, have had some previous experience in that area; that it was an interest continuing for some time is evidenced by an article he wrote that appeared in *The Atlanta* (Georgia) *Journal* in 1930: "Cattle Kings of Florida."

A return to the journal turns up references to a different form of life, however:

Fendlason Hotel, Folsom, Louisiana.

    Have just passed a night indifferent to many horrors. On going to bed I found the bed itself hard, and much too short. Had to sleep with my feet on the dashboard, so to speak. Woke at half-past one in time to hear the most damnable thunder-storm. The thunder used to reverberate for a moment and would end with a series of terrifying percussions that made the house quite jump from its piles. By and by the moon came out and shone through my shutters, a beam falling on the bed, and lighting, as I discovered this morning, the unholy festival of a bed-bug family. At five-thirty this morning my bed was so covered with flies that it looked like a great huckleberry pudding. I got up to write this and as I write there are about ten flies on each toe. As I looked out of my window I saw on the ground a large spider wearing black with silver buckles. There must be many, many bugs here. I saw the pine wood white with mist—that is something. I see it now—for the sun seems not yet to have risen, though I can vouch for one rooster, one cow, one baby and one hawking man.

To continue my notes of travel. The razor back hog looks like this ⌄´ . No account unless it can outrun a nigger. Can be changed to lard in three weeks. Cannot be starved to death so long as it can root. Long nose & sunken face.

The umbrella tree is said to have filthy habits because it so often sheds its leaves. Now, the live-oak does only once.

Yesterday I saw eight oxen drawing a heavy wagon on which was a bag of flour and a box of soap.

1 p.m.
Nigger girl's white sun-bonnet just blew into a puddle.

Fendlason, my landlord, calls a near-by town "a bad place in the road." He says a razor-back's "pow'ful disagreeable prop'ty to have 'round. Always in the way."

The next entry is headed "New Orleans. August 15, 16 or 17 something." The rest of the page, the lower quarter, has been cut off, and the page after that begins at the end of a sentence:

New-Orleans dull. Went to Audubon Park this morning and saw orange trees (2) without any oranges, a bunch of banana trees (without any bananas), a withered coffee tree, several prosperous banyan trees (nice, tangled, shady sort of things), fig & rubber trees etc. etc. Bah! A gentleman in a car while I was seeing St. Charles Avenue discoursed on the crape myrtle. There were some pretty live oaks in the park, thick with moss. Went to the head of Canal Street to see the water-front. Saw it. Slept all afternoon. Intolerable climate. One is wringing wet hour by hour. Have taken three baths already today. People look washed out—women positively rank; men no account.

August 21.   East Orange
Back again & in new quarters at 24 Halsted Place. Laundry scattered all over creation; greater part of my outfit is at the old place in a fellow's room and the landlord won't let me take it out because he hasn't the authority to do so!

When I left off about my trip, I was describing things. To continue—the sun was shining when I left New Orleans (on the 19th). I have a memo about "morning-glory" and, no doubt—yes: I remember now—trailing in the cotton; big ones.

How odd that in "Things of August" he should write, "the morning-glories grow in the egg," particularly after this August reference. The entry goes on:

> It was pleasant to get glimpses of the soft Gulf—all of it gold and dim blue and every movement a glistening one. And the fan-like, starry palms in the marsh gutters, with the innumerable reeds (like a certain Seymour [Haden]) were new. So was the japonaiserie of the pines now and then—when they were single and of strange design. At Mobile I saw a ship from Bergen. Somewhere else I saw a lumpish bird with a face like Gladstone's silhouette and a tail like a little fan. One noticeable thing down there is that, at early twilight, colors—green, I am thinking of—do not become obscure but stand out of the darkness. I remember one strange patch of mist—fields—and dead trees; I remember a group of buzzards; an orange sunset over Lake Pontchartrain; a sign at Flomaton on the Florida line with the words "Do not hitch stock to Park Fence"; an evening in New Orleans when I saw nothing unusual about the stars; a passenger with a bouquet like Elsie's; a Pullman moonrise in Alabama.

Did it become part of "Stars at Tallapoosa," where "There is no moon, no single, silvered leaf?"

> On my way back I stopped at Reading and to my delight I found Elsie there. A way she had of taking my hand made me feel wonderfully welcome.

Last Sunday in August.

> First long walk since I know not when, today. Left East Orange after breakfast—about nine o'clock. A cold morning, really; people in overcoats. Went down to Branch Brook Park (a capital thing) and struck the Morris Canal, which runs to Phillipsburg. Great pleasure to walk on a tow-path again. Lots of interesting foliage—water affairs, and reeds, and so on. Few birds—few other people. Italians fishing, Italian girl washing on a stone, young workmen sitting on bridges, occasional Delft-like reflections of sky in the water. At Richfield, I took the road to Paterson, thence to Hackensack, Bogota, Leonia (just skipping Englewood) and Fort Lee. Took all day. The leaves are beginning to come down—the morning indeed was *most* autumnal. But there are still roses, and the marsh-meadows are still charming with their big pink flowers, whatever they are.

Took lunch with Walter A[rensberg] at the Harvard Club. A fellow of most excellent fancy. Sat in Park afterwards.

September 10. Sunday morning.

Last Sunday (and Monday, since it was Labor Day) I was with Elsie. On Monday afternoon we went around the Gravity and got off at the first station beyond the Tower: "Six," on the ticket. We found a secluded path and walked down through the woods till we found an inviting spot. We returned to the station towards evening and sat there waiting for the train.

Have decided to stay out here all winter

September 15.

No letter from Elsie for nine days. If I get none tomorrow, hanged if I'll be in haste to write again. This *cannot* be a caprice—too much is excused on that ground, anyhow. I have this consolation, that we have had two inimitable nights—the moon in the trees, the sky blue all night long, and huge stars hanging in the bushes like lanterns. The feeble are wearing overcoats. Next week I move to 6 University Place—as I understand the map. Somehow I am ambitious to work. One gets the best view of New-York from a distance.

September 27.

After all, I'm living at 34 Halsted Street, and in more or less comfort, too. I am indefatigable in procrastination.

October 2.

Today, at about noon, I was twenty-six. A year hence I expect to look back at this page and take

Here the rest of the page, about one-third, has been cut off before the next one begins, at the end of a sentence:

dark. And how active, how incessant!

October 11.
Procrastinating *encore*.

November 14.

A month of bitter *far niente*. Smoking, reading [Henry] Murger's *Scènes de la Vie de Bohème*, improvising, writing and receiving love-letters, eating and drinking. The first moon of winter is among the first bare branches

Nov. 24.

A day of St. Martin—the blood warm in my cheeks—an air of truant summer. My landlady was sitting on the porch as I came in tonight, with a shawl around her. She said it was the first time she had enjoyed the porch this season. I saw others walking up and down. Next week I go home for the Thanksgiving holiday. I am full of wishes to see Elsie. How wonderful an agony it is!

December 3. Sunday.

I cannot get the idea of summer out of my head. There is still positive warmth in the air. It rained vigorously all morning. Now the weather seems changing.

December 9.

Snow and rain tonight. Elsie wrote to me today, "I do not think [the balance of this sentence, less than one line, has been excised]." She is quite right. Even reason aids her. She touches all my subtle stops.

Was this, perhaps, one of the times when they quarreled, or decided not to see each other exclusively? As my father wrote, in "Waving Adieu, Adieu, Adieu":

> In a world without heaven to follow, the stops
> Would be endings, more poignant than partings, profounder,
> And that would be saying farewell, repeating farewell,
> Just to be there and just to behold.

VIII

If there was a break in their relationship, it didn't last long.

December 27.

Have been home for Xmas. Elsie & I were together most of the time. On Xmas afternoon we walked to the top of the boulevard. Her cheeks were incomparable. In the evenings, we chatted etc. on the sofa. That "etc" means volumes. Everybody else stale as usual.

The last day in the year. Sunday.

A weighty day, of course. Walked to Montclair and back, in the morning, rather meditatively. Very mild air. My head full of strange pictures—terra-cotta figurines of the Romans, ivory figurines of the Japanese, winter birds on winter branches, summer birds on summer branches, green mountains, etc. Reflections (sic) on Japanese life, on specificness, on minute knowledge as disclosing minute pleasures, on what I should wish my wife to be, on my future. On returning, read a little of [Thomas] Hardy's "Trumpet-Major" and after dinner read more. Pulled my curtains shortly after four and lit my lamp, feeling rather lonely—& afraid of the illusions and day-dreams that comfort me—and frightened at the way things are going, so slowly, so unprofitably, so unambitiously. I hope a few things for the coming year, but resolve nothing.

Went to Humperdinck's *Haensel und Gretel* last evening. Wretched seat in side of top gallery [at the Metropolitan Opera House]. Made no effort to see the stage during the first two acts or "scenes." A somewhat rococo entertainment, I thought.

Tea at Coleman's tonight: toast in the kitchen.

January 2. [1906]

New Year's day was like Spring & Autumn combined. Walked to the Park and around the Field therein before breakfast. After breakfast went over to the Bushwings. Bob & I walked to some nearby village. Read a novel in the afternoon and evening—and wrote a little letter to Elsie. It is delightful to write to her. A letter takes me a long time—but I enjoy it.

Jan. 8.

This year's first snow. And very different it is from a snow in town. But I'd rather there was none at all. I've a desire for books tonight—obscene things, yet amusing.

Jan. 9.

Full moon & snow & perfectly clear.

January 14.

A cold rain last night covered all the branches with a coating of ice. It is something to see, at all events—but I don't know whether or not it's beautiful or strange. It was white & mauve—& now at twilight it looks like nothing more than a mist.

> Tschaikowsky at Carnegie Hall, last night—
>   Serenade in C. Major
>   Concerto, op. 1 (with Adele aus der Ohe)
>   Symphony in B Minor.

[Here five words have been crossed out and are illegible.]

Heber R. Bishop collection of odds & ends yesterday afternoon. Charming & extensive but not great.

January 23.

Last Saturday afternoon I went to the National Academy of Design. The landscapes were charming. One excellent thing by Lockwood De Forest—a pond—fairly real—black trees—faint pink clouds. That, indeed, is the only picture that I remember—with anything like pleasure. There were two or three decent portraits. One nude, evidently the work of Tom Thumb, was "nice": a delicious, pink creature—stepping from some flowers into a rather amorous-looking bit of water.

From the exhibition I went to a decorator's & bought a screen, for some irises on it. Looked up irises in the dictionary & found this line from Tennyson—

"In the spring, a livelier iris changes on the burnished dove."

Is it Virgilian, O doctors? Then went to dinner at Mouquin's. Then to another concert of Good Mozartian polyphony and Rimsky-Korsakoffish blurs.

Last night—a concert by amateurs at Christ Church: Amateur musicians are as bad as school-boy orators. It takes great powers to accomplish even the little things of Life.

February 5.

Pale moonlight.—Have been to a little dance at Miss Morehouse's. I felt like a tramp in some *maison de blanc*. Escaped by walking out of the front door as if to smoke and left my hat etc. behind. I'll get it in the morning. Had I stayed, I should soon have been blacker than Moses when the light ———.

Yesterday I was more in my element—alone on an up-and-downish road, in old clothes, quick with the wind and the cold. It is boorish, I know. Old clothes men are indescribable imposters and boors—yet I am one of them. Think of not dying to dance! But yesterday I went to Morristown and back. My brain was like so much cold pudding. First, I loathed every man I met, and wanted to get away, as if I were some wild beast. People look at one so intimately, so stupidly. Then I noticed the way patches of trees stood on hill-sides, and couldn't think even of a simile. Then I found some pussy willows, the first of the year—and some yellow river willows. Everything was dull and hard and tiresome. A bird on a telephone wire turned its tail toward the wind and seemed to enjoy the raking. Good old fellow! Saw Kahn's Jewish paradise; a good school; good hills; good roads; good towns. What I *did* enjoy was the tear on my body—the beat of the blood all over me. In the evening went to Christ Church. Full litany—sweet and melodious and welcome. They should have dark corners there. Impossible to be religious in a pew. One should have a great nave, quiet lights, a remote voice, a soft choir and solitude. Near me was a doddering girl of, say twenty—idiot eyes, spongy nose, shining cheeks. With her were two ladies—one not quite middle aged, and hungry-respectable looking, the other elderly with the same look. All three wore home-made bonnets. One sees the most painful people, wherever one goes. Human qualities, on an average, are fearful subjects for contemplation. Deceit—how inevitable! Pride, lack of sophistication, ignorance, egoism—what dreadful things! Necessity, too—. I can't make head or tail of Life. Love is a fine thing, Art is a fine thing, Nature is a fine thing; but the average human mind and spirit are confusing beyond measure. Sometimes I think that all our learning is the little learning of the maxim. To laugh at a Roman awe-stricken in a sacred grove is to laugh at something today. I wish that groves still *were* sacred—or, at least, that something was: that there was still something free from doubt, that day unto day still uttered speech, and night unto night still showed wisdom. I grow tired of the want of faith—the instinct of faith. Self-consciousness convinces me of something, but whether it be something Past, Present or Future I do not know. What a bore to have to think all these things over, like a German student, or a French poet, or an English socialist! It would be much *nicer* to have things definite— both human and divine. One wants to be decent and to know the reason why. I think I'd enjoy being an executioner, or a Russian policeman.

Homer's only a little story—and so are all the others; and yet men have not memory enough even to remember a little story. It is a tremendous mark of scholarship to know a little story.

The difference between Keats and a long-shoreman is a matter of a drop or two of blood in their brains, or of the shape of their skulls or of something of the sort. Both are quite innocent of their merit or lack of it. Both are the results of an indifferent psychopathy. —One man is a wag; another is a pessimist; another is a dreamer; another is a practical fellow. That is due to no cleverness on their parts. They are quite helpless. Fancy the Ego looking into that mirror—*plein de Hapsburgs.*

And after this sort of thing, one thinks—well, of a thousand things: whole ages at once—Carthage, Athens (of course—pooh!), Florence—Venice—and one feels like a silly child.

I pass from one thing to another. But John Doe likes music and writes his life out in it; Richard Roe pities a beggar and gives *himself* up to him; Giles is touched by a prayer and dies praying after a life-time in a monastery; Smiles likes a fight and goes through every army in the world. Each of one's passing moods has been a life-time to someone else. Grave and reverend reflection—.

May it be that I am only a New Jersey Epicurean?

February 6.
    Very cold. The river filled with ice. The moon lit the edges. Spent the evening smoking cigarettes with Sam Poole.

February 13.
    Spent Sunday & Monday (Lincoln's Birthday) at home. Nothing changed. Baked potatoes and soft-boiled eggs for Sunday morning's breakfast—a century-old arrangement. Monday morning, crept out to Riverside and back. Snow and mist. (There's still a little primitive mystery about mist.) I think that all the beautiful things in Reading wouldn't be enough to fill a trunk. I saw only one pretty thing—a lamp through a window. Elsie was very loyal to me—but not too loyal. Hummed Dvorak's "Humoresky," more or less. —The river

was heavily undulous, coming home. I noticed how the grain elevators loomed (as one says) in the Jersey shadows. —The stars are moist and large and glistening and innumerable. I'm inclined to Schopenhauer & the fine arts.

February 21. 1906.
    Read in Matthew Arnold's "Notebooks" this morning:
        "la destination de l'homme est d'accroître le sentiment de la joie, de féconder l'énergie expansive, et de combattre, dans tout ce qui sent, le principe de l'avilissement et les douleurs."
    As far as one thing by itself can be true, that is true, I think; but for the word "destination" I would substitute "virtue." Yet it is only one phase of "infinite" wisdom, like the fear of the Lord etc.

    A mild day. During the afternoon the rain came down in showers, as it does in the summer. The river was most interesting—coming home: low clouds & jumble of lights

    Have just finished Leopardi's "Pensieri" (translated by P. Maxwell—a scholarly major-general). They are paragraphs on human nature, like Schopenhauer's psychological observations, Pascal's "Pensées," Rochefoucauld's "Maximes" etc. How true they all are! I should like to have a library of such things.

We might note here that my father did accumulate "a library of such things," as well as writing his own "Adagia."

February 22.
    A Cyprian morning. It makes no difference that there are neither birds nor flowers (which, on such a morning, have a clandestine existence in irreality). A tree looks like a plant of light and shadow.

    In a note on [Joseph] Israels, [William Ernest] Henley says "But he has realised that it is man's destiny to [illegible word—"grieve"?] and to endure." That is the reverse of the Arnold medal.

Feb. 25.
    Went to a concert of the Russian Symphony Orchestra last night. Nothing could have been more entertaining—more interesting. There was a symphonic arrangement: "From the Middle Ages," by Glazunoff, that contained two most *encoreable* movements: the second (Troubadour's Serenade, *andantino*) and third (Scherzo. *Allegro assai*—Dance of Death). Josef Lhevinne of Moscow played a number of solos among them Scriabine's Nocturne (for the left hand only). Konyus' suite "From Child-life" was played entire. Part II (*Vivo e leggiero:* Playing Horses) and part IIII (*Capricciosamente:* Being Naughty, *Scherzino*) were delightful impressions. Part III (*Andante*

ma non troppo: With the Doll) was clever—very; and part VI (*Tempo di valse:* The Little Music Box) was clever, too— & enchanting in an Austin Dobsonish way. There was a roaring polonaise while people were putting their coats on.

Feb. 27.

Saw a little Cazin at the American Art Gallery today called "Departure of Night," that I liked: a step or two of road, a roadside house of white, a few trees and *just* the sky-full of *clair d'aube*—with three stars, as I remember. He had caught even in so small a painting the abandoned air of the world at that hour, that is, abandoned of humans. If there had been a light in the house—it would have been quite different. One could imagine the dewy air and the quiet. There was an Israels that I thought well of: a girl knitting by the sea. I liked her bare feet & the ordinary sand & the ordinary water. But what I liked best was that she was not dreaming. There was no suggestion even of that trite sorrow. It was a capital point—exquisite prose instead of dreary poetry. It was as if she had confidence in the ordinary sand & the ordinary water. And there was a gray-green Corot. One noticed, incuriously, an inch of enamored man and an inch of fond woman in the foreground, and one approved. Fortunate creatures to be wandering so sweetly in Corot! There was a phosphorescent Ziem, a pretty cheek by Madrazo, a bit of Henner blue, & a Bierstadt—really excellent: buffaloes, yellow sun-light & all that. But the Cazin was best!

March 3.

Apropos. This sonnet (in part) of Meredith's on "The Spirit of Shakespeare" (II):

> "How smiles he at a generation ranked
>   In gloomy noddings over life! They pass.
> Not he to feed upon a breast unthanked,
>   Or eye a beauteous face in a cracked glass.
> But he can spy that little twist of brain
>   Which moved some weighty leader of the blind,
> Unwitting 'twas the goad of personal pain,
>   To view in curs't eclipse our mother's mind—"

I am grateful for "little twist of brain."

March 4.

Phew! My head is clogged with maxims. Let me put these on record and forget the rest:

"The highest aim of art is beauty, its highest effect the feeling of pleasure."

"Le mieux est de faire contre fortune bon coeur."

"Une vie laborieuse, une succession des travaux qui remplissent et moralisent les jours."

"Il faut être amiable."

"The song seraphically free
Of taint of personality."
(G. Mer.)

Rather a striking day for clouds (as if these were little affairs of the studio or of artists' brains). But, when I was walking this morning, they came over a hill in a dull, purple troop; and this afternoon —late—from my window they were a most fashionable shade. The fields were full of puddles, there were green circles around evergreens, the tree-tops had a blurred appearance. Poor, dear, silly Spring, preparing her annual surprise!

The following page is headed "March 11," but the rest of the page has been cut off, and the following page excised. The page after that begins within a sentence:

flute, a cup, a maid—there's a Greek idyll. One likes Anacreon for his roses, too—and gloomy grasshoppers. His maidens seem to have been about sixteen, whereas those of Horace seem to have been in the early twenties. Speaking of this (and it is a subtle matter) one cannot help observing that stockings and slippers are sadly missing from Greek and Roman poetry. Undoubtedly stockings belong properly only to a decadent age. Slippers—sandals etc. are of a nobler potency, and one need not discuss them. But stockings are impossible. They're like buttons—and collars.

People are not particularly interested in humanity nowadays, as Schiller was, or Desmoulins or Shelley—or anybody. We study the individual & that individual is one's self & through one's self to one's neighbor. As for humanity at large, we are content to write Johnsonian letters to the *Post*—but never to read them. We go slumming in a quarter, we help starving Asiatics—true; but we do not pursue the ideal of the Universal Superman—at least not today. But we may the day after tomorrow.

April 5. Thursday.
Last Sunday I heard my first blue-bird. He was on a bean-pole in a muddy field. Walked to a rock near Paterson along the Valley Road & the Notch— & there I lay down and basked. Heard frogs in the woods. All week we have had velvety weather.

Russell Loines has been recommending G. Lowes Dickinson to me. A fine measured style. The "Letters from John Chinaman" (or "of")—capital—particularly respecting Christianity, Chinese morals and European economics. "Whether your religion be better than ours, I do not at present dispute; but it is certain that it has less influence on your society." The friendly Chinese pictures are interesting: "For many miles along the valley, one after the other, they (the houses) lift their blue- or red-tiled roofs out of a sea of green; while here and there glitters out over a clump of trees the gold enamel of some tall pagoda." I take from "The Greek View of Life" this partial "List of Translations Used"

Euripides—*Tragedies*—trans. by A. S. Way (Macmillan & Co.)

Pindar: *Odes*—trans. by E. Myers (Macmillan & Co.)

Plato: Jowett

Sophocles by Dr. Jebb. Camb. U. Press.

Thucydides: Jowett, Clarendon Press.

I have been specially keen after Greek matters all winter. Loines told me of the eagles at Delphi. He sketched Mahaffy snoozing on a steamer.

Arthur Symons has great weight with several fellows I know. What has always made him impossible for me is his terrible chatter about Art. The *Saturday Review* quotes him on women: "beasts of prey," and on his *raison d'écrire:* writing raised one more barrier between himself and other people. They label him perverse. Otiose, I should say. Morbid, of course-- & so concerned with intense situations. Huneker is to write him up in a newspaper on Saturday. I can imagine it in advance. Huneker is a bee—with well-covered thighs—but, after all, a bee-bug. His beating about is mere buzzing: no air whatever, no tune. He confuses me.

I saw a sentence today saying that Machiavelli had been the subject of more controversy than any other writer. That is the sort of thing that drives one insane. One says, "Really, that's news to me." In short, it's nonsense. It is akin to that other type of statement: Napoleon lost Waterloo because of a peasant's fake statement—or Rome was saved by a goose—or Holland was saved by a finger in a dyke. How much history depends on trifles! How much nonsense, too!

April 9.

Took my customary ramble yesterday—with three, for company. I detest "company" and do not fear any protest of selfishness for saying so. People say one is selfish for not sharing one's good things—a naively selfish thing in them. The devil take all of that tribe. It is like being accused of egoism. Well, what if one be an egoist—one pays the penalty.

It must be a satisfaction to be without conscience. Conscience, nowadays, invades one's smallest actions. Even in that cell where one sits brooding on the philosophy of life, half-decided on "joyousness" —one observes one's black brother in a corner, and hears him whisper, "The joyous man *may* not be right. If he dance, he *may* dance in other people's ashes." It is the *may* that dashes one. Professor Woodberry remarks in "The Torch" that Milton in all his studies, sought beauty—as the origin of nobility. But why not holiness, temperance, justice etc. The truth is that beauty without conscience, holiness, temperance, justice etc. without conscience, are—all of them—triumphant. While saying so, that voice in the dark corner says: "But may not any defeat be as much a victory as any triumph?"

Professor Woodberry has his disciples. I do not consider him distinguished, either as a thinker or writer. The same is true of Paul Elmer More.

My father obviously reread this entry in September 1909, for he has interjected the comment, "No longer my opinion—far from it 9-9-9," between that sentence and the next:

Both men are capable—but they lack vigor, life, originality. —In European criticism, as contrasted with American—indeed in European thought in general, as contrasted with American, vigor, life and originality have a kind of easy, professional utterance. American—on the other hand, is expressed in an eager, amateurish way. A European gives a sense of scope, of survey, of consideration. An American is strained, sensational. One is artistic gold; the other is bullion. To be sure, this may be only as it seems to me.

The rest of this page, about one-third, has been cut off, and the next page begins at the end of a sentence:

death. The Christian fears life and loves death.

April 22.
"Où trouverez-vous, dans l'océan des littératures, un livre surnageant qui puisse lutter de génie avec cet entrefilet:
"Hier, à quatre heures, une jeune femme s'est jetée dans la Seine du haut du pont des Arts."

Le Peau de Chagrin—Balzac

Somehow, in this season, I like to get my pipe going well, and meditate on suicide. It is such splendid melancholy, and, mixed with a little beer and whiskey—divine. If only one could look in at the window when they found one's body—one's blood and brains all over the pillow. How terrible the simple books would look, —and the chairs and the curtains so carefully drawn! How empty, for a moment, the lawns would seem, —the Sunday twittering of the birds! How impotent all the people! Such a death is a death to everything— Then one would tap on the window and laugh and say, "It is all a mistake. Let me come in again. I know how foolish it all is. But what is one to do?"

There is a robin's nest nearby and at twilight the trees are full of music. —*There* are three women I know—one in gray, one in purple, and one in green. I wish I could bury them all during the afternoon, and, after tea, listen to the robin again.

The next page has been excised, and the page following that begins in the middle of a sentence:

are one: and one must begin to live out a certain, definite life. The horror of it is to be able to see the end of that life. That takes away all desire to live it. A clerk ends as a clerk—and so on. In ignorance of this plain destiny, a clerk, too often, imagines marvels for his old age, or even has some hallucination that supports a present pimp. At least, romantic clerks do. What a bore it would be not to!

Finally (for today) my opinions generally change even while I am in the act of expressing them. So it seems to me and so, perhaps, everyone thinks of himself. The words for an idea too often dissolve it and leave a strange one.

Has there ever been an image of vice as a serpent coiled round the limbs and body of a woman, with its fangs in her pale flesh, sucking her blood? Or coiled round the limbs and body of a man? Fancy the whole body fainting, in the distorting grip, the fangs in the neck—the victim's mouth fallen open with weakness, the eyes half-closed. Then the serpent triumphing, horrible with power, gulping, glistening.

Did this image dissolve, over the years, into the opening lines of "Auroras of Autumn"?—

> This is where the serpent lives, the bodiless.
> His head is air. Beneath his tip at night
> Eyes open and fix on us in every sky.
>
> Or is this another wriggling out of the egg,
> Another image at the end of the cave,
> Another bodiless for the body's slough?

This is where the serpent lives. This is his nest,
These fields, these hills, these tinted distances,
And the pines above and along and beside the sea.

This is form gulping after formlessness,
Skin flashing to wished-for disappearances
And the serpent body flashing without the skin.

April 27.

Clear sky. The twilight subtly mediaeval—pre-Copernican. A few nights ago I saw the rim of the moon, and the whole black moon behind, just visible. The larger stars were like flares. One would have liked to walk about with some Queen discussing waves and caverns, like a noble warrior speaking of trifles to a noble lady. The imagination is quite satisfied with definite objects, if they be lofty and beautiful enough. It is chiefly in dingy attics that one dreams of violet cities —and so on. So if I had *had* that noble lady, I should have been content. The absence of her made the stealthy shadows dingy, atticy— incomplete.

There are no end of gnomes that *might* influence people—but do not. When you first feel the truth of, say, an epigram, you feel like making it a rule of conduct. But this one is displaced by that, and thus things go on in their accustomed way. There is one pleasure in this volatile morality: the day you believe in chastity, poverty and obedience, you are charmed to discover what a monk you have always been—the monk is suddenly revealed like a spirit in a wood; the day you turn Ibsenist, you confess that, after all, you always were an Ibsenist, without knowing it. So you come to believe in yourself, and in your new creed. There is a perfect rout of characters in every man —and every man is like an actor's trunk, full of strange creatures, new & old. But an actor and his trunk are two different things.

April 29.

If men studied men, as they study women, they would probably involve themselves in an equal enigma. —I wonder, on the other hand, whether or not it would be interesting to collect studies of men by women.

It would be curious to establish, in a slum, two parks, the first with flowers and rambles but without seats; the second without flowers or especial rambles but with seats. The curiousness would be in seeing who used each, and how. —Parks (excepting the drives in them) are, generally, filled with the lower classes. Our park here, today, was thick with Italians and negroes. So, too often for the aesthete, museums etc. are visited by the lower classes, to the exclusion of the upper. Undoubtedly these things are important in modifying the natures of those who frequent them; & are, thus, a phase of that police system upon which order, very largely, rests.

The rest of the page, about three-quarters, has been cut off. The next page begins:

May 2.
     A half-misty, Fantin-La Tourish night. The moisture and new leaves together fill the streets with a sweet, earthy perfume. —In town, I lunched with Walter Arensberg at the Harvard Club. Finished with brandied peaches and cream. Felt like licking the saucer. Borrowed a pile of books. —As I came indoors a moment ago, a cat stole over the porch, much like a mote in one's eye.

Again the rest of the page, about one-half, has been cut off. The following two pages have been excised. The journal resumes on the page after that, within a quotation:

what is beautiful & good—the facetious, sensational, sentimental, and all the other varieties of distorted commonplace." I like that coupling of the facetious and sentimental.

May 7.
     The trees stand up tonight like charcoal daubs. The eastern side of the house is yellow with moonlight. —I have written to Elsie, and am the happier for it. It is so pleasant a thing—this mood of not knowing whether or not one is in love, just because one does not feel sure of knowing what love is—and because one does not feel like doing the things normally accredited to lovers.

May 29.
     Been reading poetry. What strikes me is the capable, the marvellous, poetic language; and the absence of poetic thought. Modern people have never failed to crown the poet that gave them poetic thought—and modern people have had to crown Hafiz and Omar— just as the ancients crowned Shelley, Browning, Tennyson. We get plenty of moods (and like them, wherever we get them, whether in novels, or poems, or talk, or paintings); and we get figures of speech, and impressions, and superb lines, and fantastic music. But it's the mind we want to fill—with Life. We admit now that Truth is the warrior and Beauty only his tender hide, as one might say. Santa-

yana's Sonnets are far nobler and enduring in our eye than [Stephen] Phillips' tragedies.

The next dozen or so pages, at the center of the notebook, have been excised. Following that, the journal continues with an undated entry written, presumably, while Stevens was home for a visit, or just afterwards.

Reading got quite on my nerves. It is a terrible place except to the native. The country is adorable. Yesterday I walked over the hills—down Easter Egg Way and over Oriole Road and up Stone Hill and by Eglantine Hedge. The bell at Spies church clattered as I passed. Looked out over Oley and went round the Lake of the Beautiful Lady and so—home. Elsie was in everything.

The rest of the page, about one-half, has been cut off. The next page begins in mid-sentence:

Clerk's Office today I thought of the smell of peaches, and the smell of wheat, of the wind on the porch at the Country Club, of the tendency of my mind to make sketches, when I am in Reading, and of the exercise of the fond imagination when I am here, filling out those sketches, of mist and fire-flies, of Elsie's taking a rose out of my button-hole because its color was in conflict. —It struck me that our letters were like an instrument full of delicate & endearing music —music just a little haunting. Tonight I shall play that instrument for the first time after this dreadful break. —I want to note that the lily pond at home with the pigeons was worth while; & that I picked up two more fragments of Sappho:

πάρθενον ἀδύφωνον
(sweet-voiced maiden)   and

γλύκεια μᾶτερ, οὔτοι δύναμαι κρέκην τὸν ἴστον,
πόθῳ δάμεισα παῖδος βραδίναν δι' ᾿Αφροδίταν.

(Sweet mother, I cannot weave my web, broken as I am for longing for a boy, at soft Aphrodite's will.)

The Epicurean motto   ἔχω οὐκ ἔχομαι
(I hold and am not held.)

The balance of the page, about one-half, has been cut off. The next entry begins as a sentence ends:

Lodge & Haeckel. These fellows lose themselves in the technology of philosophy and science. For example, I have been thinking lately that men & women were the precipitates of some force—well, that turns out to be Monism. Perhaps, one ought not to think of such things without reading, too: but the thinking is superb, the reading preposterous.

Solomon muttered in his whiskers,

"As in water face answerable to face, so the heart of man to man." Yes: in both art and Life. That's the mirror affair again—smirking Nature. But there's a kind of Art from which Nature is excluded—the Art of the Unreal—Affectation. The heart does not answer that—the brain follows; and the brain is a tremendous Artist. There are other brains—*they* answer. There's your circle.

Poverty is loathsome—not sad; misanthropy is loathsome—not sad. A boy with a new penny is gorgeous.

July 22.

Homer said—nothing crushes a man's spirit more than the sea and "like most of the Greeks he probably dreaded it." (Collins, Ephem. Crit.) How jealous the Greeks were of their humanity!

Dr. Johnson on Addison's verses—

Polished & pure, the production of a mind too judicious to commit faults, but not sufficiently vigorous to attain excellence."

July 26.

Sappho is like apples.

July 29. Sunday.

Rather a picturesque time of it. Walked out from New York yesterday afternoon. Through Hoboken, Jersey City etc. Broken down place—vile shops—saw an advertisement of a pic-nic of the something or other "Hog-Slaughterers Association"—mountain of manure along the turnpike, scrap-yard of the Pennsylvania Railroad —hundreds of Italians at work building a street-railway, some of them working in the most farcically useless way. I rode several miles on the floor of a plumber's wagon. Rain—lightning etc. Dropped into public library in Newark and found some translations of somebody or other from the anthology by Phillimore in the *Dublin Review*. Walked up from Newark. Saw a child eating melting ice-cream from a paper and trying to pick up the drops on the pavement with its fingers. This morning I found a few new paths on the hill and a puddle to swim in. Watched four boys—interested in their ribs—wonderful to consider them as intelligent creatures. In the same class with all this are the cats I've been noticing in town, along West Twenty-Second Street and the like. Such starved, nonchalant, dingy things! I saw one with a predatory foot in a garbage can blinking at a cloud of flies buzzing around its nose. Another was so depressed about something that it showed positive reluctance in getting out of the way of a horse and carriage. Others skulk here and there; others lie curled on stoops dreaming, no doubt, of *Harzreise*.

Aug. 3.

Engaged at the office all day on a sonnet—surreptitiously.

August 17. Thursday.

Tuesday night at Sheepshead Bay with Carrell. Rowed out to sea and bathed from the boat. There were rose waves and gold—and gnats.

Last night Poole & I went to a band concert in Branch Brook Park at Newark. [Here about seven words have been crossed out and are illegible.] I liked the stars & warm air and the beat of the music.

Tonight—after dinner a harp, a violin, a bad piano, Mrs. Yeager and Louise singing hymns, my rusty guitar in vindictive opposition, bawling crickets, Poole, & Gillis piled up—I fled to the Park. There a mist was forming—and the lamps sought me out—and my feet crunched on the pebbles—and there were young men and women in erotic grips. Well, I tried to think whether or not life was worth living—I cannot think. My object was to determine whether or not it is worth while improving one's condition as they say. Of course it follows that it is if life be worth living. The answer is, *ça depend de cas*. Life is worth living under certain conditions. And there's a circle. At all events beauty and use are two good things irregardless of either question; and in default of a satisfactory answer, beauty and use still point a way. Prima facie, life is not worth living unless you do it well.

On the reverse of this page my father has written three double-spaced lines:

> Oh, Leonardo, paint with ghostly brush
> Subtle Melpomene, with slow regard
> To so much beauty be a little kind

before going on to the next page, where the first date seems out of sequence, unless the dash indicates that he wasn't sure of the date.

August 2—

G. de Nerval:

"j'ai pris au serieux les inventions des poetes."

—*Le Rêve et la Vie*

"Werther, moin les pistolets, qui ne sont plus de mode"

—*Les Filles du Feu*—Sylvie

Pythagoras:

"Eh quoi? tout est sensible"

E. Verhaeren:
   "L'homme qui pense est un héro silencieux"
—Les Forces Tumultueuses.

September 4.
   Been to Reading over Labor Day. With Elsie practically all the time. Went driving around Womelsdorf yesterday; and up to the Tower—in the evening. Usual moon.

Sept. 5.
   "Read such things as may rather yield compunction to thy heart, than occupation to thy head."
—Dear old T. à Kempis
And in his 3rd book, the 5th Chapter thereof, he writes (3)
   "The noble love of Jesus impels a man to do great things, and stirs him up to be always longing for what is more perfect."

Sept. 15.
   Out of work.

October 10.   Sedgwick avenue, Fordham Heights.
   Have been living here for a little more than a week. After leaving Philbin's office the idea occurred to me to try to start for myself and I beat up the bushes for a chance. In that process, I ran into an opportunity to make an advantageous connection with Eaton & Lewis of 44 Broad-Street, where I am now—since October 8. —Once it was settled that I was to go there, I ran off to Boston, just to renew my acquaintance with things. Spent a night with Horace Stanton at Millis, in a most interesting little house. Knocked about Cambridge a little, on foot and in an automobile. (By the way, Stanton drove us in an automobile from Millis to Providence, "whence" I returned to Boston.) —Am settling down to this new arrangement: new office, new room—everything new.

December 5th.
   I am afraid to review the last two months. They seem to have changed me—I no longer read, and no longer think. The brain is like a worm that tunnels its way through everything—and leaves everything crumbling behind. Busy with many things—that's it, I'm *busy.* A walk now and then, a little music, a few pages, a trip home at Thanksgiving time—there's no Iliad in that. I feel strenuous, not lyrical.

Jan. 4. [1907.]
   My letters to Elsie usurp the chronicles that, but for them, I should set down here. —There is so little in reality. My office is

dingy, and I go to and from it, underground. —But sometimes I get glimpses of Washington Bridge and its neighborhood, and I think it is all very impressive and Roman and wonderful, in its way. —And on Sundays I take walks here and there: one, lately, through Yonkers Park, Scarsdale, along Weaver-Street to New-Rochelle, and then down Pelham Road to Bartow. Twilight clings to the shores of the Sound like mist to a wood. There is no country here. That's one trouble. —Occasionally I hear a little music. Once it was Camille Saint-Saens and once Alexander Scriabine. —Home at Christmas and again at New-Year's. As usual, Reading reveals the perspective of New York & I return from it indifferent. —I dream now of writing golden odes; at all events I'd like to read them.

Although it is far from being a golden ode, it seems appropriate to quote a poem that my mother copied from a letter she received from my father about this time:

> If I love thee, I am thine;
> But if I love thee not,
> Or but a little—let the sun still shine
> On palaces forgot.
>
> For me: be thou no more
> Attendant on my way.
> My welcome one will not, like thee, implore
> No never! He will play
>
> Brave dulcimers and sing
> In darkness, not repine;
> And I shall leave all dreams and closer cling
> And whisper, "I am thine."

—for my collection of "Songs for Elsie."

In the journal, there is one more entry before his letters to Elsie truly do begin to "usurp" his "chronicles" there.

Jan. 21.
    And here pompous record should be made of an agreeable dinner at Ramsay Hognet's last night. There were two pièces montées on the table—very Fragonard: candied fruit in candy baskets full of candy straw. My tongue felt as large as a bull's.

IX

Although the first extant letter to Elsie was not written until March 7, we must assume that the correspondence had been regular for months, if not years. But now these letters began to come with few days intervening; after the 7th, the next was written on March 10; then he wrote again March 12, 14, 19, 20, 21, 24, 26, etc. Rather than include the letters in their entirety here, I shall excerpt only some portions that otherwise might have been journal entries.

[March 10, 1907.]

I've been shovelling snow and it made my arms so tired that now my hand shakes as I write. It has been snowing all day—confound it! This morning I thought I should have to stay indoors all day and so, after breakfast, I put on my loafing outfit and began to read a volume of new poems that I bought yesterday. But shortly after ten o'clock there was a lull and I started out. Good Lord, how I needed it! My blood leaped. I wanted to wash my face in the snow—to hold it there. I *did* let the wind blow through my hair. Then I ran a long way and towards noon, when it had started to snow again, I was on Bronx River, or rather, along it. It was enchanting there. What is known as the Hemlock Forest was a huge clump of green and white. I stopped under an oak still covered with dead leaves and noticed a whispering noise as the snow fell on the leaves. And it was so quiet and lonely there.

Then I bounced out of that into the Green Houses, and there it was midsummer. All the larger palms, some of them much higher than your house, are gathered together in one room, under a dome. Some sparrows have built nests in the dome. When I got there they were just coming out of the sparrow church (probably in a banana tree) and they were all chattering at once—"So glad Spring is here!" —and outside there was a blizzard. In another room there is a collection of camelias. One bush from Japan was in bloom. It would have made you sing to see it. In the last room I shall tell you about, instead of a floor there is a pool, crossed by a little rustic arch. I stood on the arch and watched the fish flick their gold backs—it was almost insane . . .

I am not in the least religious. The sun clears my spirit, if I may say that, and an occasional sight of the sea, and thinking of blue valleys, and the odor of the earth, and many things. Such things make a god of a man; but a chapel makes a man of him. Churches are human. —I say my prayers every night—not that I need them now, or that they are anything more than a habit, half-unconscious. But in Spain, in Salamanca, there is a pillar in a church (Santayana told me) worn by the kisses of generations of the devout. One of their kisses are worth all my prayers. Yet the church is a mother for them—and for us . . .

[March 21, 1907.]

I am so full of misery tonight that I am ridiculous. Every Spring I have a month or two of semi-blackness and perhaps the mood is just returning. Perhaps, it is simply a revulsion against old things— habits, people, places—everything: the feeling the sun must have, nowadays, when it shines on nothing but mud and bare trees and the general world, rusty with winter. People do not look well in Spring. They seem grimy and puffy and it makes me misanthropic.

Spring fills me so full of dreams that try one's patience in coming time. One has a desire for the air full of spice and odors, and for days like junk of changing colors, and for warmth and ease, and all the other things that you know so well. But they come so slowly. —Earth and the body and the spirit seem to change together, and so *I* feel muddy and bare and rusty. —I'd like to wear a carnation every morning and I'd like to see other people decorating themselves like good children . . .

[March 24, 1907.]

. . . It is nearly time for me to move again. Yesterday it was fairly warm and my room, when I came home, was like an oven. What will it be in July and August? If I can find a pleasant place on Long Island, not too far from town, I might try it, as soon as affairs at the office become settled. As they are now, I don't know whether I shall be there one week after the other; and it is a very difficult thing to make an advantageous change late in the season . . .

A week later, he returned briefly to his journal:

April 1.

Just back from a trip to Reading for Easter. Family about as depressing as usual; Elsie more or less unmanageable. Spring on the calendar but nowhere else—except that the wheat fields look sharply green. Last night there was snow, and tonight there is wind. —I suppose if I turned my glass back on the last few months I should find something to record—but tremendously little. I am drifting.

In a letter the next day he noted:

> . . . I happened to see in a bowl of odds and ends on my table the carnation you took from the table in your dining-room the last time but one that I was home—and that you gave me . . .

And, in line with his comments on the weather that spring, it seems natural to turn to the first of "The Poems of Our Climate," written in 1938—

> Clear water in a brilliant bowl,
> Pink and white carnations. The light
> In the room more like a snowy air,
> Reflecting snow. A newly-fallen snow
> At the end of winter when afternoons return.
> Pink and white carnations—one desires
> So much more than that. The day itself
> Is simplified: a bowl of white,
> Cold, a cold porcelain, low and round,
> With nothing more than the carnations there.

—and then to turn to the journal again.

April 4.

Of course, the season is inevitable. This evening as I walked up Sedgwick Avenue the birds were noisy in the trees of the grounds of The Convent of the Sacred Heart. There are buds on the trees, too— and I have laid aside my gloves, too—too—too.

A few Sundays ago I noticed a number of pigeons sitting out the rain on one of the ledges of Washington Bridge; and as I passed there this morning I heard their rou-cou-cou.

April 7.

One of my maladies is to rub the freshness off things and then to say, "So, how commonplace they really are!" But the freshness was not commonplace.

I must be gallant. One loses too much in going under the surface. Besides, it is all what one imagines, there. Take a lacquered cheek—why not let it go at that?

I must think well of people. After all, they are only people. —The conventions are the arts of living. People know. I am not the only wise man. —Or if I cannot think well, let me hide my thoughts. —It is of no consequence to explain or to assert one's self. —Nice people are nice. —Egoists are witches. —It's all a comedy, if you're in the humor. —It's a sore delight to insist on the tragedy. —Life is not important. —At least, let's have it agreeable.

That same day he also wrote to Elsie:

A day of Spring sun and Winter wind. Arthur came up at noon and took dinner with me. In the afternoon we walked North and South criticizing all the architecture in the little world we saw. Home again in time for tea—and a crimson and yellow and blue sunset—and here I am, sitting in a new chair, with the wind crying around the chimneys and rattling the windows. Next Sunday I am going to the country, and on the Sunday following I am going to the country, too—your country and mine, God willing, as the sailors say—to see you. Last night I was home (Saturday nights down town are out of the question) and I read the "Letters of John Keats" until early this morning; and there is a page full of news. I have been wanting to read Keats' letters ever since I knew there were such things. They are mere chatter (as they ought to be) with only a little observation here and there. The other evening I bought Boswell's "Life of Johnson," an enormous affair in three volumes. Have you ever read it? It is one of those books one is always going to read, but which one never does. Lately, I have been buying almost any book that struck my fancy. I wish I might line my walls with them and devote myself to study, or rather, reading; for if I have ardor left for anything at all, it is for books. The book-stores in New-York are a distress to me: they are so *un*-bookish. I like to drop into a dusty-looking basement shop and find odd volumes of the old English poets or of the old French ones for all that. I'd like to find a volume of [Clément] Marot or Villon, but the books one does find are the most utterly common-place, trashy things under the sun . . .

[April 9, 1907.]
. . . The love of books for the thoughts in them is like the love of the earth for its seas and distances. We must talk about books sometime when we are together. That will be quite as good as a walk on the hill, if we talk about the right ones.

Yesterday I bought a little volume called the "Note-Books" of Matthew Arnold. It is made up of quotations jotted down by him from day to day, and of lists of books to be read at various times. The quotations are in a half-dozen different languages. (It gives me a sort of learned delight to guess at the Latin ones; and last night I hunted all through Dante for translations of several Italian ones.) Here is a

Latin one: "Angelica hilaritas cum monastica simplicitate"; and here is what I guess it to mean: "Angelic hilarity with monastic simplicity." And here is an English one: "A merry heart doeth good like a medicine, but a broken spirit drieth the bones."

I also bought a volume of lectures on Greek subjects. . . . The impression of Greece is one of the purest things in the world. It is not a thing, however, that you get from any one book, but from fragments of poetry that have been preserved, and from statues and ruins, and a thousand things, all building up in the mind a noble conception of a pagan world of passion and love of beauty and life. It is a white world under a blue sky, still standing erect in remote sunshine . . .

Two days later he made an entry in his journal:

April 11.
On the 9th it snowed all day, and when I came home in the evening there were six inches of soft snow on the ground. —Today it is gone again, or most of it.

Turning back to the letters, one written April 16 includes the following:

Late at night mice run about my room and make a rustle among my papers. I hear them now—their rustle and the hissing of an engine and the abstracted buffeting of the wind on the windows. How full of trifles everything is! It is only one's thoughts that fill a room with something more than furniture. Startling reflection!

Perhaps the mice led him to the opening topic of the next letter.

[April 19, 1907.]
Last night was house-cleaning night with me. I went through my things . . . and threw away a pile of useless stuff. How hard it is to do it! One of the things was my Bible. I hate the looks of a Bible. This was one that had been given to me for going to Sunday-school every Sunday in a certain year. I'm glad the silly thing is gone. There are still a few odds and ends that I keep for sentimental reasons: my college books, my father's copy of Burns' poems, and so on. They'll go, too, when my courage is at its height. Everything looks prim and old-maidish tonight and I half like it for a change.

Meanwhile, the journal has another comment on the weather.

April 21st.
On the 19th, snow all day. —But today it was blue & gold again. Have been to Darien, Connecticut, walking with dogs, loafing along the Sound. Mrs. Dana very attractive. Beautiful little house.

A letter written Monday evening tells us more about his day in the country.

> This might well be a wonderful letter because Sunday was a wonderful day. The house, where I visited, is in the midst of a wood, but the house was quite as fascinating as the trees. On Saturday evening, we sat by the fire and talked and read until almost midnight. The room was full of pretty things—every picture, every lamp, every chair. We slept late. When the church-bells began to ring at nine o'clock, I was still dozing, or else half-listening to the frogs whistling, or whatever it is they do. After lunch, we walked to the Sound with two dogs, passing all manner of pleasant houses on the way. We basked in the sand, and loafed on a point of rocks, looking out over the empty water, blue and tumbling. It makes me feel now as if I had been away for a month or two. My room was unwelcome when I returned. So, at noon today, I ran up-town and (to do what I could) bought a large photograph of one of Rembrandt's paintings. It is a portrait of himself and of his wife, Saskia—*and she is sitting in his lap!* I might just as well have chosen a Madonna, but now I am glad I chose this, because it is just what I needed. And of course I bought a few more books: some pamphlets of lectures delivered at Oxford, and a translation from the Greek—Propertius. (Maybe it's from the Latin—I know it's about love, and that is really all I know.) Thus, you see, I have been having an exciting time. After dinner tonight, Professor Lamb and I took a walk (to Hop Sing's for some collars of mine) and we noticed a cloudy ring around the moon. Therefore, it will rain tomorrow. But, at all events, it is not raining now, and that is something to be thankful for in April. I came home alone, through the grounds of the University, not at all a bad place at night. There is a dome there, and there are pillars and arches and quiet shadows and a suggestion of dark nobility . . .

Here the correspondence ceases temporarily, at least in what is extant; the next letters that have been found are dated in December 1908, and all we have for the intervening period are some excerpts that my mother copied out to save. We must, therefore, return to the journal.

> April 23rd.
>   Paul Bourget in "Une Idylle Tragique," p. 65—Je me dis: Il n'y qu'une chose de vraie ici-bas, s'assouvir le coeur, sentir et aller jusqu'au bout de tous ses sentiments, désirer et aller jusqu'au bout de tous ses désirs; vivre enfin sa vie à soi, sa vie sincère, en dehors de tous les mensonges et de toutes les conventions, avant de sombrer dans l'inévitable néant.
>   ("farouche nihilisme")

April 30.
The Nation No. 7 (London) p. 255
> We must leave it to the aesthetic critics to explain why that is—why it is easier for nearly everyone to recognize the meaning of common reality after it has passed through another's brain— why thousands of kindly people should have contemplated negro slavery day by day for years without emotion, and then have gone mad over "Uncle Tom's Cabin."

It is because common reality is being exhibited. It is being treated objectively.

May 22.
> This morning I walked down Aqueduct Avenue to the bridge. There were lilacs, gray and purple, in the convent garden. The corner of a stable was hung with wisteria. —This evening, as I passed the same way, a warm scent drifted out to me.

> At noon I ran up to Cottier's to see a collection of Monticellis. They are singular, captivating things—out of a dark, carnival fancy, all color. One, "La Danse," was worth remembering. —Lutes, indistinguishable dancers at a *fête champêtre*, a red dress as large as one's hand to the left. —Downstairs there were Rodins, one of a Danaid, one Le Matin. The face of Le Matin was a subtle marble veil of features. —But, after all, both the Monticellis and the Rodins were only what ought to exist in abundance. Such things are what they are because it is a poor world.

June 6.
> I am in the mood for suddenly disappearing.

The next line in the journal reads "July 25th—Reading," and then the rest of the page, about one-half, has been cut off. The next page begins with the ending of a sentence, "and rugged." All the rest of that page has been cut off; the next page begins within a sentence:

> old road to Lancaster—catching sight of Livingood in a car at Adamstown, and eating six buns outside the post-office at Reamstown for lunch. The distance from Reading to Lancaster is thirty-one miles. There are a number of quasi-ancient milestones on the road: one of brown sandstone—"17 M. to L. 14 M. to R. 1774". One is illegible. So that I may remember them, let me recall from the Hamburg walk —the quaint Forney barn along the Maidencreek (locally, "along the Maidencreek" is classical), the seclusion of Evansville with its business street of three or four houses (the [illegible word—"clever" or "clover"?] hill rises behind it—that's obscure except to my spirit),

then the unvirginal air of Virginsville—not much to remember along the way—the near approach to the Blue Hills or Blue Mountains, and finally, most excellent Hamburg, where, it is said, the pavements are scrubbed on hands and knees. While waiting for the train at (strictly, near) H. I climbed a high field and meditated on the mountains—how like the Palisades! Only in meditation. Then when the train

Here about three-quarters of the page has been cut off, and the following page excised, before the journal goes on, again within a sentence:

usual, I am scornful of the people around me—so many of them almost bestial. But it is just that they are "plain." Very—incomparably.

August 31.

In a few days I shall be [here a word has been crossed out and is illegible] back in New-York. I am just coming to like to be here. Yet there is no special reason—except that I have walked to so many interesting places:

(1) To Morgantown and Joanna. Morgantown "supine upon a bed of carbonate of lime"! Graveyard full of pleiocene Morgans and things. Sunny, afternoon-ish neighborhood. Waited an hour for a train at Joanna. Sat on a machine in a field; ate peanut bars and smoked a wild cigar; listened to three voices droning hymns; saw a man who had kicked a mule (with soft shoes) and had blackened his big (magna) toe. To start all over again: the road to Morgantown is more like "the road" than any other that I know of. It winds towards distant upland spires—or rather to *one* (1) distant upland spire. That particular spire stands up on a height that overlooks the whole country. Just under it there is a cemetery full of soldiers and Dutchmen born long ago. All the sandstone tombstones are illegible; but one can imagine: [here he has drawn a headstone decorated with a daisy wearing a face, and underneath it the words "Hier Robet etc."] —It is a Northern walk in a Southern direction.

(2) Up the Tulpehocken to Van Rud's, to Sinking Spring, Fritztown, Vinemont, over the hill (with a view at the top and many on the way) to Adamstown then home. I came from Adamstown to Reading, say eleven miles, in two hours exactly.

(3) From Blandon to the Maidencreek at the Stone Bridge and then to Lenhartsville. At Len. I found some friends (all girls) and I stayed over night at "Bench" Leidig's "Washington House"—a good enough country hotel. We climbed a field and sat on a fence fumbling constellations till the moon rose—over the corn. Then we went down to the creek and watched the mist on the water. On the following day we climbed to Pulpit Rock via the Blue Rocks. These latter (!) are really greenish and grayish and form part of a terminal moraine.

(4) Temple, Leesport, then to a church on the Bernville road and a grove where I rested under tall trees on a picnic table and listened to chickens scratching in the leaves, then to a farm where I drank like a camel, past the Half-Way House, Leinbach's,—and home —finally riding under a big umbrella advertising haberdashery in a wagon that picked me up.

(5) An orchard talk with Levi Mengel; a vegetable and art talk with Christopher Shearer. Shearer has a new truck farm near Stoudt's ferry. I ate onions, tomatoes, turnips, carrots and radishes. Saw celery, asparagus, lima and string beans, rhubarb etc. etc. Had a roadside bake in the sun.

(6) Sunday mornings at the Tower—with Elsie and without.

(7) Days at Wyomissing with the Lances.

The rest of the page, about one-half, has been cut off. The next page has two quotations on it:

Balzac à Honoré Daumier:
"Si vous voulez devenir un grand artiste, faites des dettes."

Rabelais:
"Mieux vaut de ris que de larmes escrire, pour ce que rire est le propre de l'homme."

The rest of the page has been cut off. The following page has been ex-cised, and the page after that opens within a sentence:

any lunch. But I begged some bread and milk from her. We sat at a little table on the porch. Mrs. Reininger's bread is a thing of her own. With some of her butter on it, one would rather eat it than—there's nothing to be mentioned with it. There was a "Tannenbaum" near us. The sun dazzled in it.

And one cool, blue morning I walked to the top of the Boulevard and sat there reading the *Sun*.

Moselem (: mō-sĕl-em!) Springs is an abandoned place. There was a furnace there, which is now in dilapidation. The houses of the work-men are empty. The shutters are closed. The little gardens are full of weeds—and hollyhocks. One dismal hotel with a lifeless look survives. Imagine sitting at the window of that hotel on a rainy day.

While there is no indication of an excised page before the next entry, it begins with a lower-case letter:

a room with brown furniture and blue rugs—with gray paper con-taining a blue design *might* be nice.

Sept. 13.

De l'avant Propos par M. Charles Louandre au "Discours de Nicholas Machiavel Sur La Première Décade de Tite-Livre":

"A Athènes on causait des crieux, de l'âme, de la nature, des mystères éternelles, et tout citoyen libre, eût-il même un manteau trouvé, pouvait s'asseoir auprès du maitre et se mêler à ses discours. A Florence, au contraire, quelques citoyens riches et privilégiés assistaient seuls au cénacle dans les magnifiques jardins *Ovicellari;* et comme si déjà le monde trop vieux avait désespéré d'atteindre cet idéal que poursurvaient les sages de la Grèce, on quittait les études abstraites et rêveuses que marquent la jeunesse des peuples, pour s'arrêter a celle qui marquent leur virilité, l'histoire et la politique."

During the last few days, the leaves have begun to turn. In the mornings I walk down to the Viaduct; and in the evenings I walk home from there. In the evenings the gold crosses on the churches shine in the high sunlight.

September 23.

A gale from the South-East. A good, rough day.

The half-page after that entry has been cut off. The next page begins within a sentence:

imagination is quite nothing at all. They are *un*-Italian. —On the contrary they are really human—with the humanity, more or less, of the bête humaine. They know a green field, and a golden sun, and a sweet face, and sad face, and the face of the working-man and working-woman. Their moonlight falls on friendly cattle and comfortable villages. Life is very much in their minds—as it is. Their fancies are the fancies of children. They are in general intensely bourgeois. —After all, it appeals to one. It leaves one content. It is, somehow, masculine—not in the bounding virile way—but just masculine.

Notes made at the Astor Library:

Catullus is not illimitable. One or two of the "Carmina" are the things commonly known. The one on the death of his brother with "ave atque vale" and this:

Odi et amo, quare id faciam, fortasse requiris,
Nescio, sed fieri sentio et excrucior.

(I hate and I love. Wherefore do I so, peradventure thou askest. I know not, but I feel it to be thus, and I suffer.)

This has been quoted as an incomparable expression of that state of mind. But it is hardly so. It is the state of mind that is incomparable. —Most men, who can, quote Latin in such cases. Some pedants would quote Latin to say "Good morning." —I read the privately printed translations by Sir Richard Burton and Leonard Smithers. Burton's mind is like Justice Maclean's—ungoverned. —It seems that scholars debate the balance of merit between Catullus and Horace—and generally between the poets of the Republic and those of the Augustan age. I favor the Augustans. —So they couple Lucretius and Haeckel. It is like coupling a star-gazing shepherd with an astronomer. —Pliny the younger wrote to Lucretius—"Pass through life unnoticed;"—"do not wish to be known even while living." That seems worth noting. How one wishes one could pass through life unnoticed—unnoticed by Necessity—by Nature, itself! —Then this: passion is not an Hellenic trait. In reality, that is superficial. Could one say of the "grave" Romans that they were passionate? Then it was not a Roman trait.

à cet âge heureux qui suivant l'expression d'Aristote, n'a pas été encore humilié par la vie.

Boissier: Tacite: 26.

and on p. 188 this:
"Néron lui-même, quoiqu'il n'eût qu'un filet de voix."

Vespasien—C'était un bon bourgeois de [illegible word—"Réacte"?], d'une famille de soldats et de petits banquiers, qui détestait l'étiquette et les cérémonies pompeuses, qui n'était jamais si heureux que quand il allait revoir la maisonette où il était né, et qu'au lieu de des vase murrhins qui contaient des fortunes, il buvait dans le gobelet d'argent qui avait servé à sa grand'mère et lui rappelait sa modeste enfance.

Suètone: Vespas., 1 et 2 quoted by Boissier.

Is it possible that a "vase murrhin" (a glass vase, with its capability for reflection) became a "jar of Tennessee"? Stevens' comment on the quotation hardly argues against that possibility:

The last extract illustrates Boissier's method of padding the known facts. Vespasian may have used the goblet but it is purely fanciful to say that it "rappelait sa modeste enfance." It might have, of course.

[William Young] Sellar's "The Roman Poets of the Republic" p. 273:
    "the natural exuberance is carelessness of the rhetorical faculty."
—Professor Sellar had an understanding of characteristics. For example: "the rhetorical faculty" was a quiet enough thing to observe. But it took understanding. Sellar's pages abound in that sort of thing. —Professor [J. W.] Mackail (the present professor of Poetry at Oxford) was one of his pupils. How they must have delighted one another! I have just completed a careful reading of Mackail's "Select Epigrams from the Greek Anthology"—a beautiful book, full of

appreciation and skill—and poetry. Compare Richard Garnett's "Idylls and Epigrams." The Garnett book is full of verses by Garnett himself, the authorship of which is mentioned only in the Index—so that one reads Garnett and Meleager without knowing which is which. Very stupid. —The attitude towards Meleager is much of the charm of his poems. Garnett must not steal that. —I was pleased by the verses (in Mackail) of Paulus Silentiarius, as much as by those of any one other poet. His mental light was silver twilight—a little cold and most delicate. —I must have the Mackail book.

On the page above this (the reverse of the previous page), another French quotation has been copied, under which my father has written, within brackets, "Usury of time":

> La doctrine de l'Art pour l'art—c'est la doctrine qui professe à la fois ces deux principes, que le but de l'art est de réaliser la beauté par la forme, que l'objet de l'art est la représentation du vrai.

October 15.
Metchnikoff in the "Nature of Man" says that religion for the most part consists of meditation upon death—a good thing to think of in bed. Metchnikoff is rather a specialist.

Elie Metchnikoff's *The Nature of Man: Studies in Optimistic Philosophy* includes a quotation from another writer; as footnoted by Metchnikoff, the quotation is from "Jean Marie Guyau, *L'Irreligion de l'Avenir*, Sixth Edition (Paris, 1895), p. 449." If we think of "Sunday Morning" as we read the full passage from Metchnikoff we find a relationship between the meditations on death.

> Far worse is the disharmony of the instinctive love of life which manifests itself when death is felt to be near at hand. It is then incomprehensible and particularly terrible, and humanity, from time immemorial, has sought the key to the tragic puzzle, and tried by all the means in its power to unravel the mystery. The religions of all times have been concerned with the problem. "Religion," says Guyau, "consists for the most part of meditation upon death. If we had not to die there would probably be still more superstitions among men, but there would probably be no systematised superstitions nor religions."

The entry immediately following the Metchnikoff reference changes the scene abruptly:

> English public buildings, in particular, are heavy, massive affairs. How far is this intentional—symbolic?

The first stanza of "St. Armorer's Church from the Outside" (1952) indicates that the transition might not be quite so abrupt as it seems:

> St. Armorer's was once an immense success.
> It rose loftily and stood massively; and to lie
> In its church-yard, in the province of St. Armorer's,
> Fixed one for good in geranium-colored day.

Returning to the journal, and to 1907, we find a comment on the death of René François Armand Sully-Prudhomme, which had occurred September 6.

I read everything I see about Sully-Prudhomme. He leaves a composed impression—a man like any other. There is something *piquant* about a poet who leaves the feeling of reticence.

This for heartsease:

"L'art pour l'art est aristocratique. Fidèle en cela à son hérédité romantique, l'artiste pourra le mépris et la haine des bourgeois, de leurs idées, de leur goûts, de leurs institutions et, par suite, ces critiques en de la presse qui sont à leur service, ainsi, il se replie sur lui-même, s'enferme dans son argueil et son individualisme. Il dédaigne la foule et les genres littéraires qui lui plaisent, comme le théâtre: il se met au-dessus d'elle, elle n'est que la matière vile dont il tirera l'oeuvre d'art."

Journal des Savants, Juillet. 1907.

"Who knows, Euripides had long ago asked, if life be not death, and death life?" That seems pathetic now.

Fénélon. —The name is enough.

Three months of idleness. I do not know what to think. I am intent on getting something of consequence, and it seems to be impossible. But I'll get it or leave New-York. New-York is more than repugnant to me and I should be glad to go. —The weather and good habits keep me in high spirits. One day after the other has been clear and neither cold nor warm. Yesterday I walked down to the old office for my mail. Where haven't I walked?

November 6.

I take a temporary "situation" with Eustis and Foster, 80 Broadway, in the morning, while my other plans simmer.

Last week I went to Boston. Hardly worth revisiting. Visited Fish Wharf on the way to the boat for New-York and laid up twenty raw oysters and three Martini cocktails. —Walked the hurricane deck of the boat. How fearful the stars seem at night at sea!

Next I went to Washington, on the 2nd. Saw [Theodore] Roosevelt and [Charles Joseph] Bonaparte, and talked with both. —Went up Washington Monument—a very important thing to do, it seems. Ran through the Capitol and Congressional Library. The library is excellentissimus.

Why my father had access to the President and Attorney-General of the United States during the financial panic of 1907 remains a mystery. He is not listed as one of the White House callers in the New York *Tribune*, which ran a regular column listing such persons. One possible connection is that the newspaper did report a presidential conference on November 1 with Paul Morton, formerly Secretary of the Navy and, at this time, head of the Equitable Life Assurance Society. Seven years later, in 1914, Stevens became vice-president of the Equitable Surety Company. The journal goes on:

Then home to Elsie. She is my strength. —Walked out to Wily's near Leesport. After lunch—we went out to climb a little hill. The clothes they wore made the leaves fall from the trees. A tragedy: Sally and Rose (I think) and I were in Sally's room looking at her flowers. I opened a door leading to the attic. A few steps up glittered a wicked [here a word has been crossed out and is illegible] you could hear yourself breathe. —I admired the flowers violently for a moment, and the curtain fell.

This is the first mention we have had of Elsie for some time, and although we do not have my father's letters to her, one of the excerpts she copied out begins: "I've been writing some verses to put in the first 'Vagabondia' book. Here they are: . . ." and goes on with three four-line stanzas that may well have been included in the letter. But I have recently discovered that they also appear in his handwriting on the flyleaf of *Songs from Vagabondia*, by Bliss Carman and Richard Hovey, as follows:

To Elsie, Xmas 1907.

FROM A VAGABOND.

I.

For us, these little books contain,
(as if, like flowers, we put them here,)
Three odorous summers of delight,
(With withered leaves of day and night.)

II.

These poets Vagabondian airs
Recall how many of our own,

That sang themselves, without a rhyme,
To stirrings of some secret chime.

III.

Our oriole sings, our wild-rose blooms
Our azure river chimes again
Our moon returns. Dear Elsie, hark!
Once more we whisper in the dark.

WS

Carman and Hovey's *More Songs from Vagabondia* has an undated Stevens inscription on its flyleaf:

> With a heart of one's own,
> In a world of one's own,
> Clinging, or loath to cling,
> Why should one cease to sing?

The third volume in the series, *Last Songs from Vagabondia,* bears the following in my father's hand on its flyleaf:

> Night stopped them here,
> One singer fell,
> Dark Vagabondia
> Lost her spell.

The latter two inscriptions do not appear in my mother's letter excerpts, or elsewhere. The excerpts do include two more poems, however, the first of which may not have been written by my father, but merely copied from a book he had been reading:

> Quick, Time, go by—and let me to an end.
> To-morrow, oh to-morrow! But today
> Poor draggling fag,—insipid, still delay.
> Flat drudge. Now let my feeble earth descend
> To violent night and there remend
> Her strength, not for a dream's affray
> But 'gainst slow death. Then up the sounding way
> Where vivid reaches of new blue attend.
>
> And many shadows of the whirling sun
> To greet her exultation thunderously!
> Let me be first of living men to throw
> The weight of life aside, and there outrun
> Even the magic light—so swift to know
> Some passionate fate accomplished wondrously.

The other poem is found not only in my mother's copy, but in my father's hand in his red folder of miscellaneous manuscripts, where there are a few differences in wording and punctuation.

The house fronts flare
In the blown rain;
The ghostly street lamps
Have a pallid glare.

A bent figure beats
With bitter droop,
Along the waste
Of vacant streets.

Suppose some glimmering
Recalled for him,
An odorous room—
A fan's fleet shimmering.

Of silvery spangle—
Two startled eyes—
A still trembling hand,
With its only bangle.

Although the next entry in his journal says "1909," it is followed by an entry dated 1908, and we can assume that he made a New Year's error and meant 1908.

January 2.
Since early in December I have been living with Horace Mann in The Benedick, Washington Square East—Feeding at the Judson, Billy the Oysterman's, Fran Maurer's and so on.

And for a little longer time I have been reading in the evenings to Robert Collyer, the old Unitarian preacher, of whom more anon.

Home both at Xmas and for New Year.

Jan. 5.
The holidays were noteable for the mild weather. Until today, we have had a most mild season. On Xmas day Elsie and I climbed up the hill and found a dandelion.

So on New-Year's Day we walked, as if it were only autumn, over to Antietam and Stony Creek. We found a hill-side of spruce, I think that we made note of, to visit next summer—and loaf there.

Today I made a second visit to the exhibition of the National Academy of Design. It does not wear well. At a glance it seems brilliant—but it is meaningless, unless, possibly, technically. Thus the landscapes, largely impressionistic in a half-decided way, are only transcripts of common-place Nature—lovely in itself, but, as Art, common-place. There is no revelation. There are no remarkable styles. It might happen anywhere.

Then I walked around the Reservoir and down the Avenue to the Square. A new moon and the evening star were near to each other and specially keen—and people were speaking to them.

August 17. 1908.

Since January 13, I have been with the American Bonding Company of Baltimore.

X

One of the excerpts that Elsie copied from Wallace Stevens' letters to her reads:

> It would only be proper for you to have your own private book of verses, even if it were very small and if the verses were very bad.

On her twenty-second birthday, June 5, 1908, this "Book of Verses" was presented to her.

I.

One day more—
But first, the sun,
There on the water,
Swirling incessant gold—
One mammoth beam!
Oh, far Hesperides!

II. NEW LIFE

Noon, and a wind on the hill—
Come, I shall lead you away
To the good things, out of those ill,
At the height of the world to-day.

I shall show you mountains of sun,
And continents drowned in the sea;
I shall show you the world that is done,
And the face of the world to be.

III. AFIELD

You give to brooks a tune,
  A melody to trees.

You make the dumb field sing aloud
  Its hidden harmonies.

An echo's rumor waits
  A little while, and then,
I hear the water and the pine
  Take up their airs again.

IV.

Hang up brave tapestries:
Huntsman and warrior there—
Shut out these mad, white walls.
I hate a room so bare.

And all these neighbor roofs
With chimney and chimney above—
Oh! let me hear the sound
Of soft feet that I love.

Then fetch me candles tall,
Stand them in bright array,
And go—I need such lights
And shadows when I pray.

V. IN A CROWD

So much of man,
The wonder of him goes away!
The little art of him returns again
To struggling clay.

Come one, alone,
Come in a separate glory keen;
And sing, on shores of lapis lazuli,
A song serene.

VI. ON THE FERRY

Fog, now, and a bell,
A smooth, a rolling tide.
Drone, bell, drone and tell,
Bell, what vapors bide.

Lights, there, not of fire,
Unsensual sounds, yet loud,
Shapes that to shape aspire,
In that encumbered cloud.

Toll, now, a world resolved
To unremembered form.
Toll the stale brain dissolved
In images of storm.

VII. TIDES

These infinite green motions
Trouble, but to no end;
Trouble with mystic sense
Like the secretive oceans—
Or violet eve repining
Upon the glistening rocks;
Or haggard, desert hills;
Or hermit moon declining.

VIII. WINTER MELODY

I went into the dim wood
    And walked alone.
I heard the icy forest move
    With icy tone.

My heart leapt in the dim wood
    So cold, so bare—
And seemed to echo, suddenly,
    Old music there.

I halted in the dim wood,
    And watched, and soon,
There rose for me—a second time—
    The pageant moon.

IX. SONNET

Explain my spirit—adding word to word,
As if that exposition gave delight.
Reveal me, lover, to my self more bright.
"You are a twilight, and a twilight bird."

Again! For all the untroubled senses stirred,
Conceived anew, like callow wings in flight,
Bearing desire toward an upper light.
"You are a twilight, and a twilight bird."

Burn in my shadows, Hesperus, my own,
And look upon me with a triumphant fire.
Behold, how glorious the dark has grown!

My wings shall beat all night against your breast,
Heavy with music—feel them there aspire
Home to your heart, as to a hidden nest.

X. SONG

A month—a year—of idle work,
    And then, one song.
Oh! all that I am and all that I was
Is to that feeble music strung,
        And more.

Yes: more; for there a sound creeps in,
    A second voice,
From violet capes and forests of dusk,
That calls me to it without choice,
        Alone.

XI. AFTER MUSIC

The players pause,
The flute notes drop
To the song's end,
And, trembling, stop.

The harper's hand,
Reluctant, clings
To the hushed strain,
Of muffled strings.

The sounds die out,
And dying, free
The thoughts of all
You are to me.

XII. TWILIGHT

Here the huge moth
Whirled in the dusk,
The wearied mammoth reared
His reddened tusk.

The rank serpent stole
Down golden alleys,
To the envenomed trees
Of jasmine valleys.

Lark's clangor rang,
In haggard light,

To giants, crouched in fear
Of fearful night.

XIII. ADAGIO

Drone, dove, that rounded woe again,
    When I bring her to-morrow.
The wood were a less happy place,
    But for that broken sorrow.

Tell her in undertones that Youth
    With other times must reckon;
That mist seals up the golden sun,
    And ghosts from gardens beckon.

XIV.

There is my spectre,
Pink evening moon,
Haunting me, Caliban,
With its Ariel tune.

It leads me away
From the rickety town,
To the sombre hill
Of the dazzling crown.

Away from my room,
Through many a door,
Through many a field
I shall cross no more.

After man, and the seas,
And the last blue land,
At the world's rough end,
If, perchance, I should stand

To rest from long flight—
Pale evening moon,
I should never escape
That wild, starry tune.

XV. DAMASK

You need not speak, if that be shame.
    I need no voice.
Nor give to bright cheeks brighter flame:
    I can abide my choice.

For mutely to my muter call,
    Come magic means.
Now the enchanting measures fall—
    A spirit intervenes.

XVI. REST

Glimpses of Eden for the tired mind,
    The misty vale, for the bending palm,
Bright Orient reefs in Orient oceans rolled,
    That never lose their flooded calm.

Oh! large and glorious, the quiet star
    Lighted beyond the half-seen trees.
Sweet is their comfort, but for dear repose,
    You by my side are more than these.

XVII. IN TOWN

It's well enough to work there,
When so many do;
It's well enough to walk the street,
When your work is through.

It's night there that kills me,
In a narrow room,
Thinking of a wood I know,
Deep in fragrant gloom.

XVIII. MEDITATION

There were feet upon the waters in the morning,
Like a golden mist that came from out the deep—
The feet of spirits lost in many a circle
Of winding dance, as if in wavering sleep.

They move away in quiet in the evening,
Lingering yet in a slow-ending round,
Faint lustres, rose and gray and purple,
That vanish soon in the devouring ground.

XIX. HOME AGAIN

Back within the valley—
Down from the divide,
No more flaming clouds about—
Oh! the soft hill side,
And my cottage light,
And the starry night!

XX.

What have I to do with Arras
　　Or its wasted star?
Are my two hands not strong enough,
　　Just as they are?

Because men met with rugged spears,
　　Upon the Lombard plain,
Must I go forth to them, or else
　　Have served in vain?

And does the nightingale, long lost
　　In vanished Shalott's dew,
Sing songs more welcome, dear, than those
　　I sing to you?

There are many echoes here of material already found in the journals; we find, as well, forerunners to Stevens' adult poems in many of the verses. "A matin gold from gold of Hesperus," in "Of Ideal Time and Choice," reflects the "incessant gold" of I; the candles in IV clearly light the way to "Carlos Among the Candles." We can also compare the "hermit moon" in VII with the "hermit's candle" and "hermit earth" in "Three Travelers Watch a Sunrise," and the "huge moth" in XII augurs "that monstered moth" in "Hibiscus on the Sleeping Shores." Surely, "Ariel was glad he had written his poems." "Home Again," XIX, was the only poem of those in the "Book of Verses" to be published, but not until six years later, when it appeared as the second of "Two Poems," in the November 1914 issue of *The Trend*.

By November 1908 my father was neglecting his family on his visits to Reading; a postscript to a letter from his mother to his sister Elizabeth says, "Wall was in town, didn't come home." He was spending his time with Elsie, and when they were apart he was writing her letters; the one bearing the postmark December 3, 1908, reads in full:

A Winter Night

Dear Lady:
　　Behold this sheep at your cottage door again—after a ramble through many a dark 'n gloomy valley; for Monday night was sacred to Blackness and last night I wept at my forlornness (as I looked down from the gallery at all the wonderful people—on the stage and off—at one of the theatres). "I am better now," as the old man said in the story—except, of course, for this sheepish feeling.
　　Yet I wonder that I am better. I wonder that I am anything at all after an argument I had at the table tonight. The subject of the debate: Why is it that school-boys who win gold-medals (the little

Jews!) never amount to anything afterwards? Pop out of the box they brought up Lincoln. Groans from my end of the table end. I denied that gold-medal boys never amounted to anything afterwards, said that so-and-so was a nobody. Everybody horrified—a tempest among honest minds.

It is such an odd thing that bright boys should be expected to be successful men. Brightness is so small an element of success. Brightness disillusions.

Shall I go into it? Fiddlesticks! The educated man or woman is simply that. People look for so much more, just as if knowledge involved ambition, tenacity, character.

I think only the learned know the uses of learning—they alone understand their own position.

The fact that Cromwell or Napoleon were dull scholars is not an argument for dull scholars. It is not an argument for anything at all. It is an idle fact.

But these school-teachers and clerks gauge everything by brains. Is there nothing in the world but the weariness of brains? Whatever is active makes its mark: industry, desire, temper; and so on.

But they are all smug in their dingy rooms now, saying, "Mr. Stevens will learn"; and here am I saying to myself, "The dunces!" The proper thing to do is to read one's paper at the table and pay no attention to them.

Poor old Lincoln (the boarding-house Lincoln, not the historic one) drives me out of my wits with his anecdotes. He caps everything with a story. Tonight he said, "Well, Mr. Stevens, Stephen Douglass thought that Lincoln had no ability, but he changed his mind. When Lincoln was inaugurated he stood beneath him and held his hat." At that, all the school-marms glared. Piffle, piffle, piffle! What had Lincoln's immense ability to do with gold-medals?

When I came up-stairs, I noticed a dispatch in the *Sun* about the typhoid epidemic at Reading. I had heard about it before but did [not] know it was so serious. Is anyone down with it in your neighborhood? Please tell me, dear. I think you ought to boil all your drinking-water. Do you? Let me know what care you take. I never drink anything but spring or distilled water. I always have several bottles of distilled water in my room and have now. Don't run any risk. Tell me in just what parts of town people are being taken sick. Above all, don't drink any milk. That is one of the most common sources of infection. If you want to take something to build you up (nearly everyone "takes something to build them up") let it be eggs, or plenty of meat and potatoes, and the like.

Don't forget to write to me on this, because I shall think about it until you do.

It was pleasant to have you speak of the saxophone. It whisks one away to a kind of German or, rather, Dutch Arcadia. I have no doubt that Dutch satyrs play the saxophone.

And then that being afraid. You deserve a kiss for being so nice and timid. But, my dear, I know all about that—not only about the frightful next room, but also about the fat men that chase around the wall, and the skinny men that chase around the ceiling—and the two men downstairs putting the silver in a great, big bag—and the footsteps in the yard—and most of all the delicious relief of the family finally coming home, when you say, "Hello!" and they say, "Were you afraid?" and you say, "Afraid? What a silly question! Did you have a good time?"

I haven't always been the abandoned animal I am now, you know—living in a corner of a hostile house. There used to be halls and stairs and vacant rooms—and a cellar *full* of tramps and people prowling around, waiting to *jump out!*

But I haven't told you about "The Prima Donna"—except to say that I wept, and that my tears looked like a chandelier. You know they rub it in here: Fritzi Scheff, and an unsurpassed chorus; book by Henry Blossom; music by Victor Herbert; wigs by Hepner; shoes by Dazian; scenes by Perlstein, Goldstein, and Katzenstein; Mme. Scheff's pearl dress by Mrs. Osborne; her pink dress by Henriette, her black dress by Hélène; hats by Cobber and Dobber; gowns for the chorus by Fobber and Gobber; the programme by Nobber and Popper; the house perfumed by Ed. Pinaud; doctors in the audience will please leaves their names at the box office; carriages for 10.45.

Well, it was *very* tame. Mme. Scheff trills and trills and trills and the chorus marches and sits around and there is a joke to each act. At all events, it passes the time; and last night I was too tired to think of anything else.

There has been only one truly great event and that is the cold wave. It was the chatter of the breakfast table. When I went out I found it to be an ordinarily brisk day with a high wind—no more. I hate high winds. They blow up one street and don't touch the cross-streets. You walk along—zip!

In Martinique, the wind breaks down iron doors. Here it blows your hat into an ash-barrel.

Why, I must be an ill-natured crow to quarrel so with everything. (That is one of the things that moved my self-contempt last night.) Tell me that I am not ill-natured—so that I have some solace from my own thoughts.

On Saturday evening, I am going to take old Mr. Maitland to the Murray Hill for dinner. We have been planning it for a week or more. He is going to bring some of his cigars—oh, they are as dry as dust, and perfect.

I wish you would write me a letter telling me everything you do some day from the time you get up until you go to bed. Don't take a special day, but just one out of a hundred—take Friday. Tell me what you wear—what time you get my letter—where you read it—every little thing. I want to have a peep into one of your ordinary days—as if I were watching you without your knowing it. No embellishing, mind you.

Couldn't you have a photograph taken for me for Christmas? It need not be a large one—just one of those inexpensive small ones, because they are all the same when framed. I shall have it framed here afterwards. I should like it to have you facing me but not looking right out of the picture—and (if I may suggest it) in the simplest dress you have. There is something disturbing about pictures that look right out, just as there is in too formal dresses. Will you do it? I should like to have that most of all.

You may even have a hat on, if you wear the one with the black thing-a-ma-jig on it—not the one with the wide brim. There is something quaint about hats as they go out of fashion—when people no longer wear anything like them. They get to be like the clothes one sees in groups of college classes fifteen or twenty years ago—strange, curious. They mark an era.

What a to-do about a little picture! Do you realize that it is only three weeks to Christmas? It falls on a Friday, I believe. No doubt, I shall be able to come on Thursday evening and stay until Monday morning—three whole days. Write me long letters in the meantime, Elsie, so that we may forget how long it is since we have been together. Upon my soul—it is half-past one. I have been writing since a little past seven—so that you know how I have spent one evening at least. Tomorrow evening there is going to be a musicale at a house nearby at which all our artists are to perform. Do you think I shall go? On the contrary, I shall be just where I am now—drat 'em. (Forgive the 'em.) I must keep myself in good form for Saturday evening, of course.

I've a notion to run over to the Library some night and take a look at the *Journal des Débats*. One must keep in touch with Paris, if one is to have anything at all to think about.

There is an old church on my favorite Varick street which the *Post* announces is to be torn down. The organ, which is a hundred years old, was built in Philadelphia and while being sent to New-York on a vessel, was captured by the British in the war of 1812 and taken to London, where it was kept for two or three years. So that I was not wrong, after all, in taking a fancy to Varick street.

With much love,
Sambo

Bearing in mind that the writer had been a gold medal winner himself in high school, the first part of this letter may well reflect many of his self-doubts. His comment that "Dutch satyrs play the saxophone" is of particular interest, in view of his use of that instrument in "A High-Toned Old Christian Woman" (1922); it is most unfortunate that my mother's reference has been lost.

But she did have a photograph taken. It shows her facing to the right, though not full profile, wearing a simple white, high-collared dress and a gold locket, with her long blond hair drawn to the back of her neck, where it is bound with a ribbon. It was as my father had wished (apparently it was taken almost immediately after she received his letter), and it was used as her wedding photograph in the local papers when my parents were married the following September.

Once again the letters to Elsie usurped the journal, and the following excerpts from them are portions that might have been journal entries.

[December 7, 1908.]

. . . I spent the evening reading the last volume of "La Chartreuse de Parme." In the afternoon Walter Butler and I took our usual walk, up to Grant's Tomb and back. It was beastly cold—my hands were swollen with it. But the air poured into us like light into darkness. In the morning, I read the newspapers—mountains of them. On Saturday evening I had old Maitland out to dinner. He is a fine old fellow—outrageously polite. His grandfather was vice-president of the Bank of New-York when Alexander Hamilton, who founded it, was President. Maitland has a portrait of him painted by Gilbert Stuart, who, as you know, painted Washington and numbers of other important people of the days of the Revolution. I remember a whole wall full of Stuart portraits in the Academy at Philadelphia. In fact, when I was there last summer I made rather a study of them, observing, as the ignorant and untutored amateur always does, a ridiculously unimportant thing that pleased me—that is, the manner of giving expression to the eye; of putting light and intelligence into it. Stuart paints his eyes blue or black or whatever the color may be. That, of course, leaves the eye blank. Then he adds a little white dot —and that makes all the difference in the world.

I should like to see if Maitland's grand-father's eyes have the white dots. No doubt.

And on Saturday afternoon (you see, I am progressing backwards) I walked hard for two hours to drive the smoke out of my blood. All my valleys were lost in mist and my sparkling hill-tops were miles in the dark. They remained so.

But the moon of the external world was sparkling enough; and, in the vivid twilight, the early stars were like incessant scintillations. The sky was June; the air was deep December.

The rest of the week before that—after the writing of my last letter, was nothing at all, except routine days and evenings in my room.

Only one thing of interest appeared. J. P. Morgan, the banker, has a very celebrated collection of manuscripts. Among them is the original of Keats' "Endymion." This is now (or was last week) on exhibition in the library of Columbia University. You know the beginning—

"A thing of beauty is a joy forever."

I wanted to get up to look at it on Saturday afternoon, but was unable to get away from the office before four o'clock and then a walk was imperative. If I can manage it next Saturday afternoon, I shall do so.

The winter pressure begins to make itself felt at the office. Business is at a high pitch and I have my hands full. There is a little law business, too, now and then, but law is mostly thinking without much result. It consists of passing one question to take up another.

. . . Tonight, after dinner, for example, I thought I should like to play my guitar, so I dug it up from the bottom of my wardrobe, dusted it, strummed a half-dozen chords, and then felt bored by it. I have played those half-dozen chords so often. I wish I were gifted enough to learn a new half-dozen.

Some day I may be like one of the old ladies with whom I lived in Cambridge, who played a hymn on *her* guitar. The hymn had thousands of verses, all alike. She played about two hundred every night—until the house-dog whined for mercy, and liberty.

Alas! It is a sign of old age to be so full of reminiscences. How often I have spoken of Cambridge and Berkeley! Here are two of my college notebooks that came to light with the guitar. You know the things one writes—scribbles—in margins. Mine are abominably serious—I can't find any fit to copy. Yes: here's one:

> Jack and Jill went up the hill
> To fetch a pail of water.
> Says Jack, "I think we ought have beer,"
> Says Jill, "Why so we oughter."

Here is a verse I wrote because I liked it, read it somewhere, and remembered it:

> "As the lone heron spreads his wing
>   By twilight, o'er a hunted spring."

Let *that* mirror be black. I have not looked into it for a long time . . . . [*sic*]. I have been far afield, wandering through my eternal journal. It is the most amusing thing in the world—that long record of states of mind—and of historic events, like the famous night when I read "To Have and To Hold" until half-past three in the morning. . . .

This letter contains my father's first mention of Walter Butler, a man I was unable to identify until, quite recently, I met his sister, Frances, through a stroke of good luck and friendship. Walter had been a close companion of my father's from the time they first met, *ca.* 1905, when the Butler family lived in East Orange, New Jersey, not far from where my father lived. Walter and Wallace shared long walks together, both there and when they again became neighbors, in 1909, in downtown New York, although Walter was younger by eleven years.

The previous letter is noteworthy not only for its mention of Butler, but as it relates to a note Stevens wrote to William Jay Smith in 1954, after receiving a copy of Smith's *Typewriter Birds.* Using a postcard reproduction of a Modigliani "Cariatide," he added three "o"s: two for eyes, and one for a navel; he then wrote, on the obverse:

> Thanks for yr typewriter birds. But just see what one can do with a single letter—used three times: O'Merry Xmas and a Happy New Year.

How close this comes to adding a white dot to blank eyes—with a bonus! We also note his mention of owning a guitar, and that one of the Misses Parsons in Cambridge had also owned one, on which she played hymns, "thousands of verses, all alike." Certainly Stevens' poem "The Man with the Blue Guitar" plays more on repetition than on any analogy with Picasso's "The Old Guitarist," which had been painted in 1903.

The next letter, written December 8 and 9, is noteworthy because it contains a "list of Pleasant Things to drive dull care away": "black-birds, blue-birds, wrens, crocks of milk, pumpkin custards, hussars, drum majors, young chickens." The most obvious analogy is with "Thirteen Ways of Looking at a Blackbird," but there are others. The blue-bird is mentioned in "In the Northwest"; the first play I remember seeing was Maeterlinck's *The Bluebird*, in a production for children by the Clare Tree Major Company, a roving repertory troupe that came to Hartford during the late 1920's and '30's. The wren takes on rather awful aspects in "Notes Toward a Supreme Fiction," but was also a familiar bird in our garden as I was growing up. "Crocks of milk" obviously separates the farm product from what might be bought in local stores; when I was a child we had certified milk delivered directly from a farm to our house, and it was far superior to the milk I tasted at school and in other people's homes. Pumpkin custards were something I suffered through, with my son, in my mother's later years—I do not remember them from my childhood, but after my father's death they made frequent appearances. Hussars—heroic figures. Drum majors—a quick reference in my father's title "The Drum-Majors in the Labor Day Parade"; we often went to parades together when I was small. Was it patriotism, or the drum majors? Young chickens? Surely they do "drive dull care away."

[December 20, 1908.]

. . . It was an exceptional day. The dark blue wintry clouds seemed to be tinged with crimson all afternoon. The water in the reservoir blew against the wall as if it were full of icy needles. There was the usual parade of carriages and machines in the Park. —In one smart Victoria there were four fat chorus girls with their lips carmine— and furs and feathers and everything else. No doubt they had all "chipped in." —We saw a parakeet in a tree. It must have escaped from one of the houses. It sat high up, pure red, making a slight clack. . . .

When he went home to Reading for Christmas, Stevens took with him several bundles; one of them probably contained an engagement ring, for he had purchased a diamond one at Tiffany's. But there is no mention of it in the letters. After Christmas he returned to New York, but he was back in Reading for the New Year holiday. The first letter after that visit opens, in the place where the date ordinarily would be: "Here begins the year 1909. And a voice cried in the Wilderness, saying:" The letter was postmarked January 6. It establishes the fact that Wallace and Elsie planned to marry the following autumn; he refers to "the Inky Pilgrimage—through snow, through wind, through rain, through early warmth, through May and June and summer—until the Pilgrimage is over," when correspondence between them would no longer be necessary in the form of letters.

He wrote again on January 7, 10, and 12; on the 13th he wrote, and added a postscript on the 14th. The next letter, written January 17, while not exactly resembling a journal entry, is quite à propos:

Sunday Evening

My dearest girl:—

The Park was turned to glass today. Every limb had its coating of ice and on the pines even every needle. The sun made it all glitter, but then the sun did not shine directly and it was twilight before it was really clear. —It would have been wonderful if there had been a moon tonight. —At a distance clumps of trees looked like winter clouds. —And the wind made the trees jingle. —Very bad walking, however—in spite of the snow-plows. There were pools over your ankle. We went through them, depending on a change when we reached home.

At twenty minutes to six it was still fairly light—a visible lengthening of the day, which makes one indifferent to hateful February, whose end is signified before it has begun. —Call this the thirteenth month of the year, February the fourteenth, and so on.

Yesterday afternoon I went a-Parking, too. The snow was just commencing to fall, blowing from the North, the direction in which I was going, so that my cheeks were, shortly, coated with ice—or so they felt.

It would be very agreeable to me to spend a month in the woods getting myself trim; for while I enjoyed that flow of North wind and the blowing snow, I felt as if I did not enjoy it quite as much as possible—as if (in so short an experience of it) it did not go the deepest possible. There is as much delight in the body as in anything in the world and it leaps for use. I should like to snow-shoe around our hills—from Leesport to Adamstown, from Womelsdorf to East Berkeley—long trips made at a jog that would pull the air down and give one life—all day trips, hard, fast; and I could do it very well except for the need of being here.

Last night, sitting at home, with a file of the *Law Journal*, with the snow blowing gustily against the window, I wanted very much to be in your parlor with you. I had intended not to say so; but I want you to know, dear, that I do not accept these fearful absences without feeling. They call for absolute faith in each other; and particularly, on your part, for faith in me. Do not let any doubt, even the smallest, creep in, Elsie. It is simply extraordinary that I cannot see you more often; but let us make the most of what we have and be happy with that. Fight the thought of absence. I have both your pictures in front of me, and they are there every evening. The new picture has changed considerably for me. I can see one of your smiles flicker over it every now and then. I do not think you know that if you have looked at it only critically. And when that happens, it is just as if you were here and had said something or other.

About a trifle: I am rather glad that you do not want that song. It isn't really pretty enough, notwithstanding it gets into one's ears. There is something else that I have heard of. I may send you a package in two or three weeks.

The "Washington Square" [by Henry James] was not specially good: altogether an exhibition of merely conflicting characters. It is such an old story that the neighborhood was once suburban but that with the growth of the City has come to be very much "downtown"—the very last place, in fact, in which people live, all below it being exclusively business, except for the tenement intermissions.

Yet it was balm to me to read and to read quickly. I have such difficulty with Maeterlinck. He distracts by his rhetoric. Indeed, philosophy, which ought to be pure intellect, has seldom, *if ever*, been so among moderns. We color our language, and Truth being white, becomes blotched in transmission. —I think I'll fall back on Thackeray.

There is a celebration of Poe in the air. He lived at Fordham

Heights, you know, for a period and the people up there have gone in for a tremendous ceremony on Friday, I believe, of this week. My friend Lamb sent me an engraved invitation as big as a bill-board.

By the way, did I ever tell you that Poe once wrote to somebody in Reading offering to lecture there and that the original letter is on sale at Richmond's now? The committee was unwilling to pay what he asked, so that he never came.

Nowadays, when so many people no longer believe in supernatural things, they find a substitute in the stranger and more freakish phenomena of the mind—hallucinations, mysteries and the like. Hence the revival of Poe. —(I have just interrupted my letter to you to thank Lamb for his prodigious invitation.) Poe illustrates, too, the effect of stimulus. When I complain of the "bareness"—I have in mind, very often, the effect of order and regularity, the effect of moving in a groove. We all cry for life. It is not to be found in railroading to an office and then railroading back. —I do not say the life we cry for is, as a question of merit, good or bad. —But it is obviously more exciting to be Poe than to be a lesser "esquire." You see the effect of the railroading in my letters: the reflection of so many walls, the effect of moving in a groove.

But books make up. They shatter the groove, as far as the mind is concerned. They are like so many fantastic lights filling plain darkness with strange colors. I do not think I complained for myself, but for the letters. Do you remember—(if it matters)? —I like to write most when the young Ariel sits, as you know how, at the head of my pen and whispers to me—many things; for I like his fancies, and his occasional music.

One's last concern on a January night is the real world, when that happens to be a limited one—unless, of course, it is as beautiful and as brilliant as the Park was this afternoon. I did not tell you that we counted eight ducks flying rapidly through the air. Walter said, "I wouldn't have missed that." It was just what was needed. A squirrel chasing a sparrow over the snow, which we had seen before, was tame by comparison.

Wild ducks! We followed them. A policeman shouted and we came meekly back to the walk. The police are as thick as trees and as reasonable. But you must obey them.

Now, Ariel, rescue me from police and all that kind of thing. —"She doesn't like to be called Bo" he whispers. Don't you? Is that why you signed your last letter with "Elsie"? Oh, but Elsie is always a sweet name to me—and I will not call you Bo. It had no reason and no appropriateness, for where were the sheep you had lost—what were we to think of when we thought of the sheep? Perhaps, the folds of hair in the old picture. I can see now why that way of doing your hair would possibly look a little out of place now; although sometime you must do it that way just once more for us both to see and only for us. It looks perfectly old-fashioned already, in so short a time—and, after all, it was only a way for a girl not yet in her twenties. I like it immensely. "She doesn't like you to talk too long about that," comes this small voice. "But, my dear fellow," I reply, "that is not talk, but meditation."

There is a creaking and rattle of trucks in the streets and shouts of "Gid-dap!" Already, the week has commenced. An incalculable element in the activity and variety of the town is made up of the traffic. During the day, on Sundays, one seldom sees a wagon and, no doubt, it is because of the carriages in the Park and on the Drive that people, missing something elsewhere, go there in such droves.

Now, it is quiet again, as a valley in Eden—our old Eden, deep in snow and ice.

I expect to read violently all week, but what—remains to be seen —and to stay at home every night. It is the easiest way to be content in winter. Write to me as often as you can, and I will to you—no matter what just so I hear from you. It is half-past eleven and time for me to stop.

I send you a real kiss.

And more—
Wallace

A letter of January 19 mentions that "Last night I wrote two poems," and goes on:

> Do you remember the last walk along the ridge north of Mc-Knight's gap when the first warmth made us both so languid and heavy? I felt like an old horse, going up the side of the hill . . .

But there is little in it to rival the reminiscences of his letter of January 21, and its picture of Stevens' childhood.

Thursday Evening.

Dear Bo-Bo:—

Secret *memoires:* go back to the bicycle period, for example— and before that to the age of the velocipede. Yes: I had a red velocipede that broke in half once going over a gutter in front of Butcher Deems (where the fruit store is now, beyond the Auditorium)—and I hurt my back and stayed away from school.

On Sundays, in those days, I used to wear patent leather pumps with silver buckles on 'em—and go to Sunday school and listen to old Mrs. Keeley, who had wept with joy over every pap in the Bible.

It seems now that the First Presbyterian church was very important: oyster suppers, picnics, festivals. I used to like to sit back of the organ and watch the pump-handle go up and down. —That was before John McGowan, the hatter, became a deacon.

The bicycle period had its adventures: a ride to Ephrata was like an excursion into an unmapped country; and one trip to Womelsdorf and back was incredible.

In summer-time I was up very early and often walked through Hessian Camp before breakfast. Sometimes I rode out to Leisz' bridge and back.

I remember a huge cob-web between the rails of a fence sparkling with dew.

And I had a pirate period somewhere. I used to "hop" coal-trains and ride up the Lebanon Valley and stone farm-houses and steal pumpkins and so on—with a really tough crowd.

Then I took to swimming. For three or four summers I did nothing else. We went all morning, all afternoon and all evening and I was as black as a boy could be. I think there are some photographs of all that at home—somebody had a camera. I must try to find them.

I could swim for hours without resting and, in fact, can still. Bob Bushing and I were chummy then—and Felix North and "Gawk" Schmucker. —We used to lie on the stonewalls of the locks and bake ourselves by the hour, and roll into the water to cool.

I always walked a great deal, mostly alone, and mostly on the hill, rambling along the side of the mountain.

When I began to read, many things changed. My room was the third floor front. I used to stay up to all hours, although I had never, up to that time, been up all night. I had a pipe with a very small bowl and a long, straight stem. There never was a better.

Those were the days when I read Poe and Hawthorne and all the things one ought to read (unlike "Cousin Phillis"—the book I am reading now.)

And I studied hard—very. —You know I took *all* the prizes at school! (Isn't it an abominable expression?) No doubt, mother still has the gold medal I won for spouting at the Academy—picture in the Eagle, and all that—just as the school-boy orators of today are puffed up.

At High School, I played foot-ball every fall—left end. We generally won at home and lost when we were away. In one game at Harrisburg the score was fifty-two to nothing against us. But the other team was made up of giants. —The only other member of the team that I recall is "Tod" Kaufman, a half-back. He has something to do with the *Herald* and still calls me Pat, which was my name then. Most of the fellows called me Pat.

I never attended class-meetings and never knew any of the girls belonging to the class. Well, perhaps I did; but they do not come back to me now.

I sang in Christ Cathedral choir for about two years, soprano and, later, alto. Worked at Sternberg's for two weeks, once—at the

Reading Hardware Company for two months. (Father was an officer of the company—my working did not interfere with swimming.)

And I went to the World's Fair, and to school in Brooklyn for a while, and sometimes to the Zoo in Philadelphia.

When I was very young, "mamma" used to go shopping to New-York and we would meet her at the station—and then there would be boxes of candy to open at home. We used to spend months at a time at the old hotel at Ephrata, summer after summer, and "papa" would come on Saturday nights with baskets of fruit— peaches and pears, which would be given to us during the week.

Sometimes an uncle from Saint Paul visited us. He could talk French and had big dollars in his pockets, some of which went into mine.

Then there was a time when I went very much with Johnny Richards and Arthur Roland. They were "bad": poker (for matches) and cigarettes.

The truth is, I have never thought much about those early days and certainly never set them in order. I was distinctly a rowdy—and there are still gossips to tell of it, although Aunt Emmy Schmucker who had all the scandal at her fingers ends no longer lives to tell. When Jones', near you, moved into their new house, they gave a blow-out which Aunt Emmy attended. She ate so much that she was sick the next day and stayed in bed. After that she never got up. Soon she knew she was dying. She asked mother to ask me to see her and when I went she kissed me Good-bye. —With her, went infinite tittle-tattle. But she made the most of life, while she had it.

My first year away from home, at Cambridge, made an enormous difference in everything. Since then I have been home comparatively little and, but for you, I think I should have drifted quite out of it, as the town grew strange and the few friends I had became fewer still. —But the years at college will do for another time.

Your own recollections interested me so much that I have followed your lead. Bye!

Pat

The letters continue regularly: January 24, 26, 29; on the 31st, a Sunday, he wrote a long letter from which we may excerpt the following.

. . . By the way, I don't in the least mind what your grandmother said either about her relatives or mine. It is amusing to think of that washer-woman. Mother must be worried to death when she thinks of her. You know she is a Daughter of the Revolution and traces herself through two or three generations to an officer in the American army. You can imagine her crowding out the details. Father once told her that she was a shoemaker's daughter and that he was a farmer's son. That is true. But her father was an excellent shoemaker and his father an excellent farmer—not at all the kind of man we call a farmer at home, but a man of ability and character. They both belonged to large families and both were poor. It is very silly for people in a country town to bother about such things. Besides, you can't get around a washer-woman.

On the other hand, we all have poor relations. —And as a last refuge, we can say that individuals rise or fall on their own merits. Their families are nothing. —The whole question is one of respectability. —We both come from respectable families—you and I. What more is there to be said? The rest depends upon ourselves. —What we inherit in our characters presents a question. What we inherit otherwise is unimportant. Nothing is more absorbing than to trace back the good and evil in us to their sources. At the same time, nothing is more unjust or more ungenerous. Our spirits are what we will them to be, not what they happen to be, that is if we have any courage at all.

I hate a man that is what he is—the weak victim of circumstances. That involves occasional hatred of myself. For example, no one loathes melancholy more than I, yet there are times when no one is more melancholy. And there are other traits besides melancholy. No one likes good manners better than I, or appreciates them more, and yet when I am blue—Lord! how blue, and bearish, and ill-mannered I am. —In defense: this is, quite likely, true of everyone, in a measure. It is particularly true of idealists,—idealism being, perhaps, the most intolerant form of sentimentalism. —By contrast, one likes those plain characters, always equable, that accept things as they are. Their simplicity seems so wise. —Unfortunately such characters commonly develop only in maturity and even in age. —The young are incorrigible. Personally, I am still decidedly young—not nearly so competent as I have an idea of being some day to be superior to circumstances. But there's no end to this. Let us avoid the beginning, therefore.

At the Library yesterday, I skipped through a half-dozen little volumes of poetry by Bliss Carman. I felt the need of poetry—of hearing again about April and frogs and marsh-noises and the "honey-colored moon"—of seeing

> "oleanders
> Glimmer in the moonlight."

You remember the fragments of Sappho. Carman has taken these fragments and imagined the whole of the poem of which each was a part. The result, in some instances, is immensely pleasant—although distinctly not Sapphic. Sappho's passion came from the heart. Carman's comes from a sense of warm beauty. Sappho says, "Sweet mother, I cannot weave my web, broken as I am by longing."

Carman, on the contrary, has his morning planet, his garden and *then* his longing.

There is a sonnet of my own that I have not sent you, that I wrote last week. At Berkeley I used to jot down lines as they came to me. Looking over my diary recently I found the line

> Oh, what soft wings shall rise above this place—

And so, after ten years, I wrote the rest:

IN A GARDEN

Oh, what soft wings shall rise above this place,
This little garden of spiced bergamot,
Poppy and iris and forget-me-not,
On Doomsday, to the ghostly Throne of space!

The haunting wings, most like the visible trace
Of passing azure in a shadowy spot—
The wings of spirits, native to this plot,
Returning to their intermitted Grace!

And one shall mingle in her cloudy hair
Blossoms of twilight, dark as her dark eyes;
And one to Heaven upon her arm shall bear
Colors of what she was in her first birth:
And all shall carry upward through the skies
Odor and dew of the familiar earth.

The next letter was written on Tuesday evening, February 2, followed by letters on the 5th, the 8th and 9th, the 10th, the 15th, the 16th, the 17th, the 25th (after they had met in Philadelphia on the weekend), and the 28th. The last letter makes reference to some topics that he might have entered in his journal.

> . . . Last night I thought of you, too, and longed to have you with me. I had spent the afternoon and evening at the Astor Library looking through the books of Paul Elmer More, one of the most discriminating, learned and soundest critics of the day. He has a very marked tendency to consider all things philosophically, and that, of course, gives his views both scope and permanence. I quote a thing quoted by him—in Latin for the sound and sight of it:
> > *O vitae Philosophia dux! O virtutum indagatrix expultrixque vitiorum!*
>
> Oh, Philosophy, thou guide of Life! Oh, thou that searchest out virtues, and expellest vices! —That struck me as such an admirable inscription for the facade of a library—or of one of those temples, bound to be built some day, when people will seek in a place not specially dedicated to religion, those principles of moral conduct

that should guide us in every-day life—as distinct, say, from the peculiar life of Sundays.

My mind is rather full of such things today, and so resembles the mood that fastened me, a year or more ago, so intently on Matthew Arnold—and maxims! —But each for himself, in that respect; and I do not, therefore, make a point of what may not interest you. —To think occasionally of such things gives me a comforting sense of balance and makes me feel like the Brahmin on his mountain-slope who in the midst of his contemplations—surveyed distant cities—and then plunged in thought again.

Or, to turn to Stevens' "Le Monocle de Mon Oncle":

> Is it for nothing, then, that old Chinese
> Sat tittivating by their mountain pools
> Or in the Yangtse studied out their beards?

and in "Six Significant Landscapes,"

> An old man sits
> In the shadow of a pine tree
> In China.

The letter then returns to an old argument:

. . . In poetry, anyone sensitive to beauty or emotion feels the beauty or emotion that the poet desires to communicate. That, I mean, is the common experience. Curiously, this is not true of painting, quite probably because painting does not make an altogether objective impression: that is, instead of seeing the thing seen, you see the thing itself. The result is that the appreciation of painting is not as acute as the appreciation of poetry. It is not as common, nor as just. People's pleasure in good poetry is simple pleasure. But people's pleasure in good painting is a timid, unbelieving thing, involved somehow with the idea that the pleasure is incomplete without some understanding of the technique of art. Whispering about it—venturing remarks on the "drawing," the "color," the "composition," the "style." That is all nonsense. A good painting should give *pleasure*, like any other work of art. —The same people who consider a painting so professionally ought, logically, to consider a pretty girl's "pattern"—"design"—and so on. —I used to think that I was putting on airs to pretend to like a picture. But I am satisfied now that if it gives me pleasure, I am right in not caring about "scale," or "balance of tones" or anything of the kind; just as I can boldly enjoy the lines:
> "This then perceivest, which makes thy love more strong,
>
> To love that well which thou must leave ere long"—

without knowing that they are a Shakespearean couplet composed of decasyllables . . .

Again, there is a reference to the "giving of pleasure," which reappears in "Notes Toward a Supreme Fiction." But it is somewhat qualified in the next letter, written March 2.

> . . . I find that I was all wrong (according to my latest read-ing) in saying that the function of art was to give pleasure. It seems that "the pursuit of beauty as something unconnected with character is a most insidious danger," which "must inevitably become corrupt"; and that, in a way, art is "the desire of select spirits to ennoble and make beautiful their lives!"
>
> . . . I am still reading Paul Elmer More, and expect to do so all week. I imagine that his limitation is to be found in his learning: his philosophical bias. —One does not invariably care to have the simple pleasures of life discussed with such importance. It is always a *relief* to know that the great poets and the great artists were not such devilish scholars.

The next letter was written the following day and is an interesting "meditation":

> Wednesday Evening.
>
> My dearest Bo-Bo:—
>
> A little phantasy to beguile you—a bit of patch-work—and about music . . . What is the mysterious effect of music, the vague effect we feel when we hear music, without ever defining it? . . . It is considered that music, stirring something within us, stirs the Memory. I do not mean our personal Memory—the memory of our twenty years and more—but our inherited Memory, the Memory we have derived from those who lived before us in our own race, and in other races, illimitable, in which we resume the whole past life of the world, all the emotions, passions, experiences of the millions and millions of men and women now dead, whose lives have insensibly passed into our own, and compose them. —It is a Memory deep in the mind, without images, so vague that only the vagueness of Music, touching it subtly, vaguely awakens, until
>
> > "it remembers its august abodes,
> > And murmurs as the ocean murmurs there."
>
> But I need not solve any theme—so I drop poetry. There is enough magic without it.
>
> I hang prose patches to my introduction and say that "great music" agitates "to fathomless depths, the mystery of the past within us." And also that "there are tunes that call up all ghosts of youth and joy and tenderness;—there are tunes that evoke all phantom pain of perished passion;—there are tunes that resurrect all dead sensations

of majesty and might and glory,—all expired exultations,—all forgotten magnanimities." And again, that at the sound of Music, each of us feels that "there are answers within him, out of the Sea of Death and Birth, some eddying immeasurable of ancient pleasure and pain."

While I had always known of this infinite extension of personality, nothing has ever made it so striking as this application of Music to it . . . So that, after all, those long chords on the harp, always so inexplicably sweet to me, vibrate on more than the "sensual ear"— vibrate on the unknown . . . And what one listens to at a concert, if one knew it, is not only the harmony of sounds, but the whispering of innumerable responsive spirits within one, momentarily revived, that stir like the invisible motions of the mind wavering between dreams and sleep: that does not realize the flitting forms that are its shadowy substance. —A phantasy out of the East Wind, for meditation.

With love,
Wallace

He wrote again on Sunday, and that day he also made an entry in his journal.

March 7. 1909.

The most remarkable exhibition of pictures that has been held in New York in recent years is the exhibition of the pictures of Sorolla at the Hispanic Museum. The pictures are extraordinary for their effulgent sunshine in beach scenes and for their realism generally. But this is not the realism of every day but the realism, say, of holiday,—of the external world at its height of brilliance. The pictures make a vigorous impression, and leave one in Sparkling spirits—all of which is, psychologically, of interest—and simple.

There has been a "retrospective" exhibition of the work of John W. Alexander. It is academic, refined, of limited range, decorative, more than pretty, less than lovely, possibly effeminate, restrained, finished.

I should like to remember the Cottier sale—La Farge's exhibition of sketches etc. The word is going around that La Farge is a colorist. I do not know, yet can hardly think so. There is so little completed work exhibited by him. These sketches in the Southern Pacific are getting a bit passé.

More letters followed, on March 8, 9, 11, 14, 15, 16; on March 18 his letter included "a private exhibition . . . all from the Chinese, painted centuries ago":

"pale orange, green and crimson, and white, and gold, and brown;"

and

"deep lapis-lazuli and orange, and opaque green, fawn-color, black and gold;"

and

"lapis blue and vermilion, white, and gold and green."

He also sent Elsie a list of Chinese "aspects of nature, of landscape, that have become traditional."

> The Evening Bell from a Distant Temple
> Sunset Glow over a Fishing Village
> Fine Weather after Storm at a Lonely Mountain Town
> Homeward-bound Boats off a Distant Shore
> The Autumn Moon over Lake Tung-t'ing
> Wild Geese on a Sandy Plain
> Night Rain in Hsiao-Hsiang.

More letters followed, on March 21, 23, 26; the next one after that is dated April 6, and indicates that he will be coming to visit Elsie in Reading the next weekend, which accounts in part for the gap between that letter and the next, written on Sunday evening, April 18. It is in this letter that we find the first mention of "The Little June Book," the group of poems he was putting together for Elsie's twenty-third birthday, June 5. He went to Reading again the next weekend, and apologized for coming away with Elsie's key in a brief note on Monday, April 26.

Back in New York, he changed residence, to 117 West Eleventh Street, as we learn from his letter of April 28:

> . . . On Monday evening, with the aid of two English sailors, whom I picked up, I moved to my new room. It is almost three times as large as the old one, with a closet, *two* windows, a fire-place and so on, and altogether a great advance on the one I left. And I have a small table to write on, too—instead of a suit-case on my knees . . .

The next letter, written May 2, again contains paragraphs that might have been written in his journal.

> . . . Today I have been roaming about town. In the morning I walked down-town—stopping once to watch three flocks of pigeons circling in the sky. I dropped into St. John's chapel an hour before the service and sat in the last pew and looked around. It happens that last night at the Library I read a life of Jesus and I was interested to see what symbols of that life appeared in the chapel. I think there were none at all excepting the gold cross on the altar. When you compare that poverty with the wealth of symbols, of remembrances,

that were created and revered in times past, you appreciate the change that has come over the church. The church should be more than a moral institution, if it is to have the influence that it should have. The space, the gloom, the quiet mystify and entrance the spirit. But that is not enough. —And one turns from this chapel to those built by men who felt the wonder of the life and death of Jesus— temples full of sacred images, full of the air of love and holiness —tabernacles hallowed by worship that sprang from the noble depths of men familiar with Gethsemane, familiar with Jerusalem. —I do not wonder that the church is so largely a relic. Its vitality depended on its association with Palestine, so to speak.

I felt a peculiar emotion in reading about John the Baptist, Bethany, Galilee—and so on, because (the truth is) I had not thought about them much since my days at Sunday-school (when, of course, I didn't think of them at all). It was like suddenly remembering something long forgotten, or else like suddenly seeing something new and strange in what had always been in my mind.

Reading the life of Jesus, too, makes one distinguish the separate idea of God. Before today I do not think I have ever realized that God was distinct from Jesus. It enlarges the matter almost beyond comprehension. People doubt the existence of Jesus—at least, they doubt incidents of his life, such as, say, the Ascension into Heaven after his death. But I do not understand that they deny God. I think everyone admits that in some form or other. —The thought makes the world sweeter—even if God be no more than the mystery of Life.

Well, after a bit, I left the chapel and walked over the Brooklyn Bridge. There was a high wind, so that I put my hat under my arm. I imagined myself pointing out things to you—the Statue of Liberty, green and weather-beaten, Governor's Island, the lower Bay. Then I rambled up one street and down another until I had a fair idea of the neighborhood. It isn't very promising.

Took the Subway back to Union Square, Manhattan, and walked across Fourteenth-Street. It is lined with the windows of cheap photographers, and I must have looked at thousands of photographs. How silly people are! They curl their hair, put on large white shirts, boutonnières and the like and then have their pictures taken. Such idiot's sights!

After lunch, I walked up-town to the Exhibition of the Water Color Society. It isn't at all a good show—there's nothing fresh, nothing original—just the same old grind of waves and moonlight and trees and sunlight and so on. Yet there are some interesting etchings of New-York—pictures of out-of-the-way corners, that will be more valuable in the future than they are now. I am always especially interested at these water-color shows in the pictures of flowers— bowls of roses and the like. It would be pleasant to make a collection of them. There was one picture of a glass vase with six or seven cyclamen in it that was particularly good. There is something uncommon about cyclamen, something rare, if not exceptionally beautiful.

Then I walked down-town—catching a glimpse, on Madison Avenue, of a yard crowded with tulips. —I dropped into a church for five minutes, merely to see it, you understand. I am not pious. But churches are beautiful to see. —And then I came home, observing great masses of white clouds, with an autumnal shape to them, floating through the windy-sky.

Tonight, it is blissfully quiet—and, as I went for a cigar, I saw the moon, large and full of lustre, shining around the sky.

I fear it is too late to make history of last Sunday. I like to do it while the pageant is still in mind. But for the Muse, I note that we met early, hurried down-town, caught a car for Blandon, crossed the country to the Stone Bridge and then went Northward along the bank. We found the water green, we heard it ripple over the shallows. Bo-Bo ran across a wobbly bridge—gathered cow-slips and what-d'ye-call-'ems—heard robins—saw dandelions. We passed through Evansville on foot—left the creek—and climbed up a field to a hill-top, where there was a *very* remarkable view. But the wind took hold of Bo-Bo and shook her out of all dignity—so that we rested in a corner of a fence while the damsel fixed her hair. Next, on the road, she rode a little way on the giant's shoulder (pretending not to like it)—getting off just in time to avoid a meeting with four Italians (who would have been enormously astonished). —We crossed a field on a foot-path, and then skirted one that had been ploughed by picking our way along the fence. We inspected a lime-kiln. We climbed over a fence into a grove and there we sat with our backs against a tree and made a combined assault on a box of rolls, some with tongue, some only with butter, eggs, tangerines, pickles, and two kinds of cake.

It was a most excellent grove, well-suited to a whole day's idling. —Another fence—a kiss in the lane on the other side of it—a drink from a goblet at a farmer's pump—two immense willows (under which the cows stand in July and August switching their tails)—a bit of rough walking—a glimpse of blossoms—the trolley once more—a blue-bird racing beside the window—The End.

O, Muse, look back on that page in our Book only with kindness. (—I called you Bo-Bo when that was written. You had pink cheeks and light brown hair and soft hands. You were twenty-two. You wore a black dress—that old black dress—and slippers—I think.) It hardly seems as if that could have happened a week ago, with all the snow, and rain, and hail, and fog that we have had; but so it was. —Or have we been to Florida in our dreams? That seems most likely.

I do not think the weather will have done any damage. The mag-
nolia trees here look rather bedraggled but not injured and the
window-boxes of geraniums and tulips look none the worse.

I wish I could spend the whole season out of doors, walking by
day, reading and studying in the evenings. I feel a tremendous
capacity for enjoying that kind of life—but it is all over, and I
acknowledge "the fell clutch of circumstance." —How gradually we
find ourselves compelled into the common lot! But after all there are
innumerable things besides that kind of life—and I imagine that when
I come home from the Library, thinking over some capital idea—a
new name for the Milky Way, a new aspect of Life, an amusing
story, a gorgeous line—I am as happy as I should be—or could be—
anywhere. So many lives have been lived—the world is no longer
dull—nor would not be even if nothing new at all ever happened.
It would be enough to examine the record already made, by so many
races, in such varied spaces. —Perhaps, it is best, too, that one should
have only glimpses of reality—and get the rest from the fairy-tales,
from pictures, and music, and books.

My chief objection to town-life is the commonness of the life.
Such numbers degrade Man. The *teeming* streets make Man a
nuisance—a vulgarity, and it is impossible to see his dignity. I feel,
nevertheless, the overwhelming necessity of thinking well, speaking
well. —"I am a stranger in the earth." —You see I have been digging
into the Psalms—anything at all, so long as it is full of praise—and
rejoicing. I am sick of dreariness. —Yet if I prattle so much of religious subjects, Psalms and things, my girl will think me a bother;
and so, no more, as we used to say when we had stumbled across
something unpleasant . . .

On May 4 Wallace wrote to Elsie that the little "June-book" was
finished. His next letter was written Friday evening, May 7, followed by
one on Sunday evening, May 9, so it is obvious that he did not go to
Reading that weekend. The Sunday letter includes comments on his
journal.

You wonder why I didn't go into the country to see apple-
blossoms and the like. The truth is, or seems to be, that it is chiefly
the surprise of blossoms that I like. After I have seen them for a
week (this is a great scandal) I am ready for the leaves that come
after them—for the tree unfolded, full of sound and shade. I remember a passage in my journal written when I lived at East Orange.
It is dated April 29, 1906:

"All the orchards are white—it is fantastic. Somehow, amid so
many blossoms, one longs for dark woods, rain, iron cages. There
is a great white cherry tree just outside my window."

The following year I lived at Fordham Heights, and on May 22, I wrote:

"This morning I walked down Aqueduct Avenue to the bridge. There were lilacs, gray and purple, in the convent garden. The corner of a stable was hung with wisteria. —This evening, as I passed the same way, a warm scent drifted out to me."

That shows the difference. I am eager for the warm scents. The white and pink of blossoms is delicately beautiful, but they beautify a chilly season. Late May brings grass in luxury, and a general luxury of leaves and warmth and fragrance. If there is anything more luxurious than warmth and fragrance I do not know it. And so, long for lilacs, purple and gray.

My journal, bye the bye, is in sad neglect. I have not written two pages this year. I wish I could put into it, without too much trouble, even a small part of the notes I have made at the Library. Let me preserve one by putting it in our Annals:

> O World, be noble, for her sake!
>   If she but knew thee, what thou art,
>   What wrongs are borne, what deeds are done
>   In thee, beneath thy daily sun,
>   Know'st thou not that her tender heart,
> For very pain and shame, would break?
> O World, be noble, for her sake!

"For very pain" etc should be "For pain and very shame"—I hate erasures, just as I do corned beef—and saxophones. And since the mood to quote is here, why here's another, picked up one learnèd night:

> Ask me not, Dear, what thing it is
>   That makes me love you so;
> What graces, what sweet qualities
>   That from your spirit flow:
> For I have but this old reply,
>   That you are you, that I am I.

They are both by Laurence Binyon—a very clever chap, who is attached to the British Museum, in London.

Scraps of paper covered with scribbling—Chinese antiquities, names of colors, in lists like rainbows, jottings of things to think about, like the difference, for example, between the *expression* on men's faces and on women's, extracts, like this glorious one from Shakespeare: "What a piece of work is man! how noble in reason! how infinite in faculty!" and so on; epigrams, like, "The greatest pleasure is to do a good action by stealth, and have it found out by accident"—(could any true thing be more amusing?)—lists of Japanese eras in history, the names of Saints: Ambrose, Gregory, Augustine, Jerome; the three words, "monkeys, deer, peacocks" in the corner of a page; and this (from the French): "The torment of the man of thought is to aspire toward Beauty, without ever having any fixed and definite standard of Beauty"; the names of books I should like to read, and the names of writers about whom I should like to know something.

The quotation from Shakespeare is particularly serviceable to me now, for I have lately had a sudden conception of the true nobility of men and women. It is well enough to say that they walk like chickens, or look like monkeys, except when they are fat and look like hippopotamuses. But the zoölogical point of view is not a happy one; and merely from the desire to think well of men and women I have suddenly seen the very elementary truth (which I had *never* seen before) that their nobility does not lie in what they look like but in what they endure and in the manner in which they endure it. For instance, everybody except a child appreciates that "things are not what they seem"; and the result of disillusion might be fatal to content, if it were not for courage, good-will, and the like. The mind is the Arena of Life. Men and women must be judged, to be judged truly, by the valor of their spirits, by their conquest of the natural being, and by their victories in philosophy. —I feel as if I had made a long step in advance: as if I had discovered for myself why Life is called noble, and why people set a value on it, abstractly. It is a discovery, too, that very greatly increases my interest in men and women. One might say that their appearances are like curtains, fair and unfair; the stage is behind—the comedy, and tragedy. The curtain had never before been so vividly lifted, at least for me; and my rambles through the streets have been excursions full of amateur yet thrilling penetration. I respect the chickens; I revel in the monkeys; I feel most politely toward the hippopotamuses, poor souls.

A short letter followed, on May 11, and then my father turned to his journal and made the last entries before those he made at the time of his mother's death, three years later. Many of them have already been seen in the letters.

May 14. 1909.
    Living at 117 West 11th Street.

During the winter I have been doing considerable reading, as they say, in the evenings at the Astor Library. I have a batch of notes that I am tired of keeping. What follows is taken from them.

"An Elizabethan actor was not, like his modern successor, a

figure set in perspective in a framed picture whose conversation with
his fellows is overheard by the audience. He stood forth among the
crowd and addressed them as an orator would address them. The
Elizabethan drama, then, was of necessity a rhetorical drama." That
is from a book about the drama, published last year by Brentano's.
I forget the names.—

What I aspired to be,
And was not, comforts me—

pumpkin-coach.

La Religion, La Guerre, La Sexualité

Paul Elmer More expands in view. I read a number of his essays,
his Century of Indian Epigrams etc. He is preoccupied with Religion,
Philosophy, Psychology. Well enough—vital, but not exclusive. He
quotes

*O vitae Philosophia dux! O virtutum indagatrix expultrixque
vitiorum.*

In his Shelburne Essay on Thoreau he says:

"I sometimes think a little ignorance is wholesome in our communion with Nature, until we are ready to part with her altogether.
She is feminine in this as in other respects, and loves to shroud herself
in illusions, as the Hindus taught in their books. For they called her
Mâyâ, the very person or power of deception, whose sway over the
beholder must end as soon as her mystery is penetrated."

Malherbe's *"et rose elle a vécu ce que vivent les roses."*

This, too, is P.E.M., on Lafcadio Hearn:

Great music is a psychical storm, agitating to fathomless depths,
the mystery of the past within us. —There are tunes that call up all
ghosts of youth and pity and tenderness;—there are tunes that evoke
all phantom pain of perished passion;—there are tunes that resurrect
all dead sensations of majesty, and might and glory,—all expired
exultations,—all forgotten magnanimities— —there answers within
him, out of the Sea of Death and Birth, some eddying immeasurable
of ancient pleasure and pain.

The essential law of the theatre is thought through emotion.
—From the forgotten book.

Ninon de l'Enclos—*"La joie de l'esprit en marque la force."*

P.E.M. again. It was the mission of the new faith to promulgate
the distinctly feminine virtues in place of the sterner ideals of antiquity—love in place of understanding, sympathy for justice, self-
surrender for magnanimity,—and as a consequence the eternal femi-

nine was strangely idealised, giving us in religion the worship of the Virgin Mary, and in art the raptures of chivalry culminating in Dante's adoration of Beatrice.

Again. Art is—the desire of select spirits to ennoble and make beautiful their lives. Compare—*le tourment de l'homme de pensée est d'aspirer au Beau, sans avoir jamais une conscience fixe et certain du Beau.*

"I read of parties at which the ladies withdrew and returned seven or eight times, appearing each time with a different dress, always of the same color, but always of a new design."

monkeys—deer—peacocks.

Landscape-Gardening—another art of Chinese origin aimed at a definite influence on the beholder's mind.

Art of flower-arrangement—concerned above all with the interpretation of life and growth of the flower, not with harmonious color effects

red camellia blossoms, or pale blue convolvulus
samisen—quail

Ukiyoyé is the Japanese equivalent of genre.

"Pictures of the fleeting world"—it means—colored with the Buddhist reproach of all that appeals to the senses and belongs to the transitoriness of miserable mortality. It came to mean a recognized style.

Arab chivalry, Persian poetry, Chinese ethics, Indian thought

the glory of the Täng emperors or the refinement of Sung society

Sakyamuni—all evil resides in the individual will to live

"It is easier to illustrate the verse, 'The hand sweeps the five strings of the lute,' than the other verse, 'The eyes follow the flight of the wild goose.'"

Kakuzo Okakura is a cultivated, but not an original thinker. His "Ideals of the East" was interesting.

From Somebody or Other—"It is in landscape and the themes allied to landscape, that the art of the East is superior to our own—the art of the West excels in the human drama

For balm—"What a piece of work is a man! (or man!) how noble in reason! how infinite in faculty" etc. etc.

Alexander—gave Hellas her footing in Asia

One comes across Dr. Wilhelm Bode, like a peak in Darien. And the eye rolls at Adam Bartsch's *Le Peintre Graveur*.

"the kind of light which on certain days suffuses old brick walls, as if dyed in the sunshine of many summers"

Japanese color prints:
> Pale orange, green and crimson, and white, and gold and brown
> Deep lapis-lazuli and orange, and opaque green, fawn-color, black and gold.

Painting & Poetry
> Figure = Epic—Dramatic
> Landscape = Lyric—Elegiac

The Four Accomplishments
> Writing Poetry
> Playing Music
> Drinking Tea
> Playing Checkers

The seven traditional subjects of Chinese Painting:
> The Evening Bell from a Distant Temple
> Sunset Glow over a Fishing Village
> Fine Weather after Storm at a Lonely Mountain Town
> Homeward-bound Boats off a Distant Coast
> The Autumn Moon over Lake Tung-t'ing
> Wild Geese on a Sandy Plain
> Night Rain in Hsiao-Hsiang

Chinese landscape—
> flight of wild geese in Autumn
> willow in Spring

A poem by Wang An-Shih:
> It is midnight; all is silent in the house; the water-clock has stopped. But I am unable to sleep because of the beauty of the trembling shapes of the spring flowers, thrown by the moon upon the blind.

Chinese saying of poetry—
> The sound stops short. The sense runs on.

I have gone through the books of Laurence Binyon. There is a kind of sedateness in them, less than tranquillity. His long poem "Porphyrion" contains much that is beautiful—as—

> Then he reclined
> Deep into joy, absolved out of himself

> In her robe
> Was moonlight silvering over purple seas
>
> The charm of deeming nothing vain
>
> Out of suspended hazes the smooth sea
> Swelled into brilliance, and subsiding hushed
> The lonely shore with music
>
> Soft as moths asleep
> Come moonlit sails
>
> As with the mystic dew
> Dropping from twilight sails

In a recent *Edinburgh Review* there is an article on Venice and the Renaissance. It is by far the most striking essay I have seen during the Winter, not only for what it says of Venice, but for a distinction that it draws between the effects of light and darkness. Light disclosing form heightens the emotional faculties—"Night, dense shadows, the decaying touch of time, mist and fog, distance—tone down the exactitude of form."

"The greatest pleasure is to do a good action by stealth and have it found out by accident."

Wallace Stevens used his slips of paper not only for his journal but, as has been noted, for his letters to Elsie. His next letter to her, written on the same day that he had resumed his journal to copy out things he wanted to remember, repeats one of the items there that he had not used in a letter before.

[May 14, 1909.]
. . . Dante's "New Life" is a strange book. I have had it for a long time, looked through it often—and never read it. But I know what it is about. In copying my notes into my journal, I came across this paragraph,—

It was the mission of the new faith to promulgate the distinctly feminine virtues in place of the sterner ideals of antiquity—love in place of understanding, sympathy for justice, self-surrender for magnanimity, —and as a consequence the eternal feminine was strangely idealised, giving us in religion the worship of the Virgin Mary, and in art the raptures of chivalry culminating in Dante's adoration of Beatrice.

Thus it appears that the "New Life" is one of the great documents of Christianity. It is very strange to read, as I am reading now, the *chief* document—the New Testament—and to consider the growth of our Western religion. St. Matthew opens with a list of the families from which Jesus descended as if to impress the fact of his humanity.

And then follows, as I said the other night, a narration of the most incredible adventures that ever befell a human being. The Catholic church, for reasons of its own, has made much of the Virgin, and when I have finished my reading, I must meditate on it and try to find the reason. Twenty centuries of Christianity have made life quite different for women (as for men, too). It may be that Christianity is a feminine religion. That, too, is worth thinking about.

Two days later, on Sunday evening, May 16, he wrote again about a visit to a place that had become familiar in his walks outside the city.

. . . I lay on the edge of the Palisades basking on a rock and I thought of the top of the Pinnacle—and then of the panorama below. It must be exquisitely green—for the green now is exquisite, so young, so fresh it is. Yet it has been a half-misty day, a steamy day, a day for vegetating. I noted that the grass has come out of curl and stands high and straight. And such a multitude of flowers—wild honeysuckle, wood-violets, purple and white, strawberry blossoms white as crystals, dandelions, buttercups—wonderful to see. The dogwood trees were sheer white and the lilac-bushes sheer lilac. I shall put in this letter two flowers the names of which I do not know. I climbed a little way down the side of the Palisades to get them—because I thought that if you had been there you would have asked me to—and so here they are.

And then to lie in the sun for two whole hours in a quiet place and listen to the birds—the bold call, the sweet answer, no less bold, but softer. The woods rang with songs. It was *delicious.* —There were green beetles crawling around and red ants and fat bumble-bees and mosquitoes—and everything . . .

He wrote again on May 17 or 18; he was not sure himself, since the "dateline" reads "Monday Evening (or Tuesday morning—I'm afraid to look at my watch)." More letters followed, on May 19 and 21, before a letter on May 23 which, as has often been the case, resembles a journal entry.

Sunday Evening.

My dear Bo-Bo—

I don't think I did my share of letter-writing last week. It was a deuce of a week, anyhow—with all that cold weather and rain. For all that, it was cold all day today—and an unexampled day (at this time of year) for walking. I went out to Englewood first—a little way beyond that village I saw a redbird, or a tanager, or a cardinal-bird. At all events it was a crimsonish red with black wings and a black tail. I sat down to watch it. It seemed to be having a stupid time—rather;—once it sat on a bush for at least ten minutes and did nothing at all. By and bye, I saw a second one—the mate. They seemed marvellously tame—allowed me to walk within four feet of them without flying away. Then I made for some hills and rambled among them all day. About half-past four, when I thought I had been walking Eastward (towards home) for some hours, the sun suddenly came out just in *front* of me and I realized that I had been walking Westward. Upon inquiring, I was told that I was twenty-eight miles from New-York. I had not had anything to eat since breakfast, it was twenty minutes to five, and I had exactly forty-cents in my pockets! I managed to reach Paterson in a little less than two hours hard walking. From there I went by trolley to Undercliff and crossed the river at 130th Street—with five cents left—to get down town with and for dinner. Fortunately, I know a fellow on 121st Street. He had just paid the cook! (or so he said). Well, I scraped a little together—enough for this, that and the other—and here I am none the worse.

I had expected to find all the blossoms gone, and they were from the fruit trees. The cherry-trees, in fact, are full of green cherries so soft that you can bite through what will some-day be a stone. But the dogwood was as fine as ever. There were a number of pink trees which I took for pink dogwood—but they were on lawns and I could not get near enough to them to look at the leaves.

In some out of the way place, there was a really old-fashioned garden, a little gone to weed. Around it was a hedge of *arbor vitae* high enough to lean against—and strong enough, I really believe, to sit on. In one corner, there was a [illegible word] of shrubs—with the richest smell, a thicket of honey-suckle, and a tree hung with wisteria. —But there were many such things—and besides, I was gladder to see the farms in the valley of the Hackensack—to see the market-gardeners filling up the lettuce barrels or standing by the barn-doors smoking their pipes and looking over their farms—and to smell the odor of the cows—which I pronounce to be heavenly, nothing less.

Have you noticed how high the wheat is? A little warmth and it will ripen.

Towards evening it grew clear—wonderfully—and I noticed the new moon—like this ☾ . Can you tell which part of the crescent (without looking, of course) is toward the sunset: Does it hang this way ☾ or this way ☽ ? In other words do the horns point toward the earth or toward the sky—down or up? —And that new moon means that we shall have moonlight on both my trips—and long evenings.

During the week I come up here after dinner: it is a bore to walk the streets—and thus I have not appreciated the evenings as they passed—that long hour or two of pure tranquillity. But this evening was memorable, particularly for a reflection of orange sunset in a stretch of marshy water.

Ah! but it's Manhattan again—and four millions of us once more. How happy I should be never to see it again! I hate it with particular glee after such a day as this.

Forgive my notes of last week. It was one of those weeks when ink stands still in the bottle. Is that why I didn't have a letter yesterday? —I shall come on Saturday afternoon in time to be up early in the evening, which we can spend for the first time in the open air.

With my love, Bo-Bo,
Your Wallace

He wrote again on Wednesday evening, before his weekend visit to Reading. Only one letter is extant for the week between that visit, over Decoration Day, and his next visit for Elsie's birthday the following weekend.

Tuesday Evening. [June 1, 1909.]

Dear Buddy:

The tireless Historian traces the plot from its beginning—from the forgotten ride to Riverside and the walk home, to the walk under the locusts, odorous as Asia, under the tulip-tree, up the high hill, beside violets, over the clover-field, down to the cold spring with its roof of spiders, up to the observatory and its airy box of sunlight (a thing to think of in January) where you lay back and looked at the sun through golden eyelids—quickly towards another observatory surrounded by savage rocks (that eat shoes)—back to a wind-mill and up in the air, where we saw the shadow of the wheel whirling on the trees—toward a bush of yellow roses, guarded by a grandmother-to-stone-house building with the sandy-haired—to a tea of sardines and bottled milk (in my native land, oh, woe is me!)—to the timely descent into the Valley of Moonlight, to the tale of Big Claus and Little Claus in the arm-chair (where we say—and have said, how often,—"Adieu!" to the rest of the world—the chair of sweet forgetfulness—our Oriental Divan)—to a pleasant morning on the hill, to a pleasanter afternoon behind Mary, the fat and foamy, when we hunted Bob White, and saw and heard him—"Bob White!"—to a walk up to the dark Pagoda, black in a night full of mysterious calm and heavenly beauty (heavenly, of course, as descriptive of the scene), to a memorable smelling of black-berry blossoms that shone whitely in the shining air, to the old prose of the Springs—and back to our own old comfort—and what one day's absence makes wonderful, and not to be spoken of. I salute you, dear, distant Buddy—as Sleep struggles with me—and send you, if I may, a kiss—quick as thought.

Your own—always your own
W.

XI

While I was growing up my mother did not read my father's poems, and seemed to dislike the fact that his books were published. Questioning her about this after my father's death, she told me that he had published "her poems"; that he had made public what was, in her mind, very private. At the time I did not understand what she meant but, with the discovery that when he first began publishing in 1914, he had used some of the poems in the books he made for her birthdays, her logic becomes clear, her resentment comprehensible. Originally, she must have been charmed by the verses, slight as some of them are.

THE LITTLE JUNE BOOK
W.S. to E.V.M.
June 5, 1909.

I. MORNING SONG

The blue convolvulus,
Less flower than light,
Ghostly with witchery
Of ghostly night,

Trembles with silver
And magic and dew,
And the lark sings
On twinkling wings.

O sun, O melting star,
Some sense supreme
Flashes inglorious Life
To glorious dream.

This is the only version we have of "Morning Song," although we have already heard of the "blue convolvulus." The next poem appears not only in the June book, but in my father's red folder, where there are slight changes in punctuation.

II.

If only birds of sudden white,
Or opal, gold or iris hue,
Came upward through the columned light
Of morning's ocean-breathing blue;

If only songs disturbed our sleep,
Descending from that wakeful breeze,
And no great murmur of the deep
Sighed in our summer-sounding trees!

III.   A CONCERT OF FISHES

Here the grass grows,
And the wind blows;
And in the stream,
Small fishes gleam:
Blood-red and hue
Of shadowy blue,
And amber sheen,
And water-green,
And yellow flash
And diamond ash;
And the grass grows,
And the wind blows.

This poem, without its title, was published as part III of "Carnet de Voyage," in the September 1914 issue of *The Trend*.

The fourth poem also appears in the red folder, with minor changes, as does the fifth; neither was published later.

IV.

Life is long in the desert,
On the sea, and the mountains.
Ah! but how short it is
By the radiant fountains,

By the jubilant fountains,
Of the rivers wide-sailing,
Under emerald poplars,
With round ivory paling.

V. VIGNETTE

This, too, is part of our still world:
Night, like a cloud, upon the sea,
Far off from us, full of the stern
Possession of deep-rolling waves;
A broken ship, with empty deck,
Sinking in darkness, all night long.

When Stevens wrote, "That the lilacs came and bloomed," in "The Rock" (1950), could he have been thinking back to the next poem?

VI.

This is the lilac-bush
Full of the cat-bird's warble,
The singer drunken with song
Of his heart's distillation,
Falling from azure tuft,
From violet spray, and jade,
Down through the dusk of the bush,
To rest in a grassy shade.

Soon again, the happy sound
Will enchant the purple ground.

Among other comparisons that can be made is one between his "green locust" in "Contrary Theses (II)" (1942) and that in the following poem, where "the leafy tremors" are also reminiscent of "The leaves were falling like notes from a piano." The images have already been seen in the love letters.

VII. NOON-CLEARING

Now, the locust, tall and green,
Glitters in the light serene.

Leafy tremors shake around
Brilliant showers to the ground.

At a dart, an oriole sings,
To fluttering of yellow wings!

Sunlight in the rainy tree,
Flash Two-and-Twenty back to me.

The next poem became part VI of "Carnet de Voyage," with minor changes in punctuation. In reading it, we can compare my father's use of Cythère in "An Ordinary Evening in New Haven":

VIII.

Man from the waste evolved
The Cytherean glade;
Imposed on battering seas,
His keel's dividing blade,
And sailed there, unafraid.

The isle revealed his worth:
It was a place to sing in
And honor noble Life,
For white doves to wing in,
And roses to spring in.

My mother had several fans, at least one of them made of sandalwood,
though I cannot be sure whether any of them date before her marriage to
my father. It may well be that the next poem was only inspired by my
father's reading, but if not, we have found another reason why my mother
objected when the lines became part IV of "Carnet de Voyage."

IX.

She that winked her sandal fan
Long ago in gray Japan—

She that heard the bell intone
Rendezvous by willowed Rhone—

How wide the spectacle of sleep,
Hands folded, eyes too still to weep!

The end of the first stanza of "Credences of Summer," where "the
roses are heavy with a weight / Of fragrance and the mind lays by its
trouble," reminds me of the next poem:

X.

Only to name again
The leafy rose—
So to forget the fading,
The purple shading,
Ere it goes.

Only to speak the name
Of Odor's bloom—
Rose: The soft sound, contending,
Falls at its ending,
To sweet doom.

Just as III seems like an exercise in color, so does XI, which also appears in the red folder, with minor variations.

XI. SHOWER

Pink and purple
In water-mist
And hazy leaves
Of amethyst;
Orange and green
And gray between,
And dark grass
In a shimmer
Of windy rain—
Then the glimmer—
And the robin's
Ballad of the rain.

The next poem does not appear elsewhere, but makes us remember many references in the journal and letters.

XII. IN THE SUN

Down the golden mountains,
Through the golden land,
Where the golden forests lean,
And golden cities stand;

There I walked in ancient fire,
To many a shining place;
And found around me everywhere
A new, a burning race.

One from hidden capes come home,
One from incessant seas,
One from valleys lost in light,
And all with victories.

No man was hampered there at all,
But lived his visions out.
There was no god's necessity,
Nor any human doubt.

We find the next poem reflected in "The Beginning" (1947), where "The house is empty. But here is where she sat."

XIII. SONG

This is the house of her,
  Window and wall,
More than the house of her:
  Rare omens fall

From the dark shade of it,
  Pleasant to see;
And the wide door of it
  Opens to me.

The next poem also appears in the red folder where, at the bottom of the lines, my father has written in light pencil, "The Imagination Revised."

XIV. IN APRIL

Once more the long twilight
  Full of new leaves,
The blossoming pear-tree
  Where the thrush grieves;

Once more the young starlight,
  And a known mind,
Renewed, that feels its coil
  Slowly unbind—

Sweeping green Mars, beyond
  Antique Orion,
Beyond the Pleiades,
  To vivid Zion.

Once more there is a single version in the next poem, which was not published and does not appear in the red folder.

XV. ECLOGUE

Lying in the mint,
I heard an orchard bell
Call the ploughman home,
To his minty dell.

I saw him pass along.
He picked a bough to jog
His single, loathful cow,
And whistled to his dog.

I saw him cross a field,
I saw a window glint,

I heard a woman's voice,
Lying in the mint.

The next poem does appear in the red folder, with minor changes in punctuation. It may be considered a forerunner to "Sunday Morning," especially parts IV and V.

XVI.

He sang, and, in her heart, the sound
Took form beyond the song's content.
She saw divinely, and she felt
With visionary blandishment.

Desire went deeper than his lute,
She saw her image, sweet and pale,
Invite her to simplicity,
Far off, in some relinquished vale.

The next poem, with minor variations, became part V of "Carnet de Voyage."

XVII.

I am weary of the plum and of the cherry,
And that buff moon in evening's aquarelle;
I have no heart within to make me merry,
I read of Heaven and, sometimes, fancy Hell.

All things are old: the new-born swallows fare
Through the Spring twilight on dead September's wing.
The dust of Babylon is in the air,
And settles on my lips the while I sing.

Explaining the phrase, "an Arabian in my room," in "Notes Toward a Supreme Fiction," my father wrote to Hi Simons, in 1943, "The Arabian is the moon." That statement is enlarged by the next poem, which is also found in the red folder, with minor changes.

XVIII.

An odorous bush I seek,
With lighted clouds hung round,
To make my golden instrument's
Wild, golden strings resound,

Resound in quiet night,
With an Arab moon above,

Easing the dark senses need,
Once more, in songs of love.

The next one became part VII of "Carnet de Voyage," with minor changes in punctuation and the subtitle "Chinese Rocket."

XIX.

There, a rocket in the Wain
Brings primeval night again.
All the startled heavens flare
From the Shepherd to the Bear.

When the old-time dark returns,
Lo, the steadfast Lady burns
Her curious lantern to disclose
How calmly the White River flows.

The last poem also appears in the red folder, with no changes.

XX.   PIERROT

I lie dreaming 'neath the moon,
You lie dreaming under ground;
I lie singing as I dream,
You lie dreaming of the sound.

Soon I shall lie dreaming too,
Close beside you where you are—
Moon: Behold me while I sing,
Then, behold our empty star.

We find my father's comment on the verses in his next letter to Elsie, written Wednesday evening, June 9:

> I hope that you will read "The Little June Book," now that it is in your possession. It represents a really considerable amount of pleasant work—and poets, you know, find the greatest delight in giving it.

He did not write again until the following Monday, June 14, but he wrote the next night as well; the Tuesday letter included the following paragraph:

> I have been sitting here reading the *Athenaeum*, a weekly published in London—"a journal of—Literature, Science, the Fine Arts, Music and the Drama." London continues to be the ultimate point of romance to me. I wish there was some chap there to whom I

could write for things. I have for a long time wanted a photograph of Professor Mackail, of Oxford. And now they are having an exhibition of Japanese Prints at the Fine-Art Society's Galleries with a catalogue, with notes by Mr. Arthur Morrison, a most important authority on such things. Frankly, I would give last winter's hat for a copy of that catalogue.

By August he had obtained one, for he inscribed the date on the flyleaf. Another paragraph reads:

> Yet it is not all scholarliness with me tonight for I have been looking at a long poem full of
>
> "The yellow apple and the painted pear"
> in   "a land the fairest"
> where   "—many a green-necked bird sung to his mate."
> Don't you like "green-necked"? It is the best thing of its kind I have heard for a long time—unless "the painted pear" (however old) is better. But all that imagination—how fickle! The delights of the mind seem as little related to its resources, as, say, the windows of a cathedral to its structure. Pooh! It doesn't matter.

On Wednesday his letter included this paragraph:

> Suppose I send you a few of the things that have come into my head. I thought of an elm-bordered village-street. That means comfort and quiet and liberal thoughts. It means space to think in—and I greatly fear that young men in attics are desirous of space to think in. They do not have the mild distractions of people lower down in the house.
> —I thought, too (as often as one thinks of a tune), of "green-necked birds." Such a fascinating adjective!
> —I thought of rhymes. There are certain words that have been rhymed together so often that when you hear one you expect the other. It is considered innocent to use them still. For example, "breeze" and "trees." But the critics are too severe in that case. There is only "bees, fleas, sneeze" etc. etc. It is a point in poetical fashion, worth observing.

Letters followed on Thursday, Friday, and on Monday, June 21; most of the latter is "a chronicle," as he says himself.

Monday Evening.

My dear—Bo-Bo:—

Not a bad Saturday afternoon and Sunday. To report on the befitting home: it must, I fear, be up-town. The place I wanted to have you see in Washington Square is quite out of the question; and inquiry at neighboring places makes them seem equally prohibitive.
—It is tiresome work, especially when you know before-hand that

the nicest places are only made to look at, like baker's windows.
—So that it is only a report of progress, with nothing definite.

On Saturday evening I went to the Astor Library at seven and
read for an hour—including the definition of candy-tuft in several
dictionaries. Candy doesn't mean candy—it means Candia, which was
a name for the island of Crete. Candy-tuft is, therefore, Candian
tuft or Cretan tuft. There were pictures of the plant, of the flower,
and of the seed—and I don't care for any of 'em. A little after eight
I thought of Sir Charles Wyndham who was playing a little comedy
called "The Mollusc" at the Empire; so I hurried over to Broadway,
took a car and shortly "found myself *au théâtre.*" It was an amusing
little play, principally concerned with a woman requiring a good
deal of waiting on—and the breaking of the habit. Wyndham is over
sixty and Mary Moore: the mollusc, is about fifty-eight. There were
only four people altogether in the cast—and the same scene all the
way through.

And when Sunday morning came around I didn't in the least
feel like taking that long walk in Jersey. I loitered over breakfast
and then wandered up town until I was near the Park—entered it,
made a circle in it and came back to my room to read the papers.
—Then, after dinner (you do not mind my making a chronicle, for
a change, I hope) I went to the Park in Brooklyn. They have a rose
garden there very much worth while—like this [here he has drawn
a sketch of three circles with "things around them"]. The three
round rings are three fountains, or basins of water. The things
around them are beds of roses. The thing marked x is a rose arbor.
It is just like a long grape arbor only *covered* with roses. The whole
garden is surrounded by heavy foliage. The air is sweet—distinctly;
and it is a beautiful place to see. —Near-by is what is called the Vale
of Cashmere. In the centre is a fountain. The sides are slopes planted
—like a jungle of rhododendrons. —Again—it is a beautiful place to
see.

I crossed from the Park to the Brooklyn Museum and looked at
an exhibition of water-colors by Sargent. He is the man that painted
the lady in the brilliant dress at the Philadelphia exhibition. —They
were interesting and full of bright color—scenes in Portugal, Spain,
Italy, Turkey, Africa. But museums are stuffy at this time of year
and I didn't stay very long.

I went down to Brighton Beach (with dusty shoes) and saw two
memorable things, first: the sea full of bathers (memorable because
unexpected); and, second: a sea of green parasols (last year's perhaps) around a band-stand where a large band was grinding out
Wagner. —I followed the board-walk to Coney Island where I went

to catch a train—and incredible as it may sound I was home again in time for tea.

At the tea-table some one said that it was the longest day in the year. Today was, in fact, but I thought yesterday was until I saw this morning's paper. A celebration seemed desireable; so I went far uptown to get the long sunset—and took all evening to get home. —There was an air-ship over the Palisades. —And at ten o'clock I was home in bed trying to get to sleep. —The longest day in the year— and the first day of summer. How long a wait we have had for it to come!

Yesterday I found some cut grass that dried in the sun and, while it was warm, smelled of August—the dry season. Dryness has a welcome sound after all our showers.

And my mind turns to "Credences of Summer," and "These lovers waiting in the soft dry grass."

He wrote a letter to Elsie every day that week excepting Saturday; a short letter written Sunday afternoon, June 27, included the following:

I've started "Endymion" and find a good many beautiful things in it that I had forgotten, or else not noticed. I wonder if it would be possible for a poet now-a-days to content himself with the telling of a "simple tale." With the growth of criticism, both in understanding and influence, poetry for poetry's sake, "debonair and gentle" has become difficult. The modern conception of poetry is that it should be in the service of something, as if Beauty was not something quite sufficient when in no other service than its own.

The next letter extant is a brief note, written on Friday morning, July 2, advising his time of arrival in Reading for the Fourth of July weekend. On his return to New York, he wrote on Tuesday evening, July 6, and noted, "I would give a year of life to spend this summer at home with you—"; but of course that could not be. He promised "to write to you a little every day," and came pretty close to keeping that resolution, except when in Reading on occasional weekends; so close that it no longer seems necessary to list the dates of letters other than those being excerpted.

[July 16, 1909.]
The desire

> For to admire and for to see
> For to be'old this world so wide

was on me strong today and at lunch-time I got a map of the Provinces and spent a half-hour tonight, after reading the paper, studying rivers and lakes and steamship lines and all that. I should like to see

Quebec and the St. Laurence and the Bay of Fundy (where the tide falls seventy-five feet and people get off boats by ladders.) —What sport it would be to knock around up there for a few months—in real woods, hunting and fishing. One of these days! When I have seen London and all the rest. —We must save for London together.

[July 19, 1909.]

Then I read a few pages in a book I borrowed this afternoon. A new book is a real pleasure to me. I like to read for a long stretch at a time; and I like best to read what are called "instructive" books, or else poetry; and yet I cannot possibly read either of these for more than an hour, if that. This is a book of essays on progress, money, Hope, fashion and all that kind of thing, written from the socialistic point of view. I find it interesting. —To tell the truth, I should be glad to stumble across a good novel—not a love story—something larger.

[July 20, 1909.]

The pressure of Life is very great in great cities. But when you think of the ease with which people live and die in the smaller places the horror of the pressure seems self-imposed. —After all, a stout heart anywhere and everywhere! —Now, I wish we could rest after so much disquisition and listen to what we have never heard. The wind has fallen. The moon has risen. We are where we have never been, listening to what we have never heard. We are in a dark place listening—contentedly, to—well, nightingales—why not? We are by a jubilant fountain, like the one in the forgotten "June Book," under emerald poplars, by a wide-sailing river—and we hear another fountain—a radiant fountain of sound rise from one of the dark green trees into the strange moon-light—rise and shimmer—from the trees of the nightingales. —And is it all on a stage? And can't you possibly close your eyes and, by imagination, feel that it is perfectly real—the dark circle of poplars, with the round moon among them, the air moving, the water falling, and that sweet outpouring of liquid sound —fountains and nightingales—fountains and nightingales—and Sylvie and the brooding shadow that would listen beside her so intently to fountains and nightingales and to her? —If only it were possible to escape from what the dreadful Galsworthy calls Facts—at the moment, no more serious than that neighborly bag-pipes and a dog singing thereto—. All our dreams, all our escapes and then things as they are! But attend to that mysterious cry: "Have a stout heart against Fortune." Meditate on it long after ghostly fountains and ghostly nightingales have ceased their ghostly chants in the ghostly mind. Yes: for flesh and blood: "Have a stout heart against Fortune." —The curtain falls. The brief flight is at an end.

[July 23, 1909.]

My novel goes along well. —The Chinese say that a half-hour's reading gives savour to a whole day. —Certainly, it stimulates me. I remember that a few nights ago the little things on my table—my writing-table—seemed stale. —I read for an hour tonight. They seem far from stale: the row of books—"Tom Jones," "The History of Early English Literature," "Geological Sketches," "Whitney's German-English and English-German Dictionary"—the four or five pictures, and so on. —Observe how the things around one cease to stimulate after a while. (That is why kings are bored—and like Haroun-al-Raschid assume nocturnal disguises.) —The desire for new things—is a part of our need for stimulation. And what more restless motive is there, since that need is so constant, than the desire for new things? —When a thing is stale it is done for. —When a thing is new it has the world at its feet (I am careless of rhetoric). It stimulates—that's *why*. Hence air-ships, wireless, the morning newspaper, the "extra," the interest in the theatre, fashions, etc. —Man flies from nothingness. Not less than nature he abhors a vacuum—or what is the same—staleness. —All that speculation springs from a "known mind renewed," to cite the "Little J.B." once more (and finally, for the time being).

[August 17, 1909.]

A cricket chirps in the rain. —I walked up-town tonight with a fellow, during a lull, and he asked me to go to a Chinese restaurant. We had Chinese noodle-soup, chop-suey with bamboo and mushrooms, rice, ginger in syrup and rice-cakes. —But tonight is set apart for the Mirror of Past Events. This time it discloses, not a patch of flowers, or a colored cloud, or pigeon in the air: not a lot of little things; but a winding drive—a long, serpentine tour behind "Kate" around and around: up the Tulpehocken with a glimpse at swimming ducks and at the site of the ancient mule bridge, and across the Red Bridge, with its new roof, up hill and across country to Leinbach's and the high church there and the chestnut tree, down a dip to Stoudt's Ferry and over the blue river, Southward to Tuckerton, Northward to Ontelaunee, where we had lunch on the dry grass, Westward to Temple—no: Eastward, and then into the back-country beyond it, along a mountain road, where we had a shower of a few drops and put up the top of the wagon and pulled a checkered robe over us—when the shower stopped, along the Kutztown road, past Hampden, through the Park—and home again, laden with dust.

[August 19, 1909.]

And this evening, I drifted, in the aimless fashion of the novels, into the Astor Library, which seemed strange to me after so long an absence, and read for an hour and a half—I don't know what—but a good deal of poetry. It is astonishing how much poetry I can read with sincere delight. But I didn't see much that was "new or strange" —except an expression about rhyme being "an instrument of music" —not that that was "new or strange"—but it *struck* me as being so; and it was a pleasant thing to think about. In the "June Book" I made "breeze" rhyme with "trees," and have never forgiven myself. It is a correct rhyme, of course,—but unpardonably "expected." Indeed, none of my rhymes are (most likely) true "instruments of music." The words to be rhymed should not only sound alike, but they should enrich and deepen and enlarge each other, like two harmonious notes.

[August 23, 1909.]

I am quite shattered by the walk I took yesterday—not less than thirty miles. The walks up and down town keep me in condition: but they have been rather few and far between of late. I ought not, therefore, have gone so far yesterday; for I have been as stiff as if all my "j'ints" were rusty.

Yet it was, as you say, such a glorious day: almost a September sun (I know them all)—when the earth seems cool and the warmth falls like a steady beam. It was an old route along the Palisades, interrupted at noon for a sun-bath on a rock at the edge of the cliff— basking in full air for an hour or more—unseen. —The woods along the side of the road looked at their height. And yet at twilight, in the neutral light, as I looked over the edge, I observed, meekly, that what I had thought to be various shades of green, were, indubitably, green and brown and yellow—oh, the faintest brown and the faintest yellow, yet brown and unquestioned yellow. You see! —I did not altogether respond—my sensibilities were numb—emotion sealed up. It is true. —But when the sun had set and the evening star was twinkling in the orange sky, I passed a camp—where gypsies used to camp a few years ago. There were two or three camp-fires and at one they were broiling ham. Well, Bo, it may sound absurd, but I *did* respond to that sugarey fragrance—sensibilities stirred, emotions leapt—the evening star, the fragrance of ham, camp-fires, tents. It was worth while, by Jupiter! Not that I give a hang for ham—horrid stuff. But it was the odor of meat—the wildness or the sense of wildness. You know—when you camp in wild places—and come in at the end of the day, you always find venison over the fire, or a dozen trouts—and then, there is the hot bread, and your pipe afterwards, and then you roll up in your blanket—and the fire begins to fall together—and you fall asleep, so tired, so contented. —I am glad I passed the camp—and I am glad they were not eating boiled potatoes. —And when I reached home I was too dusty and worn out to write, which you will forgive

I know, now that you know the reason. I fell all over the bed in a hump. —Next Sunday I hope to do the same thing.

The next day (August 24) he wrote a letter that may well be included in its entirety. (Note, in the first paragraph, what he does with the word "Hades," and relate it to his use of "Haddam" in "Thirteen Ways of Looking at a Blackbird" [1917].)

Tuesday Evening.

My dear Bo-bo:—

Here's a kiss to start with. Oh, you've missed it! (Better look sharp next time.) —It is a very warm kind of evening—and I suppose you have on a white dress and are sitting on the porch—with Mr. Bell. Fe-fi-fo-fum—the sailor from Cadiz cried "Boo!" to the ladies, who wished him in Had-um-um-fe-fi-fo-fum.

I wish I was coming on Saturday. It is so pleasant to see the moon getting rounder and rounder and to think that it will probably be full then—and that the two nights will be all gold and silver and lapis-lazuli and mother-o'-pearl and all the rest:

> A caravan from China comes;
>   For miles it sweetens all the air
> With fragrant silks and dreaming gums,
>   Attar and myrrh—
> A caravan from China comes.
>
> O merchant, tell me what you bring,
>   With music sweet of camel bells;
> How long have you been travelling
>   With those sweet smells?
> O, merchant, tell me what you bring.
>
>   .   .   .
>
> The little moon my cargo is,
>   About her neck the Pleiades
> Clasp hands and sing; lover, 'tis this
>   Perfumes the breeze—
> The little moon my cargo is.

[Not by Stevens, but by Richard LeGallienne.]

(Beastly pen.)

Under my window, the little cricket that sang in the rain—so long ago, it seems—chirps, chirps, chirps—like—well, like an old clock; and I have been sitting here reading and looking at pictures

—in the "Studio," a magazine you will know and like one of these days. I have been reading about votes for women, languidly, and then—one of those malicious articles that the English like to write about the Americans: "the sheer, stark, staring madness of the Americans," "the witless Americans." Last week I read a letter by an Englishman in which he said that there were "300,000 inhabited, windowless rooms" in New-York City alone. Jove! What a fib! —I always feel sensitive to this kind of thing, notwithstanding it is such awful rot. But the kind of Englishman that makes such remarks *must* be as much of a bounder in fact as he is in print; and while the desire is to give him a black eye (if I may say so), the proper thing is to chuckle and enjoy the show.

But you can hardly care about all that; and no doubt, you wonder why I write of it. . . . The cricket must have reminded me of it—chirp, chirp, chirp, chirp, chirp, chirp, chirp. —I want you to hear it—not that buzzy thing (probably a locust)—not your katy-dids and tree-frogs on the noisy hill-side.

Last night's long rest patched me up and today I felt pretty much myself. By tomorrow I shall be all together again. —You can imagine what Sunday's walk really was—long runs—and so on. —I did not tell you of a vegetable garden I saw—rows of celery, rows of tomatoes, a patch of squashes, and the like. It was almost forgotten. —What an answer to pessimists it is to be able to point to things growing—and not only growing, but ripening, too! If the odor of ham under the evening star failed to enchant them that patch of yellow squashes would.

What a delightful poem that is, too:
A caravan from China comes;
For miles it sweetens all the air—
Good-night, my dearest Bo-bo.

With much love,
Wallace—no: —you know.

[August 26, 1909.]
It has been one of the most uncomfortable days. Tonight, the caravan from China was only half-visible through the heat mist in the sky. This is the great moon of the year and I follow its growth as a devout poet should.

The brief note of August 27 follows in full:

Friday Evening.
My dear:
The sky is purple tonight and in the East there is a great golden star. I have been up to the Park wandering around in the—moonlight.

There is a reservoir there a mile around. The water was as quiet as a mirror, and it was, in fact, very much like a mirror altogether. Then the shapes of the trees were so splendid against the sky—the flat, palm-like boughs of the pines, the round, graceful elms, the tall, slender white birches. It was after ten when I came in. Will you forgive me if I send only a word? I shall do better and deserve better on Sunday. I feel too tired to take the walk I had planned; but a cool Saturday may make a difference.

Your Buddy

Sunday Evening. [August 29, 1909.]

After tea, this evening, I pulled my chair close to the window and spent a half-hour in so-called reflection and then my crimes as a letter-writer haunted me. —The last Sunday in August: the last vacation Sunday in the minds of most people—or *many* people. I spent it here at home—in this very chair, reading the *Times*, the *Sun*, the *Studio*, the *Athenaeum*. There is such a funny story about the *Athenaeum*. It is, as you may know, a weekly devoted to literature, music, art and the drama. It is able and complete but prodigiously dull. Stevenson, the novelist, mentions a sporting man who picked the paper up and said, "Golly, what a paper!" —That amused me immensely.

The sky was too threatening to think of a walk. I waited until the last minute for breakfast, and came back here, feeling indescribably lazy and tired. In fact, the mere idea of moving made me sigh. —But that singular lethargy has been decreasing all day. At four o'clock I walked up and down the streets, getting as far north as 34th Street, before it was time to return to the house. There were many interesting things in the windows, which I made note of, although I really know, without looking, just where to go for anything I want. Yet one makes discoveries. In a general way, I know where to go for coffee machines, for example; but today I found a store that deals in them altogether. That is one of the first things we shall need, because, while we won't want to bother about little dinners for ourselves, for the present, we shall have to get our own breakfasts. Everybody does, that lives that way—and it is great fun. The coffee makes itself (in the machine), while you thrill over the morning paper.

[August 31, 1909.]

The real reason my letters were so bad last week was that I was depressed from too much smoking. Often, when there is a great deal to do at the office, lots of people to see, and so on, I smoke incessantly to quiet my nerves. The result is, that, when the day is over, and the strain is gone, I find myself in a kind of stupor and find it very difficult to do anything at all. I do not even feel like reading—unless it be the newspapers. —On the other hand, if I do not smoke, my nerves tingle and I am full of energy: yes: tingle with it. And then I want to walk violently, work violently, read, write, study—all at a bound. The trouble is, however, that I am intolerably irritable at such times and make life miserable for everybody who must assist me and am apt to be very short and sharp to people with whom I must do business. That, of course, is impossible. For example, I didn't smoke at all on Sunday. On Monday I did mountains of work and had everybody on tip-toe. Today I started my third day without a cigar and behaved outrageously; so that at lunch I smoked—and have been like a lamb all the rest of the day. —Yet if I go without smoking for three or four days at the end of that time the irritableness disappears and I am as agreeable as the next man. —I wonder if you know that I always stop smoking a few days before I come to see you. I will not smoke tomorrow, nor at all until after our holiday. —I wanted to break myself of the habit entirely, but it is a terribly insidious and seductive thing and, if one could indulge in it mildly, quite harmless. Tomorrow commences a new month and I am going to try to go through it without a single puff—or if I must smoke, at least try to limit myself to one cigar a day, which I think I could do . . . So much for a thing that causes me more regrets than anything under the sun. But was there ever a smoker who was not bidding farewell to the weed with one hand and reaching for a perfecto with the other? I doubt it.

[September 10, 1909.]

This is the very kind of rain that sets the leaves going. In Spring it brings them. In Autumn it takes them away. —Everything goes along just as it should (and as it is bound to do if one pays attention). Yet we may take a little recess tonight and not speak of plans— although anyone coming into my room would know at once that a change is pending—bare floor, pile of boxes—and so on. —I wish it was tomorrow that I was going home, instead of a week hence. Next week will hang on me like lead, because of the week to follow.

As I look over my things, there are a good many odds and ends that I want to throw away, I find; and it is the hardest thing in the world to make up my mind to do so. My old trunk, which has been through a score of boarding-houses is sure to go. It is most dis- reputable-looking piece of baggage. Then there is a batch of papers —college note books etc. which have a sentimental interest, yet ought to be sacrificed, it seems to me. I hate to throw them away. At the same time, I hate to have all that junk tagging after me. I'll make up my mind on Sunday. —I should like to start with everything fairly new—not necessarily new-looking, but fresh; and I am going to get rid of everything possible.

[September 12, 1909.]

Whenever I move I have a house-cleaning and I have been having one all day today. First I packed the books, dusting them first. They are now ready to be moved. When I get them over, and when the new shelves are ready, I am going to fill the shelves and then throw away a good many of those that remain and for which we shall have no room. The ones to be thrown away are the old ones, some of them in bad condition, and others which no longer interest me—chiefly historical and similar books.

This evening (it is after ten o'clock) I went through my trunk and threw away practically everything that was in it. Then I had a great batch of papers in connection with legal matters which I have reduced from a pile two feet high to two small packages in envelopes. It has been my habit to save everything that might be useful and the result was an appalling litter. It was high time that something was done.

For example, at college, where the instruction is given by lectures (instead of recitations) I took notes on what was said. So did everybody else. It was part of the system. —Well, my note-books were scandalous affairs, full of pen-and-ink sketches of queer noses, the backs of heads and so on. These note-books, which seemed to have a sentimental interest, have always survived previous cleanings; but today I found courage to dump them one and all in the overflowing waste-basket. —Of course, I have kept my diaries, and my priceless poetical scribblings, and other odds and ends—but the whole business can be carried now in one hand, instead of blocking up closets and corners.

XII

On Saturday, September 18, 1909, my father returned to Reading for the last time as a bachelor; my parents were married on Tuesday morning, September 21, in Grace Lutheran Church, which my mother had joined a few years earlier. There were no attendants, and the space for witnesses to sign on the wedding certificate is blank. There was a small reception at my mother's home, which was "beautifully decorated with palms and cut flowers," according to the newspaper, and then the couple left on a brief honeymoon. Their first stop was in Boston, where they also visited Cambridge; from there they went to Stockbridge and Pittsfield, Massachusetts, and then to Albany where they left by boat on September 28 to sail the Hudson to New York. Shortly after arriving there, they sent a postcard to my mother's parents; the scene was of the Chapel of the Good Shepherd at General Theological Seminary, Chelsea Square, and an arrow indicates the house, in the background on West Twenty-first Street, where the young couple was living. They both wrote messages; my father's was:

> Our house is under the mark. Our floor is the next to the top. There-
> fore, we face the chapel, which is only across the street. Chimes
> every evening. *We are not a part of the chapel*—but apart from it.
> Hence, the word apartment. Hope this is clear.

My mother wrote:

> Wallace is crazy. Don't mind him. But this is the house, as much as
> you can see of it.

My father had found what he termed "the befitting home" in August, and had described the apartment at 441 West Twenty-first Street in a letter to Elsie.

> There are two very large rooms with abundant light (they occupy
> almost an entire floor). The front room looks out over the General
> Theological Seminary—a group of beautiful buildings occupying an
> entire block. It is all freshly painted and papered—has hardwood

floors—open fire-places—electricity etc. There is also a corking kitch-
enette—clean as a whistle—white paint etc. And a corking bath-room
with a porcelain tub, a large window etc. Then I saw at least three
large closets for clothes.

According to the sons of my parents' landlord, my father used one of those
closets to stand in and recite poetry; on the other hand, it was reported that
when my mother was angry she would pace through the apartment slam-
ming doors vigorously, including closet doors. In both cases the noise was
sufficiently loud to travel downstairs where the landlord, Adolph Alexander Weinman, lived with his family.

I know very little about the first years of my parents' marriage, and
have only met one person who visited them in their New York apartment
(where they lived until they moved to Hartford in 1916), Frances Butler,
the older sister of my father's walking companion, Walter. All she was
able to remember was that it was rather sparsely furnished, and that the
evening she was there Wallace sat in a corner reading, while she talked
with Elsie. At that time, though Miss Butler was unsure of the year, my
mother told her that she wanted a child; apparently my father did not
think he could afford to take on an added responsibility. After all, it was
five years after he first met Elsie that Wallace married her, and it was not
until 1914, when he was thirty-five, that he first published noteworthy
poetry; one gets the sense that my father had to be sure that everything
was in order before going ahead. He had been brought up in an era that
placed strong emphasis on the "work ethic," on being able to provide;
and an era which also looked askance at poets, as being effeminate and/or
corrupt. Especially as an attorney, and as that role related to his occupation
in the insurance world of bond claims, involving construction work, cattle
herds, etc., it seems quite logical that, in trying to establish himself both
professionally and financially, my father would conceal—at least for a
time—his poetic aspirations. There was also the matter of energy: just as
writing letters to Elsie had usurped the time he had spent with his journal,
now living with, and needing to provide for, Elsie usurped at least part of
the time he had spent in reading and in writing: both letters to her, and
occasional verses.

It was a time of coming to maturity. Not since he had left his family
to enter Harvard twelve years earlier, in 1897, had he lived with someone
intimately, or shared his life with anyone he cared for deeply: someone
who might be critical, or adoring; someone who might love, or hate; someone with whom he would have to modify his own character in order to
get along.

At the time of his marriage Wallace was a minor officer in the insurance world: resident assistant secretary of the New York office of the
American Bonding Company, whose home office was in Baltimore. The
position must have paid a salary large enough for him to feel that he could

take on the responsibility of supporting a wife; it also was a position that involved a certain amount of travel away from home. At the same time, my mother was a delicate, fragile woman, and in those days (before air-conditioning) she was unable to suffer the summer heat of the city. Thus, although living together, there were times when Wallace and Elsie were apart.

They were together, though, and happy, five months after their marriage, in February 1910, when Wallace wrote this verse for Elsie:

A VALENTINE

Willow soon, and vine;
But now Saint Valentine,
To whom I pray: "Speed two
Their happy winter through:
Her that I love—and then
Her Pierrot . . . Amen."

In April of that year they were also together—in Annapolis, Maryland, where, according to one of the postcards my mother sent home, she "Found violets here today, and trees are in blossom." It seems possible that at this time Wallace was being considered for a "home office" job, in Baltimore, where his elder brother, Garrett, had been working for another company; a letter from their mother (to their sister Elizabeth) indicates that the boys were crossing paths, and that Garrett had just moved to New York: "their office is in same locality." This was amplified in a letter from their father, Garrett Barcalow Stevens, Sr., on April 5, 1910, when he wrote to Elizabeth: "You will find Wallace at 84 William St., and Garrett at 100 William Street. . . ." Elizabeth went to New York that week and may have found Garrett; she did not find Wallace at home, for a postcard from Elsie mailed on April 11 indicates that they were both in Baltimore, after their sojourn in Annapolis.

By the end of May, Wallace was back in New York and Elsie was in Reading for a visit. There is no further reference to a position in Baltimore. But, being alone in the city on Decoration Day weekend, Wallace wrote to Elsie and mentioned that he had revisited his old haunts on the Palisades, and had run "into the library at Columbia College, where I read for an hour or two." The following week he went back to Baltimore, and to Reading briefly, where they celebrated Elsie's twenty-fourth birthday on Sunday, June 5. Their separation was obviously amicable, and perhaps one of convenience, as can be seen from the following letter:

Tuesday Evening. [June 7, 1910.]

My dearest girl:—
    Your letter came this morning—with its house-wifely injunction about camphor etc! I had thought of it myself, but forgot to get the

camphor tonight. Moth-balls are better, since camphor sticks fast to things. I needed the blanket on Sunday night, when it stormed all night long. Tonight I went back to Mrs. Hillary's for dinner. The same people were at the table—but I felt as if I had been far away from them. Only, in the narrow life of a boarding-house, they do not change much—probably they were wearing the same clothes, with a new stitch or two.

But how much I miss you! Such a vacation makes one realize how precious a prize companionship is. We have never been in the habit of saying this or that—yet I wish I *could* say how sweet you seem to me. I don't say it, mind you—I only know that it makes me happy: I just say that I am happy, and you will know why I am.

So you sit at your old window, looking at an old scene, and thinking old-far-off-thoughts. Think kindly of your buddy. —It is an important thing to keep a true home in the world. There are so many changes—so much at which we just look on, so much we endure. And the best treasure is to have familiar things to console and encourage us. We have more of life ahead of us than after. Therefore, cherish that old scene and those old thoughts. If I wanted to think all of life over, I think I could do it best up the Tulpehocken, or sitting on a fence along the Bernville road. The Colisseum [*sic*] by moonlight would be a distraction by comparison. Native earth! That makes us giants.

There was more of Spring in the few weeks we spent in Baltimore than the whole season here has shown. Today, instead of that golden freshness of June there was a gray-blue in the air and the sunshine was autumnal. And the roses and peonies at home became little groups in florists windows. I like it so. The country is one thing, the city another—I like them well-defined, separate. It is sentimental to mingle them. —Blackberries and plums are on the stands—stony peaches—canteloupes—occasional water-melons. Those mark our "perfect days."

Have a good, quiet, comfortable time. That last bit of dress-making left you a shade pale—your mother thought so and then I did, too. And try to complete your summer things, so that you feel free. I shall send you anything you want. Everything here is in good order, except, possibly, your violet, which seems to be losing flesh. The pine is bright with new moss. The ferns are strong-looking. The ivy was never better. —But I have discovered that dust is a huge matter. It settles as calmly as "water falling down"—as continuously, as finally. A little thing—but a huge matter. Thus, one learns day by day things unexpected and amazing!

> With much love—
> Your—learner—and
> student of dust.

The correspondence indicates that my mother stayed in Reading for at least two or three more weeks, and that my father missed her intensely. His letter of June 23 must have convinced her to return, for no later letters are extant from that summer. In it he wrote:

It has been so hot here all week (and quite likely will remain so) that I hesitate to ask you to come back. Certainly, it would be a hundred times better for you to be in the country, in good air, having a good time. At the same time, I should not like you to go alone. Come and see how comfortable you can be and perhaps we can find some place near by for you to spend a week or so. As a matter of fact, New-York is no worse than Reading in the summer time. One cannot be comfortable anywhere except in the country or at the shore and since we cannot spend the time there, let's be cheerful and happy at home here. The weather does not last for more than a month or two and your long visit ought to have given you strength. Of course, if you *can* arrange a few days in the country, you know that I should be happy to have you go. Otherwise, come and give life to these quiet rooms and take care of me for a while. You can go some other time, you know. I want to have you here again. It will be like beginning anew—won't it? And now that you have had long evenings (last night was the longest in the year) and have seen Spring change into Summer, (and have finished with Dr. H) I think you'll be glad to be back in your nest. Mrs. Duff comes tomorrow to make it shine—and I hope that you will come on Saturday afternoon to see it—just the same place, but your own. Let me know in due time what train you will take and what time it reaches Jersey City and I'll meet you there and take care of your baggage—and we'll go off somewhere for dinner and enjoy ourselves. Don't forget my cap and the photographs and anything else that may have been left behind.

At Christmas, Elsie was in Reading again; perhaps they had both gone for the holiday, but Wallace was back in New York by December 28, when he noted, "It seems to be very dull around town, although, at the office, there is plenty to do as usual." At home, Elsie's grandmother died just before the New Year, and her visit was extended. Her absence gave Wallace an opportunity to write to her, once more a letter which, in part, resembles a journal entry.

[January 2, 1911.]
    A most dismal day it is—and was yesterday. On New-Year's eve, I looked at the clock in the Metropolitan Tower, (it was illuminated), at about half-past eleven, and I remember how bright the stars were. And yet when morning came there was a deluge of rain, that kept me indoors until evening. Then I went out only for dinner, and after-

wards, read and studied a little. This morning there was a heavy fog filled with mist. It was impossible to see to Tenth-Avenue from our door. Across the street, the trees were like a charcoal *sketch* of trees. However, I was in great need of a walk and, therefore, started for the Metropolitan Museum. They are showing some new things—one a small bronze by Bouchard: a girl feeding a faun, I liked particularly. There is some new Japanese armor. I have no sympathy with those who go in for armor.— There is a bronze bust of John La Farge, which I hope to see often.

Walked down Fifth Avenue to Madison Square and, after lunch, went into the American Art Galleries, where, among other things, they are showing some Chinese and Japanese jades and porcelains. The sole object of interest for me in such things is their beauty. Cucumber-green, camellia-leaf-green, apple-green etc moonlight, blue etc ox-blood, chicken-blood, cherry, peach-blow etc etc Oh! and mirror-black: that is so black and with such a glaze that you can see yourself in it. —And now that I am home again, and writing, in semi-obscurity, lights lit, boats whistling, in the peculiar muteness and silence of fog—I wish, intensely, that I had some of those vivid colors here. When connoisseurs return from the pits of antiquity with their rarities, they make honest, everyday life look like a seamstress by the side of Titian's daughter.

The summer of 1911 found Elsie in Reading again, and Wallace in New York where, as he wrote her on July 22, "I mean to spend my evenings at home reading and trying to *think* a way through the future, that will lead us all through pleasant places." Only a few days before that, on July 14, Wallace's father, Garrett Barcalow Stevens, had died; but he makes no mention of it in his letters, though we can infer that he had been in Reading for the funeral services. In thinking "a way through the future," Wallace was not considering a return to Reading, where he might have had the chance to share in his father's law practice, as we learn from his letter of August 6 to Elsie.

Sunday Morning.

My dearest Bo-Bo:—

I was so glad to get your letter last night and to find you in such good spirits. —I was in rather a low humor, to put it so; for I had learned during the day that Connie Lee had got a fairly good thing that I was after—although Lee and Kearney and Stryker do not know that I know it, yet, to be honest. You will recall that I always said that Lee stood in my way—and I know that they are all loyal friends of mine. Only now that Lee is taken care of, I should be next in line. However, the assistance of friends is at best auxiliary; and progress depends wonderfully on one's own energy.

Your dream of a home in Reading is most fanciful. To be sure, if I succeeded here, we could have an inexpensive place there in summer. I think that possibly I should have been well advanced if I had stayed in Reading. If I were to come back, I should want to go into a business—and that requires capital and experience and a willingness to make money 1-¾ cents at a time. I fully intend to continue along my present line—because it gives me a living and because it seems to offer possibilities. I am far from being a genius—and must rely on hard and faithful work.

It is not hard to see why you are discontented here. It is undoubtedly lonely—and if by nature you are not interested in the things to be done in a place like New-York, you cannot, of course, force your nature and be happy. If I could afford it, there are many things you might do. But there are many thousands of us who do not look too closely at the present, but who turn their faces toward the future—gilding the present with hope—to jumble one's rhetoric. And then you know, there is no evil, but thinking makes it so. —I hope to make next winter a little more agreeable for you. —There's the sexton announcing morning services with his bell. After an hour at church, I am going out into the country somewhere—haven't had any fresh air for a long time. I may go to Yonkers, cross the river and walk down the Palisades among the locusts.

With my love, Your Bud.

WUXTRA!

There were no locusts. I saw *one* thing distinctly pleasant. A path in some woods was surrounded by black-eyed Susans—(flowers, of course.) Three yellow birds in a group were swinging on the yellow flowers—picking seed, or something, and chattering. —But in mid-summer grandmother Nature is not specially interesting. She is to busy with her baking.

Tonight as I came out of the Earle, I saw the moon, beautifully soft over Washington Square. The Weinmans have been up on the roof—gazing. —Such nights are like wells of sweet water in the salt sea (to repeat an ancient fancy)—like open spaces in deep woods. —Why cannot one sit in such rich light and be filled with—tableaux! At least, why cannot one think of new things, and forget the old round—past things, future things? Why cannot one be moonlight through and through—for the night? —The learned doctors of men's minds know the reason why. I read it all once in the *Edinburgh Review*. Psychologically, the obscurity of twilight and of night shuts out the clear outline of visible things which is a thing that appeals to the intellect. The clear outline having been obliterated, the emotions replace the intellect and

Lo! I behold an orb of silver brightly
Grow from the fringe of sunset, like a dream
From Thought's severe infinitude—

[by David Gray]

I swear, my dear Bo-Bo, that it's a great pleasure to be so poetical.

But it follows that, the intellect having been replaced by the emotions one cannot think of anything at all. —At any rate, my trifling poesies are like the trifling designs one sees on fans. I was much shocked, accordingly, to read of a remark made by Gainsborough, the great painter of portraits and landscapes. He said scornfully of some one, "Why, the man is a painter of fans!" —Well, to be sure, a painter of fans is a very unimportant person by the side of the Gainsboroughs.

I've had one of the candle-sticks over at the table to write by and find that the wax has been melting over the table. Poor table-top —as if all its other afflictions were not enough! —Adieu, my very dearest—and many thoughts of you—and kisses.

w

In February 1912 Wallace wrote to his mother, who was not well, indicating that he would come home to Reading for his summer vacation that year. (The letter has not been found, but it is referred to in a letter from Mrs. Stevens to her daughter Elizabeth.) Apparently he made a visit late in May and then, after his return to New York, took up his journal to enter this account.

June 25, 1912.

About a year ago (July 14, 1911) my father died. And now my mother is dying. She was thought to be almost gone a month ago and I went home then to see her. I have not been able to see her often for ten years or more. During that time, she has changed, of course, but only in growing thinner. Her present sickness has aged her more than many years; and when I saw her a month ago she was much whiter than I had expected. When I went home, I saw her sleeping under a red blanket in the old blue-room. She looked unconscious. —I remember very well that she used to dress in that room, when she was younger, sitting on the floor to button her shoes, with everything she wore (of summer evenings, like these) so fresh and clean, and she herself so vigorous and alive. —It was only a change for her to be in the blue room. After a while, she walked, with assistance, into her own room and either rested in her chair by the window or in bed. Many unconscious habits appeared. She wanted her glasses to be on the window-sill by her side. She would reach out her hand to satisfy herself that they were there. This was at a time when her mental condition was such that she could not form a question: when she would stop mid-way in her questions out of forgetfulness of what she had intended to ask. She would pick up anything strange on the sill and examine it. —After some days, her mind (and body) cleared somewhat; for she was still powerful enough to resist, although to the eye she seemed so often at the point of death, with her dark color, her fitful breathing and the struggles of her heart. She liked the flowers that had been brought. She asked for Mrs. Keeley, an old friend, who came to see her. She watched the parade of the veterans on Decoration Day in a sort of unrealized way. It encouraged her to be taken to the porch and to remain there for long periods. She seemed to be perfectly conscious of her surroundings. She smiled and nodded her head, but seemed to be trying to gather her thoughts —or else to let them wander far away. —All the feelings that are aroused create a constant desire or hope of something after death. Catherine writes that mother wishes that it were over. Fortunately for mother she has faith and she approaches her end here (unless her mind is too obscured) with the just expectation of re-union afterwards; and if there be a God, such as she believes in, the justness of her expectation will not be denied. I remember how she always read a chapter from the Bible every night to all of us when we were ready for bed. Often, one or two of us fell asleep. She always maintained an active interest in the Bible, and found there the solace she desired —She was, of course, disappointed, as we all are. Surely, for example, she endured many years of life in the hope of old age in quiet with a few friends and her family. And she has never had a day of it. —In the bed she is in now all of her children, except the first (and possibly him) were born. And there are a thousand things like that in the old house—certain chairs, certain closets, the side-board in the dining-room, her old piano (she would play hymns on Sunday evenings, and sing. I remember her studious touch at the piano, out of practice, and her absorbed, detached way of singing). At one period, say twenty years ago, she made efforts to get new things and many such objects remain: things in the parlor etc. Her way of keeping things, of arranging rugs, of placing pieces of furniture, remains unaltered. A chair is where it is because she just put it there and kept it there. The house is a huge volume full of the story of her thirty-five years or more within it.

As a meditation on death, it is also a presentiment of "Sunday Morning" (1915):

> Death is the mother of beauty, mystical,
> Within whose burning bosom we devise
> Our earthly mothers waiting, sleeplessly.

A week later he made another entry in his journal.

July 1, 1912. (Monday.)

I went home to Reading to see mother on Saturday. She was so glad to see me. On Sunday morning she was very bright and natural —altogether in possession of herself: infinitely more natural than she has been since last summer; and cheerful. She had had a good-night, with "a delicious sleep" from about four o'clock in the morning, to use her own words. She spent Sunday sitting up between long naps. The beating of her heart in the veins of her throat was as rapid as water running from a bottle. It was a terrible thing to see. When she was lying down, all her covers quivered. During the afternoon, the girls were there and spoke of Dr. Blackburn, who had given her communion on Saturday morning. He had been to Williamstown, Massachusetts, and had told her how his thought had turned to the verse, "I will lift up mine eyes unto the hills whence cometh my strength." She thought this very "sweet." She quoted "The Lord preserveth all them that love him"; and this I believe is her favorite text. Catherine reads to her from the Bible. —She had a good night, Sunday night. In the morning, before I left, she saw what a bright morning it was and remarked on it. She said that she would like to have "a room right in it." She was propped up. She would not lie down until after I had gone. She kissed me when I went (as I did her) and her last words, full of affection, were "Good-bye!" —Of course, she expects to die. She wishes not to complain. She said that she had had her "boys" and asked, "Do you remember how you used to troop through the house?" After all, "gentle, delicate Death," comes all the more gently in a familiar place warm with the affectionateness of pleasant memories. —She is too weak to get out of bed. She joked about the large number of pills she has been taking. She said that whenever she had a drink of water, it was to wash down a pill. —She enjoyed a mixture of grape juice, orange juice, lemon and sugar—thought it a rich wine.

At this time Elsie was vacationing in Vinemont, Pennsylvania. Wallace wrote to her on July 7 and said, regarding a walk he had taken that day, "If you care to you can read about it when you come back, because I've taken to my journal again." Nevertheless, there is no indication that he made any entries after the two about his mother in the fourth and final notebook.

Margaretha Catharine Zeller Stevens died on Tuesday evening, July 16. Wallace was notified by telegram and left for Reading after work on Wednesday; the funeral took place on Saturday. He returned to New York on Monday the 22nd, and a week later wrote to Elsie, "For several evenings I sat around, thinking chiefly of my poor mother." Apparently, although Vinemont was not far from Reading, Elsie had not gone to the funeral, nor had Wallace stopped to see her, for the letter goes on, "But during all this, I have not forgotten you. I had many thoughts of you and wished for you often." The earliest that he thought he might be able to get away was mid-August:

> Even then, perhaps, I should stay in Reading and come up to Vine-mont for Sunday, all day. Our old home will, no doubt, be broken up for good, after thirty-five years, at the end of the summer; and I should want to spend at least a few hours there, among its familiar objects.

On August 11 he wrote again, to say, "Recently, I spoke of coming to Vinemont next Sunday; but I cannot possibly spare the money." The next letter extant is dated August 26, 1912, but makes no mention of when he and Elsie would be together again. Certainly she did return to New York that autumn, because a letter to his sister, in November, notes, "Elsie is a stunning cook," and also mentions that they had been going to the theater frequently.

The following April Wallace and Elsie spent a few days in Atlantic City, where he had some business to attend to. Then, as summer returned, Elsie went to the country again—this time to Pocono Manor, Pennsylvania —while he remained in the city. By now Wallace's friend and business associate Heber H. Stryker had moved to Connecticut, as vice-president and secretary of the First Reinsurance Company of Hartford (he later became president), and my father's letter to Elsie of July 2, 1913 (a Wednesday), opens, "I have an invitation to Hartford from tomorrow to Monday, which I have accepted. I had been wishing for it." He stayed at Stryker's home, 22 Arnoldale Road, West Hartford, just around the corner from where we would live from 1924, shortly after my birth, until 1932, at 735 Farmington Avenue. On his return to the city Wallace wrote to Elsie, describing the weekend and, more pertinently, the neighborhood where he would find himself living eleven years later:

> The walk to the house has an edge of blue lobelias on each side. Along the porch and around the front of the house are Canterbury bells and holly-hocks, in bloom, and various other things not yet in bloom. The long field which lay under the window of our room was full of newly-mown hay. Fancy how sweet the room was! And about a hundred black-birds were holding a convention in the field while I was there.

He also said that he would come to visit her the following weekend; they did not share accommodations, however, for a note on July 10 asked Elsie to reserve a single room for him.

He went to Pennsylvania again July 26–27, and complained in a note on July 30 of "the vicissitudes of two nights on a rather poor bed at Pocono." The following weekend he went to Connecticut again, this time to the New London area where he joined the Strykers as a guest at a Mr. Heublein's "place at Eastern Point." A letter written Monday afternoon, August 4, indicated they had done some sailing—to both Fisher's Island and Watch Hill, Rhode Island. The letter concluded:

> I'll be out to the mountains next Saturday afternoon. If you can arrange for a double room and bath why go ahead. It will be like forty-eight hours of home.

Just as Wallace had turned to his journal, after a hiatus of three years, the previous summer, under the stress of his mother's dying, this summer he turned to poetry.

> [August 7, 1913.]
> I sit at home o'nights. But I read very little. I have, in fact, been trying to get together a little collection of verses again; and although they are simple to read, when they're done, it's a deuce of a job (for me) to do them. Keep all this a great secret. There is something absurd about all this writing of verses; but the truth is, it elates and satisfies me to do it. It is an all-round exercise quite superior to ordinary reading. So that, you see, my habits are positively lady-like.

He was also able to find, through Stryker, a piano that he could afford to buy, and that he hoped Elsie would enjoy. He was obviously eager to find something to keep her at home and in August wrote that he thought "a piano would make more difference to us than anything. It would help you through the evenings and be pleasant any old time." On August 20 he bought the piano: "It is a beauty—a Steinway baby grand in an ebony case—a gorgeous polish etc." Labor Day weekend he went to Pocono Manor; from there they both went to Reading, where Elsie stayed for a while after Wallace returned to New York: to work and to arrange delivery of the piano.

But the brief stop in Reading, with both of his parents gone and the family house no longer the Stevens home, made him look at the place somewhat differently from the way he had before, as he noted in a letter to Elsie on September 4.

> What strange places one wakes up in! Reading was very—unsympathetic, I thought. The trouble is that I keep looking at it as I used to know it. I do not see it as it is. I must adjust myself; because I do not intend to shut myself off from the heaven of an old home. How thrilling it was to go to the old church last Sunday! I had no idea I was so susceptible. It made me feel like Thackeray in the presence of a duke . . . The nobility of my infancy, that is: the survivors, all in the self-same rows . . . For me, a mirror full of Hapsburgs.

Expecting Elsie to return to New York on September 16, Wallace busily set about having the apartment cleaned, after his "bachelor" summer, and the piano was delivered and tuned for her arrival. But there was a delay, owing to business trips that Wallace had to make, to Albany and to Baltimore. At last it was settled that she would arrive by train in Jersey City on Tuesday, September 23, two days after their fourth anniversary, where Wallace would meet her on his way back from Baltimore.

Although we have no record of that winter, we can imagine evenings with Elsie at the piano and Wallace in his chair, reading or writing. The purchase of the piano had strained his finances, and it is doubtful that they spent much time dining out or going to the theater. In the spring of 1914, Wallace made what his aunt called "an agreeable change in his business arrangements," becoming resident vice-president (in New York) of the Equitable Surety Company of St. Louis, Missouri. Things began to look up, and by August 1914, when Elsie was visiting her family in Reading, Wallace had again been invited to Hartford by his friend Stryker. By this time another business friend, James L. D. Kearney, had also left New York to join the newly formed Hartford Accident & Indemnity Company, a subsidiary (founded August 5, 1913) of the Hartford Fire Insurance Company.

It began to seem inevitable that one day Wallace Stevens would move to Hartford too. This must have been an agreeable prospect for both my parents: it would provide, for my mother, the small city environment in which she felt comfortable; for my father, it would mean that his talents as an insurance attorney were recognized, and that he could begin to think of himself as a success. Although the offer of a position, and the move, would not come until the spring of 1916, surely 1914 was an encouraging one in my father's career (though not so on the international scene). He was approaching his thirty-fifth birthday and, after his failures as a reporter and in private practice, he was doing well, he had supported a wife for five years, and had even been able to give her the possession of her heart's desire: the instrument she could play to fill her idle hours and that gave him enjoyment too, as well as the leisure for contemplation. When my father said, "The house was quiet," he never meant to rule out music, as we can see in the opening lines of "Peter Quince at the Clavier" (1915):

> Just as my fingers on these keys
> Make music, so the selfsame sounds
> On my spirit make a music, too.
>
> Music is feeling then, not sound;
> And thus it is that what I feel,
> Here in this room, desiring you,
>
> Thinking of your blue-shadowed silk,
> Is music.

Was it the element of music entering their lives that gave my father enough confidence to begin publishing some of his poetry? Or was it that he at last felt secure enough in his position to do so? Was it simply the encouragement of friends who had started "little magazines" and needed contributions? Was it that he now had time to spend on "a little collection of verses"? No doubt all of these factors entered into it, and perhaps others.

Sometime before August 1914, he sent eight poems to a friend from Harvard days, Pitts Sanborn, who was editing a journal called *The Trend*. They were published in the September issue, under the general title "Carnet de Voyage." Of the eight, five had originally been written for "The Little June Book," which Wallace had put together for Elsie's birthday in 1909, five years earlier. It is thus possible to see the "Carnet" as a transition from juvenilia to the mature poetry that began appearing shortly thereafter.

Let us take a look at the "new" verses in the collection:

I.

An odor from a star
Comes to my fancy, slight,
Tenderly spiced and gay,
As if a seraph's hand
Unloosed the fragrant silks
Of some sultana, bright
In her soft sky. And pure
It is, and excellent,
As if a seraph's blue
Fell, as a shadow falls,
And his warm body shed
Sweet exhalations, void
Of our despised decay.

Certainly this would not have been appropriate in a book of verses to one's sweetheart early in the twentieth century; certainly, too, it bears deeply on a sexual relationship that may have some resemblance to that of my parents, regardless of whatever literary connotations may be brought to it.

II.

The green goes from the corn,
The blue from all the lakes,
And the shadows of the mountains mingle in the sky.

> Far off, the still bamboo
> Grows green; the desert pool
> Turns gaudy turquoise for the chanting caravan.
>
> The changing green and blue
> Flow round the changing earth;
> And all the rest is empty wondering and sleep.

Robert Buttel has quite rightly called this "an effort preliminary to 'Sunday Morning' . . . with the chanting caravan anticipating the ring of pagan men . . ." We can also note the use of green and blue which seem, throughout my father's work, to be the colors that take on particularly important character.

VIII. ON AN OLD GUITAR

> It was a simple thing
> For her to sit and sing
>   "Hey nonino!"
>
> This year and that befell,
> (Time saw and Time can tell),
>   With a hey and a ho—
>
> Under the peach-tree, play
> Such mockery away,
>   Hey nonino!

How odd that one of my father's very late poems, written *circa* 1954, should be titled, "Farewell without a Guitar."

Two further poems by Stevens appeared in the November *Trend*: one had been written for the "Book of Verses" for Elsie in 1908 ("Home Again"); the other was "new":

FROM A JUNK

> A great fish plunges in the dark,
> Its fins of rutted silver; sides,
> Belabored with a foamy light;
> And back, brilliant with scaly salt.
> It glistens in the flapping wind,
> Burns there and glistens wide and wide
> Under the five-horned stars of night,
> In wind and wave . . . It is the moon.

Simultaneously, "Phases" appeared in the November issue of *Poetry*, a group of four poems selected by Harriet Monroe from a larger submission. Within the following year all of these were published in various magazines: "Cy est Pourtraicte, Madame Ste Ursule, et Les Unze Mille Vierges," "Tea," "Peter Quince at the Clavier," "The Silver Plough-Boy," "Disillusionment of Ten O'Clock," and "Sunday Morning" (again, selected by Harriet Monroe, who published five of eight stanzas originally submitted, in the November 1915 issue of *Poetry*).

I cannot explain the great leap from the juvenile verses to "Sunday Morning," but we have seen many intimations of its coming. We have seen Wallace Stevens in his region, we have seen him as a youth, walked with him through his woods, across his fields, and up and down his mountains. We have sat in a cathedral with him. We have seen him fall in love and marry, we have seen the death of his parents; we have been with him on many Sunday mornings through the years until they were distilled into this mature expression of his imagination that slowly brought him some recognition and, toward the end of his life, honors and awards. I hope that I have remembered the words of his journal entry in the summer of 1905, "I think human bones may be among my ashes," well enough to belie the message on one final postcard ("A Postcard from the Volcano") written when I was twelve:

> Children picking up our bones
> Will never know that these were once
> As quick as foxes on the hill;

and that I have guessed

> that with our bones
> We left much more, left what still is
> The look of things, left what we felt

> At what we saw.

As my father wrote to Ronald Lane Latimer in 1935: "The real world seen by an imaginative man may very well seem like an imaginative construction." As much as I can see of him:

> This is my father or, maybe,
> It is as he was,

> A likeness, one of the race of fathers: earth
> And sea and air.
>
> ("The Irish Cliffs of Moher," 1952)

NOTES

PAGE vi

A man's sense . . . Wallace Stevens, in "Effects of Analogy," first published in 1948. See *The Necessary Angel: Essays on Reality and the Imagination* (New York: Knopf; 1951), pp. 120–1. (Hereafter referred to as *NA.*)

The Comedian . . . First published in 1923. See *The Collected Poems of Wallace Stevens* (New York: Knopf; 1954), pp. 27–46. (Hereafter referred to as *CP.*)

PAGE vii

The image . . . Wallace Stevens, in "A Mythology Reflects Its Region," first published in 1957 in *Opus Posthumous: Poems, Plays, Prose by Wallace Stevens*, edited, with an introduction, by Samuel French Morse (New York: Knopf; 1957), p. 118. (Hereafter referred to as *OP.*)

PAGE 3

It is an illusion . . . "The Rock," *CP*, p. 525.

If there must . . . "Less and Less Human, O Savage Spirit," *CP*, pp. 327–8.

PAGE 4

wasn't a man . . . Letter to Jane MacFarland Stone, Sept. 13, 1943. See *Letters of Wallace Stevens*, selected and edited by Holly Stevens (New York: Knopf; 1966), p. 454. (Hereafter referred to as *LWS.*)

The house was . . . "The House Was Quiet and the World Was Calm," *CP*, pp. 358–9.

At home, our . . . Letter to Hi Simons, July 8, 1941. See *LWS*, p. 391.

PAGE 5

the impersonal person . . . "Things of August," *CP*, p. 494.

The son . . . "Esthétique du Mal," *CP*, p. 324.

Neshaminy . . . Letter to Lila James Roney, Nov. 2, 1942.

The wood-doves . . . *CP*, pp. 356–7.

It must have . . . Obituary of Garrett Barcalow Stevens, *The Reading Eagle*, July 14, 1911, p. 1.

PAGE 6
after three years . . . Ibid.

Mr. Stevens . . . Unidentified, undated newspaper clipping sent to Wallace Stevens by Emma Stevens Jobbins.

PAGE 7
The house . . . Letter to Thomas McGreevy, Oct 7, 1948. See *LWS*, p. 618.

That same year . . . "Our Stars Come from Ireland," *CP*, pp. 454–5.

PAGE 8
My father . . . As quoted by Jerald E. Hatfield in "More About Legend," *The Trinity Review*, VIII (May 1954), 30.

His place . . . "A Quiet Normal Life," *CP*, p. 523.

That was important . . . Letter to Babette Deutsch, Feb. 15, 1954. See *LWS*, p. 818.

We thought alike . . . "The Auroras of Autumn," *CP*, p. 419.

PAGE 9
La légèreté . . . René Taupin: *L'Influence du Symbolisme Français sur la Poésie Américaine (de 1910 à 1920)* (Paris: Librairie Ancienne Honoré Champion; 1929), p. 276.

In the Adagia . . . *OP*, p. 178.

I still think . . . Letter to Bernard Heringman, July 21, 1953. See *LWS*, p. 792.

PAGE 10
Read, rabbi . . . "The Auroras of Autumn," *CP*, p. 420.

On Monday . . . Francis Roland, Jr., compiler: *Manual and Directory of the Public Schools of Reading, Pa.* (Reading: Press of Harner & Pengelly; 1895), pp. 40–41.

having flunked . . . Letter to Byron Vazakas, May 26, 1937. See Vazakas, "Wallace Stevens: Reading Poet," *The Historical Review of Berks County*, III (July 1938), 112.

At the end . . . *The Reading Eagle*, June 29, 1894, p. 3.

Each year . . . *The Reading Eagle*, March 30, 1895, p. 2.

It is hard . . . Francis Roland, Jr., compiler: *Manual and Directory of the Public Schools of Reading, Pa.* (Reading: Press of Harner & Pengelly; 1895), pp. 41–42.

will hereafter . . . *Dots and Dashes*, I, 2 (February 1895), 4.

breezy personals . . . *Dots and Dashes*, I, 3 (March 1895), 4.

PAGE 11
Whenever Ned . . . Louise Seaman Bechtel: *The Boy with the Star Lantern* (New York: privately printed; 1960), pp. 23–4.

teacher of . . . Ibid.

he had . . . Op. cit. (New York: n.p.; 1956), pp. 206–7.

absent from . . . *The Reading Eagle*, June 27, 1896, p. 3.

The curriculum . . . Francis Roland, Jr., compiler: *Manual and Directory of the Public Schools of Reading, Pa.* (Reading: Press of Harner & Pengelly; 1895), p. 42.

At the end . . . *The Reading Eagle*, March 28, 1896, p. 5.

It was at this time . . . *The Reading Eagle*, March 12, 1896, p. 2.

PAGE 12

The curriculum . . . Francis Roland, Jr., compiler: *Manual and Directory of the Public Schools of the City of Reading, Pa. for 1896–97* (Reading: Press of Harner & Pengelly; 1896), p. 44.

a dark-haired . . . *A Poet's Life: Seventy Years in a Changing World* (New York: Macmillan; 1938), p. 43.

Wallace Stevens . . . *The Reading Eagle*, Dec. 23, 1896, p. 5.

The newspaper . . . Ibid. (The next day the *Eagle* included a sketch of Stevens on p. 4, the first published "likeness" of him known.)

Six months . . . *The Reading Eagle*, June 24, 1897, p. 3.

PAGE 13

The menu . . . *The Reading Eagle*, July 2, 1897, p. 4.

Grandmother . . . For other parts of this letter, see *LWS*, pp. 14–15.

PAGE 14

When I went . . . Letter dated April 26, 1948. See *LWS*, p. 588.

The Sabbath . . . See Elma Loines, editor: *Russell Hilliard Loines 1874–1922: A Selection from His Letters and Poems with Biographical Sketch and Recollections by His Friends* (New York: privately printed; 1927), p. 171.

PAGE 15

I recall . . . Letter from Arthur Pope to Holly Stevens, June 16, 1964.

Don't you . . . Letter dated Oct. 31, 1897.

When I was . . . Letter dated Sept. 10, 1951. See *LWS*, p. 728.

All the other . . . Letter dated Dec. 8, 1897.

Years ago . . . Letter dated Jan. 22, 1948. See *LWS*, p. 575.

PAGE 16

first year . . . See *LWS*, p. 126.

Autumn . . . *The Red and Black*, I, 3 (January 1898), 1.

Miss Parsons . . . Letter from Garrett Barcalow Stevens to Wallace Stevens, postmarked Jan. 21, 1898.

PAGE 17

Glad to see . . . Letter from Garrett Barcalow Stevens to Wallace Stevens, Feb. 22, 1898.

a real . . . Letter dated March 6, 1898. For other parts of this letter see *LWS*, p. 18.

I have . . . Letter postmarked June 10, 1898.

It has been said . . . See Michael Lafferty: "Wallace Stevens: A Man of Two Worlds," *Historical Review of Berks County*, XXIV, 4 (Fall 1959), 110–11.

Nevertheless . . . Op. cit., July 30, 1898, p. 1.

After a few . . . The binding has broken away from the pages, and it may be that none are missing, though I cannot be certain.

(Jowett . . .) Evelyn Abbott and Lewis Campbell, editors: *The Life and Letters of Benjamin Jowett, M.A. Master of Balliol College, Oxford*, two volumes (New York: Dutton; 1897), vol. I, p. 165.

Benjamin Jowett . . . Oxford: Clarendon Press; 1871.

. . . *next journal entry.* Undated.

VI. I find the . . . Abbott and Campbell, editors: op. cit., vol. II, p. 153, from Jowett's introduction to the *Gorgias*.

Of poetry . . . Ibid., from Jowett's *Plato*, vol. II, p. 314.

I dare say . . . Letter dated Jan. 10, 1936. See *LWS*, p. 305.

The next entries . . . The rest of the page on which the Jowett quotations were written has been cut off, and the three following pages have been excised, as has all of a fourth page except the heading "December 1898."

Dec. 4 . . . *Journal et Fragments.* This book is not in my father's library. In the 11th edition (Paris: Didier; 1864) the quotation appears on p. 91 (entry for August 24, 1835).

Dec. 8 . . . This is the first entry from the Journals to appear in *LWS* (pp. 20–1). Because of the ease in comparing the entries in *LWS* with the entire journal, which appears in this book, no further indication of previously published excerpts will be made.

Now, a poet . . . "The Relations Between Poetry and Painting," *NA*, p. 163.

Stevens had written . . . Letter dated Jan. 10, 1936. See *LWS*, pp. 305–6.

Note these . . . *CP*, p. 17.

There is something . . . *CP*, pp. 355–6.

Who lies dead . . . *The Harvard Advocate*, LXVI, 4 (November 28, 1898), 57.

With fear . . . *The Harvard Advocate*, LXVI, 5 (December 12, 1898), 78.

PAGE 24

Your lines . . .   Letter postmarked Dec. 16, 1898. See *LWS*, p. 21.

Credences . . .   *CP*, pp. 373–4.

PAGE 25

In the evening . . .   Parts of this entry were revised during its writing.

PAGE 26

A Day . . .   *The Harvard Advocate*, LXVI, 9 (March 6, 1899), 135–6.

PAGE 28

Another version . . .   *CP*, pp. 254–5.

She loves . . .   *The Harvard Advocate*, LXVI, 10 (March 13, 1899), 150. As published there the third line ends with a comma.

PAGE 29

I strode . . .   *The Harvard Monthly*, XXVIII, 5 (July 1899), 188.

Come . . .   *East & West*, I, 7 (May 1900), 201. For a comment on *East & West*, a "Monthly Magazine of Letters," see *The Harvard Monthly*, XXX, 3 (May 1900), 126–7.

PAGE 31

If we . . .   *The Harvard Monthly*, XXVIII, 1 (March 1899), 31. There the fourth line ends with a comma, and the eighth line is punctuated "Of Death, and by our side its last, keen sound;".

There shines . . .   LXVII, 2 (April 10, 1899), 18. There the second, third, sixth, seventh, tenth, and thirteenth lines are indented two spaces; the twelfth and fourteenth lines are indented four spaces; and the thirteenth line ends with a comma.

PAGE 32

Cathedrals . . .   XXVIII, 3 (May 1899), 95.

PAGE 34

The next sonnet . . .   Robert Buttel: *Wallace Stevens: The Making of* Harmonium (Princeton: Princeton University Press; 1967), p. 12 *n*.

And even . . .   LXIX, 6 (May 23, 1900), 86. There the first line reads "Lo, even as I passed beside the booth", and the eighth line ends with a period.

PAGE 35

No wonder . . .   Letter dated Feb. 16, 1950. See *LWS*, p. 667.

PAGE 37

I used to . . .   Up to the ellipsis, letter from Seasongood to Holly Stevens, June 29, 1964; after the ellipsis, as quoted in Samuel French Morse: *Wallace Stevens: Poetry as Life* (New York: Pegasus; 1970), p. 27.

I suppose . . .   As quoted by Jerald E. Hatfield in "More About Legend," *The Trinity Review*, VIII, 3 (May 1954), 30.

Glad to hear . . .   Letter dated March 19, 1899. See *LWS*, p. 24.

PAGE 38

In 1941 . . .   *NA*, pp. 3–36.

PAGE 39

Could he . . .   Part III of "Owl's Clover." See *OP*, p. 58.

Part of His . . .   LXVII, 3 (April 24, 1899), 35–7.

PAGE 40

Just what . . .   Letter postmarked May 21, 1899. See *LWS*, p. 26.

One more story . . .   *The Harvard Advocate*, LXVII, 8 (June 12, 1899), 123–4.

PAGE 42

Those thoughts . . .   *The Harvard Advocate*, LXIX, 8 (June 16, 1900), 119–20.

PAGE 47

Surely . . .   New York: Macmillan; 1899.

The Course . . .   *OP*, pp. 96–7.

The mind . . .   Ibid., p. 155.

PAGE 49

Again, this entry . . .   *The Harvard Advocate*, LXVIII, 2 (October 18, 1899), 19–20.

PAGE 51

These images . . .   *OP*, p. 10.

And these lines . . .   *CP*, p. 68.

PAGE 52

Compare this . . .   *CP*, pp. 404–5.

. . . and with . . .   *CP*, p. 405.

PAGE 54

The genus Dicentra . . .   *Others*, II, 3 (March 1916), 173. Only book publication in Alfred Kreymborg, editor: *Others: An Anthology of the New Verse* (New York: Knopf; 1916), p. 128. (A copy of the poem is in Stevens' red folder.)

PAGE 58

Quite possibly . . .   *The Harvard Advocate*, LXIX, 2 (March 24, 1900), p. 18.

PAGE 60

We have already . . .   *The Harvard Advocate*, LXVIII, 2 (October 18, 1899), 19–20.

It was followed . . .   *The Harvard Advocate*, LXVIII, 4 (November 13, 1899), 54–6.

Go not . . .   Ibid., p. 63.

Another story . . .   *The Harvard Advocate*, LXVIII, 6 (December 6, 1899), 86–7.

To the Morn . . .   XXIX, 3 (December 1899), 128. Published over the pseudonym Hillary Harness. As published, the word "heaven" in the eleventh line is spelled "heav'n," and both the twelfth and thirteenth lines end with a comma.

PAGE 61

Ah, yes! . . . *The Harvard Advocate*, LXIX, 1 (March 10, 1900), 5.

Two weeks later . . . *The Harvard Advocate*, LXIX, 2 (March 24, 1900), 18. Published over the pseudonym R. Jerries.

The first . . . *CP*, p. 17.

PAGE 62

The adolescent . . . *The Harvard Advocate*, LXIX, 3 (April 3, 1900), 42–3.

There were three . . . Ibid.

Sunday Morning . . . *CP*, pp. 66–70.

PAGE 63

Wallace Stevens: . . . Princeton: Princeton University Press; 1967. See especially pp. 30–7.

I remember . . . Letter from Floyd Du Bois to Wallace Stevens, Jan. 28, 1942.

A night in May! . . . The ode was published in a keepsake distributed at the dinner, which also included a poem by William Bond Wheelwright. The only known copy is in the archives at Harvard University.

PAGE 65

As an example . . . *The Harvard Advocate*, LXIX, 5 (May 10, 1900), 65–6.

PAGE 66

I stand upon . . . Ibid., p. 66.

I pray thee . . . *The Harvard Advocate*, LXIX, 6 (May 23, 1900), 82.

PAGE 67

The short story . . . Ibid., pp. 83–6.

It would seem . . . Note from Witter Bynner to Michael H. Lafferty, dictated Oct. 27, 1958.

PAGE 68

I should say . . . Ibid. Confirmed in letter from Witter Bynner to Wallace Stevens, Dec. 11, 1954, where Bynner said: "Do you remember, as I remember, Copey's asking you when you left Cambridge, what you were going to do, and upon your reply, 'I am going to be a poet,' his ejaculation, 'Jesus Christ!' "

No matter . . . As quoted by Jerald E. Hatfield in "More About Legend," *The Trinity Review*, VIII, 3 (May 1954), 30.

Before leaving . . . George Santayana: *Lucifer: A Theological Tragedy* (Chicago and New York: Herbert S. Stone; 1899). My father's copy of this book is now owned by Patricia Adel Smith, and was made available to me by Thomas M. Greene; I am grateful to both of them. The flyleaf is inscribed "W. Stevens. May 1900. Camb."

I tried to answer . . . George Santayana: *A Hermit of Carmel and Other Poems* (New York: Scribner's; 1901), p. 122. Santayana's holograph copy of this sonnet, laid into my father's copy of the book, together with a holograph copy of his own sonnet, is dated May 1, 1900.

"*Cathedrals . . .*" See *The Harvard Monthly*, XXVIII, 3 (May 1899), 95.

"*Then the wild . . .*" Santayana, op. cit., lines 9 and 10.

PAGE 69

I doubt if . . . Letter to José Rodríguez Feo, Jan. 4, 1945. See *LWS*, pp. 481–2.

I never took . . . Letter to Bernard Heringman, May 3, 1949. See *LWS*, p. 637.

It is obvious . . . Letter to Henry Church, Oct. 15, 1940. See *LWS*, p. 378.

To An Old . . . First published in *The Hudson Review*, V, 3 (Autumn 1952), 325–7. *CP*, pp. 508–11.

I grieve . . . Letter to Barbara Church, Sept. 29, 1952. See *LWS*, pp. 761–2.

PAGE 70

He sought . . . The Harvard Advocate, LXIX, 7 (June 2, 1900), 110. Published over the pseudonym Henry Marshall.

PAGE 73

That entry . . . First published in 1923. See Holly Stevens, editor: *The Palm at the End of the Mind: Selected Poems and a Play by Wallace Stevens* (New York: Knopf; 1971), p. 84, and note, p. 402. (Hereafter this book will be referred to as *PALM*).

Gray Room . . . First published in 1917. See *PALM*, p. 23.

The elysium . . . "The Shape of the Coroner," *OP*, p. 30.

PAGE 75

Have just been . . . An ellipsis of Keats' line "But, in embalmed darkness, guess each sweet," in the fifth stanza of "To a Nightingale."

PAGE 76

One can't help wondering . . . *OP*, pp. 21–2.

PAGE 77

The next entry . . . See *The Works of W. E. Henley, Vol. I, Poems* (London: David Nutt; 1908), pp. 168–9.

A Window . . . See *LWS*, p. 40 and *n.*

PAGE 79

It's interesting . . . New York and London: Harper & Brothers; 1895.

And hear . . . There is no evidence that this sonnet was written.

outwinged . . . Preceded by "Unhappy dreamer," these are the first two lines of Santayana's sonnet "On the Death of a Metaphysician." See his *Sonnets and Other Verses* (New York: Stone and Kimball; 1896), p. 56.

PAGE 81

This last is reminiscent . . . *CP*, pp. 134–6.

PAGE 84

Psychologically . . . Letter dated August 6, 1911. See *LWS*, pp. 170–1.

One's first . . . See David Gray, *The Luggie and Other Poems* (Cambridge and London: Macmillan; 1862), p. 90.

PAGE 86
How keen . . . This sounds like Keats or Shelley, but I have not been able to identify the line.

PAGE 88
It seems likely . . . New York *Tribune,* October 17, 1900, p. 1.

The poem . . . CP, pp. 158-9.

PAGE 91
Never suppose . . . CP, p. 381.

The lower half . . . First published in *Zero,* II, 7 (Spring 1956), 28. See *OP,* p. 115.

PAGE 93
In the North American Review . . . Elizabeth Robins, "On Seeing Madame Bernhardt's Hamlet," in *North American Review,* CLXXI, 529 (December 1900), 908-19.

PAGE 94
Long ago . . . *NA,* pp. 56-7.

PAGE 95
Now in midsummer . . . "Credences of Summer," CP, p. 372.

PAGE 96
There is also . . . Letter from William Carlos Williams to William Van O'Connor, August 22, 1948.

I do not know . . . Note from Witter Bynner to Michael H. Lafferty, dictated Oct. 27, 1958.

PAGE 97
The four murderers . . . New York *Tribune,* Jan. 30, 1901, p. 4.

PAGE 101
As the season . . . CP, pp. 411-21.

Again. . . . CP, p. 414.

PAGE 102
After leaving you . . . Letter dated Dec. 1, 1950. See *LWS,* p. 700.

The Eberharts . . . Letter from Lowell Tozer to Holly Stevens, March 9, 1971.

Sybil told me . . . Ibid.

PAGE 103
Knowing my father's . . . OP, pp. 99-105.

What is the shape . . . Ibid., p. 104.

PAGE 104
He knelt . . . CP, p. 32

PAGE 105
In 1953 . . . Letter dated June 3, 1953. See *LWS,* p. 778.

PAGE 107

In my room . . . *CP*, p. 57.

It may be . . . *CP*, pp. 479–80.

As the journal . . . *CP*, p. 222.

PAGE 108

Stevens, looking . . . See "Variations on a Summer Day," *CP*, p. 233.

There it . . . *CP*, p. 512.

PAGE 112

A poem like . . . *CP*, pp. 177–8.

A hawk . . . Letter to Renato Poggioli, June 25, 1953. See *LWS*, pp. 783–4.

PAGE 117

One of his . . . See *The Century Association Year-Book 1956* (New York: Century Association; 1956), p. 206. Anonymous memoir, probably by Edwin De Turck Bechtel.

PAGE 132

Noting the reference . . . *CP*, p. 534.

That scrawny . . . Ibid.

PAGE 134

Here, then . . . *CP*, p. 443.

Richard Ellmann . . . *NA*, pp. 131–56. See Richard Ellmann and Robert O'Clair, editors: *The Norton Anthology of Modern Poetry* (New York: W. W. Norton; 1973), p. 242.

the great poems . . . *NA*, p. 142.

PAGE 135

Or, perhaps . . . *CP*, pp. 462–3.

My bar exams . . . See *LWS*, pp. 73–4.

PAGE 138

It's odd, . . . Taped interview with Claire Tragle Bauer, Jan. 19, 1973.

PAGE 140

ragginess . . . Thomas Cadwallader Zimmerman: *Olla Podrida, consisting of Addresses, Translations, Poems, Hymns and Sketches of Out-Door Life,* two volumes (Reading, Pa.: Times Publishing Co.; 1903). Zimmerman, a friend of Garrett Barcalow Stevens, was editor of *The Reading Times.*

There is another . . . *OP*, pp. 144–50.

was one of . . . Letter to Ronald Lane Latimer, Nov. 5, 1935. See *LWS*, p. 291.

PAGE 141

the sun . . . See Sarah Tyson Rorer: *Mrs. Rorer's New Cook Book: A Manual of Housekeeping* (Philadelphia: Arnold; 1902), and other cookbooks by Mrs. Rorer. (The title cited is the one still in the family library.)

PAGE 143

In other respects . . . I have not been able to identify this quotation, but it has been suggested that my father was misquoting Virgil, and that the lines are a parody of Tennyson. In a book that we know my father read, Arthur Colton's *Harps Hung Up in Babylon* (New York: Henry Holt; 1907), we find the line "Oh, Fons Bandusiae, babbling spring," on p. 39.

PAGE 145

I am reminded . . . OP, p. 58.

One of the things . . . Telephone conversation with Claire Tragle Bauer, Jan. 18, 1973.

PAGE 146

By this time . . . See *LWS*, pp. 79–81.

"caverns . . ." Samuel Taylor Coleridge: "Kubla Khan," lines 4 and 5.

The Spring . . . Sonnet 66.

PAGE 148

The geography CP, p. 3.

My father's poem . . . CP, p. 270.

PAGE 150

I placed . . . "Anecdote of the Jar," first published as part of "Pecksniffiana," *Poetry,* XV, 1 (October 1919), 1–11. CP, p. 76.

PAGE 151

He was there . . . Letter dated April 27, 1918(?). See *LWS*, pp. 206–7.

"Cattle Kings . . ." The Atlanta Journal, Dec. 14, 1930, p. 11. I thank Mr. and Mrs. Frank Doggett for discovering this article.

PAGE 153

How odd that . . . CP, p. 490.

Did it become . . . CP, pp. 71–2, where "no" has been transposed to "on" before the word "single." I am grateful to Donald E. Stanford for calling this error to my attention.

PAGE 155

In a world . . . CP, p. 127.

PAGE 157

"In the Spring . . ." "Locksley Hall," line 19 (which immediately precedes the more famous line "In the spring a young man's fancy lightly turns to thoughts of love.").

PAGE 160

"la destination . . ." See Howard Foster Lowry, Karl Young, and Waldo Hilary Dunn, editors: *The Note-Books of Matthew Arnold* (London and New York: Oxford; 1952), p. 34. The source is given there as Senancour, *Obermann,* letter xxxviii, p. 158. (As printed there the penultimate word is "des" instead of "les.")

We might note . . . See OP, pp. 157–80.

PAGE 161
March 3. Apropos . . . See George Meredith: *Poems* (New York: Scribner's; 1901), p. 190.

PAGE 163
Russell Loines . . . G. L. Dickinson: *Letters from John Chinaman* (London: R. Brimley Johnson; 1904), p. 5 (from "Letter I").
"For many miles . . ." Ibid., p. 18 (from "Letter III").

PAGE 165
Did this image . . . CP, p. 411.

PAGE 168
πάρθενον . . . See Edgar Lobel and Denys Page, editors: *Poetarum Lesbiorum Fragmenta* (Oxford: Oxford; 1955), fr. 153.

γλύκεια . . . Ibid., fr. 102. I have been told that the adjective modifying Aphrodite is more likely to mean "slender" than "soft" here.

ἔχω . . . Apparently not attributed to Epicurus himself, according to Thomas Gould, Professor of Classics at Yale University, who advised me that the full meaning "is likely to be 'I am master of my destiny; I am not mastered,'" or something similar (letter dated May 28, 1973).

PAGE 169
"As in water . . ." Proverbs, 27:19.

PAGE 172
Although it is far . . . See *LWS*, pp. 93–4 (letter excerpts, 1906–7).

PAGE 175
Clear water . . . CP, p. 193.

PAGE 176
Yesterday . . . No early edition of the *Note-Books* remains in the Stevens' library.

PAGE 177
"Angelica . . ." See *The Note-Books of Matthew Arnold*, ed. by Howard Foster Lowry, Karl Young, and Waldo Hilary Dunn (London and New York: Oxford University Press; 1952), p. 277. The source is given there as Fulbert of Chartres, quoted in Montalembert: *Les Moines d'Occident*, I, XCV, *n.* 4.
"A merry . . ." Ibid., p. 139. *Proverbs*, 17:22.

PAGE 182
"Odi et amo . . ." The *Carmina of Catullus*, LXXXV.
This has been quoted . . . London: 1894.

PAGE 183
Is it possible . . . See "Anecdote of the Jar," CP, p. 76.

PAGE 184
Elie Metchnikoff's . . . New York and London: G. P. Putnam's Sons; 1903.
If we think . . . CP, pp. 66–70.
Far worse . . . Op. cit., p. 133.

PAGE 185
The first stanza . . . *CP*, pp. 529–30.

PAGE 186
Why my father . . . *New-York Daily Tribune*, Nov. 2, 1907, p. 6. (Dateline, "Washington, Nov. 1.")

Here they are . . . See *LWS*, pp. 106–7.

Songs from Vagabondia . . . Boston: Small, Maynard; 1907.

PAGE 187
More Songs . . . Boston: Small, Maynard; 1905.

Last Songs . . . Boston: Small, Maynard; 1905.

The excerpts . . . See *LWS*, pp. 107–8.

PAGE 190
One of the excerpts . . . See *LWS*, p. 107.

New Life . . . A copy of this poem is in the red folder, without a title. There are minor changes in punctuation and, in the third line, the word used is "these," not "those."

Afield . . . A copy of this poem is in the red folder, without line indentations and with a comma at the end of line 5.

PAGE 191
IV . . . A copy of this poem is in the red folder, omitting the middle stanza, and with minor changes in punctuation.

PAGE 192
Tides . . . A copy of this poem is in the red folder, with minor changes in punctuation.

Winter Melody . . . A copy of this poem is in the red folder, where it is titled "Ancient Rendezvous." There are minor changes in punctuation.

PAGE 195
Home Again . . . This poem was published as the second of "Two Poems," in *The Trend*, VIII, 2(November 1914), 177. There are minor changes in punctuation.

PAGE 196
Of Ideal Time . . . *NA*, p. 88.

Carlos . . . *OP*, pp. 144–50.

Three Travelers . . . *OP*, pp. 127–43.

Hibiscus . . . *CP*, pp. 22–3.

Ariel was glad . . . "The Planet on the Table," *CP*, pp. 532–3.

By November . . . Letter dated Nov. 22, 1908.

PAGE 200
Bearing in mind . . . *CP*, p. 59.

PAGE 201

Only one thing . . . My father's copy of Sidney Colvin's edition of *Letters of John Keats to His Family and Friends,* has laid in it an undated page from a catalogue of rare books issued by Geo. D. Smith, 48 Wall St., New York, offering a first edition of "Endymion" at $500.

Let that . . . By Mary Johnston (Boston and New York: Houghton Mifflin; 1900).

PAGE 202

This letter contains . . . Early in 1971 Miss Butler was in the Gotham Book Mart in New York, and introduced herself to Andreas Brown, who had recently become proprietor. Mr. Brown very kindly put me in touch with her.

The previous letter . . . New York: Caliban; 1954.

Thanks for yr . . . Card postmarked Dec. 22, 1954.

We also note . . . CP, pp. 165–84.

The next letter . . . See LWS, pp. 112–5.

Thirteen Ways . . . CP, pp. 92–5.

The blue-bird . . . See "Poems from 'Primordia,' " OP, p. 7.

Notes Toward . . . CP, pp. 380–408, esp. pp. 394 and 405.

PAGE 203

The Drum-Majors . . . OP, pp. 36–7.

When he went home . . . See LWS, pp. 115–6.

PAGE 209

oleanders . . . See Bliss Carman: *Sappho: One Hundred Lyrics* (London: Chatto and Windus; 1907), p. 19 (Lyric XIII, "Sleep thou in the bosom,").

PAGE 210

Oh, what soft . . . See journal entry, August 1, 1899.

"O vitae . . ." Cicero: *Tusculan Disputations,* 5.2.5.

PAGE 211

Is it for . . . CP, p. 14.

An old man . . . CP, p. 73.

"This then . . ." William Shakespeare: Sonnet 73 ("That time of year thou mayst in me behold,"), lines 13 and 14.

PAGE 212

"it remembers . . ." These lines, from Walter Savage Landor: *Gebir,* Book I, are also quoted by John Freeman, the English poet, in a letter to John Haines, May 10, 1927. See Gertrude Freeman and Sir John Squire, editors: *John Freeman's Letters* (London: Macmillan; 1936), p. 231. A copy of this book is in my father's library.

PAGE 214

"*pale orange* . . ." The first two lists of colors are included in a journal entry for May 14, 1909; they are also in manuscript form in Stevens' red folder. The third group does not appear elsewhere.

PAGE 217

My chief objection . . . *Psalms,* 119:19.

"*All the orchards* . . ." This entry no longer appears in the journal where part of the appropriate page has been excised.

PAGE 218

"*This morning* . . ." See journal entry, May 22, 1907.

"*O World* . . ." Laurence Binyon: "O World, Be Nobler." Stevens has made minor punctuation changes in copying this, as well as changing "nobler" to "noble."

"*Ask me not* . . ." The first stanza of Binyon's "Ask Me Not, Dear" (no. xxviii in *Lyric Poems* [London: Elkin Mathews; 1894], p. 62).

Scraps of paper . . . *Hamlet:* II.ii.315 ff.

PAGE 219

A short letter . . . See *LWS,* pp. 172–4.

PAGE 220

"*O vitae* . . ." See letter to Elsie, Feb. 28, 1909.

"*I sometimes think* . . ." See More's essay, "Thoreau," in *Shelburne Essays,* First Series, Vol. 1 (New York and London: Putnam's; 1909), p. 4.

Great music . . . See letter to Elsie, March 3, 1909.

P.E.M. again . . . See letter to Elsie, May 14, 1909.

PAGE 221

For balm . . . See letter to Elsie, May 9, 1909.

One comes . . . Note the imagery here, taken from John Keats: "On First Looking into Chapman's Homer."

PAGE 222

Pale orange . . . See letter to Elsie, March 18, 1909.

I have gone . . . See Laurence Binyon: *Porphyrion and Other Poems* (London: Grant Richards; 1898). The first two lines quoted are from Book III, lines 129–30; the next two lines are from Book III, lines 232–3; the three lines beginning "Out of suspended hazes" are from Book IV, lines 56–8. The other lines are not from "Porphyrion" and have not been identified elsewhere.

PAGE 223

"*The greatest* . . ." See letter to Elsie, May 9, 1909.

"*It was the mission* . . ." By Paul Elmer More.

PAGE 228

III. The Trend, VII, 6 (September 1914), 744.

IV. In the red folder, the second line reads "On the sea, on the mountains."

PAGE 229

That the lilacs . . . *CP*, p. 526.

VI. A version of this poem appears in the red folder with minor changes in punctuation.

green locust . . . *CP*, p. 270.

The leaves . . . Ibid.

VII. The version of this poem in the red folder omits the third couplet, and the first word of the last line is "Bring" instead of "Flash."

An Ordinary Evening in New Haven . . . *CP*, p. 480.

PAGE 230

Credences . . . *CP*, p. 372.

PAGE 231

XI. The version in the red folder has minor changes in punctuation, the tenth line is omitted, and the eleventh line begins with "Then" instead of "And."

The Beginning. CP, p. 427.

PAGE 232

XIV. In the red folder, the title is "April," and the eighth line ends with a comma.

PAGE 233

Sunday Morning. CP, pp. 68–9.

XVII. As published, the fourth line reads "I nod above the books of Heaven or Hell," and there are minor changes in punctuation.

an Arabian . . . *CP*, p. 383.

my father wrote . . . January 12, 1943. See *LWS*, p. 434.

XVIII. In the red folder, the second line reads "And lighted clouds around," the fourth line ends with a semicolon, and the sixth line begins with "To" instead of "With."

PAGE 235

could write for . . . A bound copy of the catalogue (London: Fine Arts Society; 1909) is in my father's library, inscribed on the flyleaf, "W. Stevens / August 1909 / N.Y."

PAGE 239

My novel . . . William Dwight Whitney: *A Compendious German and English Dictionary* (New York: Henry Holt; 1887). Two volumes, both remaining in my father's library.

PAGE 241

The next day . . . *CP*, pp. 92–5.

PAGE 246

On Saturday . . . *The Reading Eagle*, Sept. 21, 1909, p. 5.

There are two . . . August 9, 1909. See *LWS*, pp. 155–6.

PAGE 247
According to the sons . . . Letter from Robert A. Weinman, March 26, 1974; telephone conversation with Howard Weinman, May 19, 1974.

Frances Butler, . . . Interview, July 7, 1971.

PAGE 248
Found violets . . . Postcard to Dorothy LaRue Moll, postmarked April 3, 1910.

their office . . . Letter from Margaretha Catharine Zeller Stevens to her daughter Elizabeth, postmarked April 3, 1910.

into the library . . . May 30, 1910.

PAGE 253
Lo! I behold . . . Op. cit.

a letter from Mrs. Stevens . . . Letter from Margaretha Catharine Zeller Stevens to her daughter Elizabeth, postmarked February 9, 1912.

PAGE 254
Death is . . . CP, p. 69.

PAGE 255
For several evenings . . . July 29, 1912.

PAGE 256
Elsie is . . . Letter to Elizabeth Stevens, November 30, 1912.

The walk . . . July 7, 1913.

The following weekend . . . August 1, 1913.

PAGE 257
I sit at home . . . Letter to Elsie at Pocono Manor, Pennsylvania.

PAGE 258
an agreeable change . . . Letter to Elsie from Anna Carle, April 20, 1914.

The house was quiet . . . See "The House Was Quiet and the World Was Calm," CP, pp. 358–9.

Just as my fingers . . . CP, pp. 89–90.

PAGE 259
Carnet de Voyage . . . The Trend, VII, 6 (September 1914), 743–6.

PAGE 260
Robert Buttel . . . See Robert Buttel, *Wallace Stevens: The Making of* Harmonium (Princeton, 1967), p. 156.

Farewell without a Guitar . . . OP, pp. 98–9.

Two further poems . . . The Trend, VIII, 2 (November 1914), 117.

Phases . . . Poetry, V, 2 (November 1914), 70–1.

PAGE 261
Cy est Pourtraicte . . . Rogue, I, 1 (March 15, 1915), 12.

Tea . . . Ibid.

PAGE 261

Peter Quince . . .   *Others*, I, 2 (August 1915), 31–4.

The Silver . . .   Ibid.

Disillusionment . . .   *Rogue*, II, 2 (September 15, 1915), 7.

Sunday Morning . . .   *Poetry*, VII, 2 (November 1915), 81–3.

Children picking . . .   "A Postcard from the Volcano," *CP*, pp. 158–9.

that with . . .   Ibid.

As my father wrote . . .   Letter to Ronald Lane Latimer, Oct. 31, 1935.

This is my father . . .   "The Irish Cliffs of Moher," *CP*, p. 502.

INDEX

NOTE: *Unless otherwise attributed, titles are of works of Wallace Stevens. First lines of untitled poems are in italics.*

A NOTE ABOUT THE AUTHOR
AND THE EDITOR

Wallace Stevens was born in Reading, Pennsylvania, on October 2, 1879, and died in Hartford, Connecticut, on August 2, 1955. After attending Harvard University and working for a time as a newspaper reporter in New York, he secured a law degree from the New York Law School and was admitted to the bar in 1904. In 1909 he married Elsie Kachel of Reading. From 1916 to his death he was associated with the Hartford Accident & Indemnity Company, of which he became vice-president in 1934.

Although he began writing poems and stories while still in school, and published a number of pieces in the *Harvard Advocate*, it was not until 1915 that "Sunday Morning," his first major poem, appeared in Harriet Monroe's magazine, *Poetry. Harmonium*, his first volume of poems, was published by Alfred A. Knopf in 1923; it was followed by *Ideas of Order* (1936), *The Man with the Blue Guitar* (1937), *Parts of a World* (1942), *Transport to Summer* (1947), *The Auroras of Autumn* (1950), *The Necessary Angel* (a volume of essays, 1951), *The Collected Poems of Wallace Stevens* (1954), *Opus Posthumous* (1957), *Poems* (a paperback selection, 1959), *The Letters of Wallace Stevens* (1966), and *The Palm at the End of the Mind* (1971).

Wallace Stevens was awarded the Bollingen Prize in Poetry in 1950. He won the National Book Award in Poetry twice—in 1951 and 1955—and the Pulitzer Prize in Poetry in 1955.

Holly Stevens, the daughter of Wallace Stevens, edited *The Letters of Wallace Stevens* and *The Palm at the End of the Mind*.

A NOTE ON THE TYPE

This book was set on the Linotype in Janson, a recutting made direct from type cast from matrices long thought to have been made by the Dutchman Anton Janson, who was a practicing type founder in Leipzig during the years 1668–87. However, it has been conclusively demonstrated that these types are actually the work of Nicholas Kis (1650–1702), a Hungarian, who most probably learned his trade from the master Dutch type founder Dirk Voskens. The type is an excellent example of the influential and sturdy Dutch types that prevailed in England up to the time William Caslon developed his own incomparable designs from them.

This book was composed, printed, and bound by
American Book–Stratford Press, Inc.,
Saddle Brook, New Jersey.

The book was designed by
Earl Tidwell.